Identity Studies in the Social Sciences
Series Editors: **Margaret Wetherell**, Open University; **Valerie Hey**, Sussex University; **Stephen Reicher**, St Andrews University

Editorial Board: **Marta Augoustinos**, University of Adelaide, Australia; **Wendy Brown**, University of California, Berkeley, USA; **David McCrone**, University of Edinburgh, UK; **Angela McRobbie**, Goldsmiths College, University of London, UK; **Chandra Talpade Mohanty**, Syracuse University, USA; **Harriet B. Nielsen**, University of Oslo, Norway; **Ann Phoenix**, Institute of Education, University of London, UK; **Mike Savage**, University of Manchester, UK

Titles include:

Will Atkinson
CLASS, INDIVIDUALIZATION AND LATE MODERNITY
In Search of the Reflexive Worker

Mary J. Hickman, Nicola Mai and Helen Crowley
MIGRATION AND SOCIAL COHESION IN THE UK

John Kirk, Sylvie Contrepois and Steve Jefferys (*editors*)
CHANGING WORK AND COMMUNITY IDENTITIES IN EUROPEAN REGIONS
Perspectives on the Past and Present

John Kirk and Christine Wall
WORK AND IDENTITY
Historical and Cultural Contexts

Janice McLaughlin, Peter Phillimore and Diane Richardson (*editors*)
CONTESTING RECOGNITION
Culture, Identity and Citizenship

Ben Rogaly and Becky Taylor
MOVING HISTORIES OF CLASS AND COMMUNITY
Identity, Place and Belonging in Contemporary England

Susie Scott
TOTAL INSTITUTIONS AND REINVENTED IDENTITIES

Ruth Simpson, Natasha Slutskaya, Patricia Lewis and Heather Höpfl (*editors*)
DIRTY WORK
Concepts and Identities

Margaret Wetherell (*editor*)
IDENTITY IN THE 21ST CENTURY
New Trends in Changing Times

Margaret Wetherell (*editor*)
THEORIZING IDENTITIES AND SOCIAL ACTION

Valerie Walkerdine and Luis Jimenez (*editors*)
GENDER, WORK AND COMMUNITY AFTER DE-INDUSTRIALIZATION
A Psychosocial Approach to Affect

Identity Studies in the Social Sciences
Series Standing Order ISBN 978–0–230–20500–0 (Hardback)
978–0–230–20501–7 (Paperback)
(*outside North America only*)

You can receive future titles in this series as they are published by placing a standing order. Please contact your bookseller or, in case of difficulty, write to us at the address below with your name and address, the title of the series and the ISBN quoted above.

Customer Services Department, Macmillan Distribution Ltd, Houndmills, Basingstoke, Hampshire RG21 6XS, England

Migration and Social Cohesion in the UK

Mary J. Hickman
London Metropolitan University, UK

Nicola Mai
London Metropolitan University, UK

and

Helen Crowley
London Metropolitan University, UK

© Mary J. Hickman, Nicola Mai and Helen Crowley 2012

All rights reserved. No reproduction, copy or transmission of this publication may be made without written permission.

No portion of this publication may be reproduced, copied or transmitted save with written permission or in accordance with the provisions of the Copyright, Designs and Patents Act 1988, or under the terms of any licence permitting limited copying issued by the Copyright Licensing Agency, Saffron House, 6–10 Kirby Street, London EC1N 8TS.

Any person who does any unauthorized act in relation to this publication may be liable to criminal prosecution and civil claims for damages.

The authors have asserted their rights to be identified as the authors of this work in accordance with the Copyright, Designs and Patents Act 1988.

First published 2012 by
PALGRAVE MACMILLAN

Palgrave Macmillan in the UK is an imprint of Macmillan Publishers Limited, registered in England, company number 785998, of Houndmills, Basingstoke, Hampshire RG21 6XS.

Palgrave Macmillan in the US is a division of St Martin's Press LLC, 175 Fifth Avenue, New York, NY 10010.

Palgrave Macmillan is the global academic imprint of the above companies and has companies and representatives throughout the world.

Palgrave® and Macmillan® are registered trademarks in the United States, the United Kingdom, Europe and other countries.

ISBN 978–0–230–24355–2

This book is printed on paper suitable for recycling and made from fully managed and sustained forest sources. Logging, pulping and manufacturing processes are expected to conform to the environmental regulations of the country of origin.

A catalogue record for this book is available from the British Library.

A catalog record for this book is available from the Library of Congress.

10 9 8 7 6 5 4 3 2 1
21 20 19 18 17 16 15 14 13 12

Printed and bound in Great Britain by
CPI Antony Rowe, Chippenham and Eastbourne

Contents

Acknowledgements vi

Introduction 1
1 Community Cohesion and the Backlash against Multiculturalism in the UK 32
2 Social Cohesion in the New Economy 56
3 Place, Belonging and Social Cohesion 80
4 Housing and the Family 113
5 Education and Social Cohesion 133
6 Social Cohesion and the Politics of Belonging 162
7 Conclusions 188

Appendix 199
Bibliography 206
Index 216

Acknowledgements

The research upon which this book is based was funded by the Joseph Rowntree Foundation, who were very supportive throughout its delivery. In particular we would like to thank JRF's Director of Policy and Research, Emma Stone, for a very productive working relationship. The research would not have been possible without the participation of the 320 people we interviewed across the UK and our local partners and researchers in each place. Their contribution and the dialogue we had with them greatly enriched our analysis and the book we have now written. The following were our partner organisations: MENTER (East of England Black and Minority Ethnic Network), Cambridge; Church of the Sacred Heart, Quex Road Community Centre, London; The Complete Works Theatre Company, London; Al-Khoei Foundation, London; South Tyrone Empowerment Agency (STEP), Dungannon; New Link, Peterborough; Lewisham Refugee Network, London; Overseas Nurses Network, Glasgow; Soft Touch, Leicester; and Downham Youth Centre, London. A special thank you to all involved in these organisations. We would also like to thank Dr Umut Erel, Open University, who undertook the research in Peterborough and wrote the site report while a member of the Working Lives Research Institute, London Metropolitan University; and our research partner in Northern Ireland, the Institute for conflict Research, Belfast, who did most of the interviewing in Dungannon and delivered the site report. We thank as well the members of the Project Steering Group and the members of the Advisory Board for their valuable contributions. Many thanks to Liz Kwast who provided excellent transcriptions of the interviews throughout the research; to Jude Bloomfield who gave us invaluable assistance in coding the interviews; and to Nicola Simpson for providing her home as a retreat for a writing week to work on the book. Finally we would like to thank all our colleagues in the Institute for the Study of European Transformations, at London Metropolitan University, for considerable support throughout the conduct of the research and the writing of this book.

Introduction

The relationship between migration and social cohesion in the United Kingdom is a live and divisive political issue featuring regularly in the media and in politicians' speeches. Newspaper headlines have ranged from 'Muslim Europe: The Demographic Time Bomb Transforming our Continent' (*Daily Telegraph* 8 August 2009) to 'Don't listen to the Whingers – London Needs Immigrants' (*Evening Standard* 23 October 2009) to 'Ethnic Minorities to make up 20% of UK Population by 2051' (*Guardian* 14 July 2010). Politicians' comments on the subject have varied from the then Secretary of State for Communities and Local Government, Hazel Blears 'White working class feels ignored over immigration' (*Guardian* 2 January 2009), to the then Prime Minister, Gordon Brown's 'Immigration is not out of control' (*Irish Times* 1 April 2010) to the current Prime Minister, David Cameron's, 'The challenges of cohesion and integration are among the greatest we face' (*Observer* 13 May, 2007).

All political parties were agreed that immigration was a crucial issue on the doorsteps in the 2010 General Election. In that election the Conservatives came to power promising to put a cap on non-European Union immigration; the Liberal Democrats came to power promising to change the immigration system to make it firm and fair so that people could once again put their faith in it; and the New Labour government lost power refusing to put a cap on immigration because it would be detrimental to employers, while insisting that various measures were systematically reducing annual immigration rates. In truth there is little between these statements as the Coalition government's efforts to amend their cap on immigration in the face of protests from business leaders demonstrates.

There is no more febrile issue in British politics than immigration, apart maybe from terrorism (and the two are often linked), and part of the explanation lies in the widespread acceptance of a taken-for-granted relationship between migration and social cohesion. Migration and the impact of the employment and settlement of immigrants are represented as the key issues to be addressed when discussing cohesion. Social cohesion in this way is constituted as a matter central to nationhood in an uncertain and fast-changing world. So not only national immigration policy but also debates about rights to support from the welfare state, about the acceptability of new citizens and about multiculturalism are framed in terms of assumed relationships between migration, cohesion and society. This book challenges these common sense views and argues for the centrality of discussing, on the one hand, the social forces and socio-economic outcomes of neoliberal restructuring, and on the other hand, the pressures and resiliencies of everyday life, for public debates about social cohesion.

The current hyper-sensitivity about migration and social cohesion in the UK is part of a wider crescendo of critiques of the impact of multiculturalism on society across Europe. Debates about cohesion became dominant throughout Europe in the first decade of the twenty-first century. This formed part of a backlash against multiculturalism in part sparked by the upsurge in global migration since the 1990s and the focus on 'global terrorism' since 11 September 2001. The backlash involves the criticism of multicultural policies developed to accommodate the major immigrations into (western) Europe from the 1950s to 1970s. The main features of the backlash are that multiculturalism fosters accentuated or preserved cultural differences; such differences lead to communal separateness; and separateness intensifies the breakdown of social relations and provides an incubator for extremism and possible terrorism (Vertovec and Wessendorf, 2010). Part of the purpose of this book is to examine this backlash and mount a critique of it based on research in the UK about what works and what does not work in terms of social cohesion.

A critical feature of European societies is that they do not conceive their national populations as historically constituted by immigration (see Robinson, 1983; Gilroy, 1993), and thus issues of national identity and social cohesion are usually syncopated with debates about immigration and minority ethnic groups. This is in part because Western nation states are characterised by a tension between universalistic liberalism, with its expectation of equal rights and liberties for all its members, and particularistic nationalism, which is predicated upon excluding from these privileges all non-members (Joppe, 2005). Blaming multiculturalism inevitably entails blaming immigrants and long-term settled minority ethnic groups and masks the existence of a complex class structure and the impact of neoliberal restructuring on cohesive relations. Instead immigrants' desire to maintain their cultural traditions and distinct identities, supported by multiculturalism, is perceived as leading to negative consequences (Vertovec and Wessendorf, 2009). Central to the perceptions that inform this backlash against multiculturalism is a perceived 'excess of alterity' (Grillo, 2007), that is, a growth in difference, and the threat it is taken to constitute for social cohesion. The fear underpinning the backlash against multiculturalism is that the homogenising force of industrial-society nationalism has been fatally undermined by the dissipating and heterogenising forces of late-twentieth century globalisation (Hannerz, 1996).

The intrinsic heterogeneities of contemporary societies are often presented as the 'problems' of a plural society and the implicit question becomes: how much, or how little, can people have in common at the cultural level and still retain a sense of solidarity, equality before the law and a sufficient degree of equal opportunity to remain loyal? (Eriksen, 2007). Eriksen (2007) argues that the majority of (west) European societies have always contained considerable cultural variation but this has been accompanied by a high degree of social cohesion. This is because Western individualism has been compatible with great cultural variation in the private sphere and therefore it is so much easier 'for the majorities in Western Europe, to accept immigrant food and immigrant music than immigrant family organization and gender roles' (Eriksen, 2007: 1064). This plus the inevitable tendency of immigrants to adapt, integrate and struggle for equality, combined with varying assimilatory policies, largely delivered the integration of mid-twentieth century immigrants. At the beginning of the twenty-first century, however, a new crisis was perceived. This was seen to stem from: fears of political violence, at a time when nation states were increasingly porous; from second- and third-generation descendants of the immigrants of the 1950s–1970s who were problematised; and from new globalised migratory flows passing into, within and through Europe.

Immigrants were and still are typically understood to hail from beyond the naturalised boundaries of the nation. There continues to be therefore an understanding of social and geographical space as the natural home of a native population (defined in terms of biology or culture) and possessed of finite social and material resources (Pitcher, 2009). Vertovec and Wessendorf (2009) argue that the backlash against multiculturalism has been accompanied everywhere by a re-emphasis on the integration of immigrants and minority ethnic groups. Their examination of these policies leads them to the conclusion that apart from the avoidance of the word multicultural in policy documents there has arguably not been a massive change. They note the growing use of the term 'diversity' and that minority cultural recognition remains prevalent within public policy. The implication of their analysis is that policies and programmes once deemed multicultural continue everywhere under another name. This is true in one sense because the official discourses of multiculturalism implied that differences could be reconciled through the legislative framework, which has historically defined Western values as neutral and universal. This use of difference as a form of reconciliation is possible because 'differences' have been set up as expressive, private or a matter of appearance and are not defined in terms of difference in values or ways of being (Ahmed, 2000). However, as Ahmed (2000) points out this leads to a disavowal of differences deemed incommensurable. The 'problem of difference', as opposed to diversity, is a problem of power: who decides what amount of difference is too much?

The lens of difference, unlike that of diversity, observes how persistent power structures unevenly shape lives but also complicates the picture by spotlighting the ways in which such structures in turn are shaped by the contingent circumstances of specific groups in specific settings (Jacobs and Fincher, 1998). Society is irrevocably heterogeneous and 'difference' is a useful lens with which to uncover how any given set of power relations constitutes the phenomenon of 'sameness' and therefore of 'difference'. The concept of diversity is used as a signifier of the difference of immigrants, of minority ethnic groups, in other words of a national community that includes 'Others'. Encapsulated in the term 'diversity' is a form of cultural fundamentalism.

> To accept that which is different from the 'standard' is already, in some sense, to accept difference *into* the standard. Those who do not fit into a standardised pattern must still fit into the nation: they fit, not by being the standard, but by being defined in terms of their difference. The nation still constructs itself as a 'we', not by requiring that 'they' fit into a 'standardised pattern', but by the very requirement that they 'be' culturally different.
>
> (Ahmed, 2000: 96)

In other words 'diversity' is always already speaking of a 'host' or core constituency that is being subject to diversification and (re)constructs itself by identifying that difference. Underlying this notion is the assumption that formal political equality presupposes cultural identity and hence cultural sameness becomes the essential prerequisite for access to citizenship rights (Stolcke, 1995).

In the research project that informs this book most of the places we explore are urban, although they range from inner city areas in large cities to small rural towns. One thing that urban spaces share in common is that difference is a sustained feature. Cities, in particular, represent the being together of strangers and city life is structured around relations between 'both seen and unseen strangers' (Young, 1990: 237). The point we want to stress here is that it is important not to constitute city life as 'community' but as 'a site structured around the actual, not imagined, "being together of strangers" joined through uneven power relations (Jacobs and Fincher, 1998: 17). Jacobs and Fincher (1998: 2) conceptualise the interlinking of power and identity in this context as a 'located politics of difference'. From the perspective of the argument being developed here the key point is that to aim at a transcendence of group difference is missing the point. Mutual empathy is not possible across all strangers in urban localities especially as urbanisation may reinforce group solidarity and differentiation (Young, 1990). Consequently our research addressed the question: do people have to get on well together? We also asked: how do people live together? This entails addressing 'the multicultural question' (Hall, 2001) rather than multiculturalism. Answering these questions is what will help us explore and understand the dynamics of social cohesion.

In this book we bring together many issues often addressed separately. We combine an examination of how people relate or interconnect together with the key structural forces and processes relevant when considering the social cohesion of societies. The impact of the social and economic transformations embedded in neoliberal restructuring of the state and economy and the resulting widening gap between rich and poor are critical for discussing the rhythms and realities of everyday life and cohesive social relations. We focus attention both on the specificities of place when exploring the significance of identifications in a globalised world and on the historical particularities of ethnic and national belongings. We bring together an examination of the contemporary backlash against multiculturalism, exploring its relationship to strategies for the management of community relations, and a macro-perspective on the social and economic transformations that are changing home, work and belonging for everyone.

Our analysis of migration, cohesion and society is based on in-depth research in six places which represent the heterogeneous contexts of social cohesion across the United Kingdom today. In these places we explore the everyday lives and practices of both new immigrants and the long-term settled population. Our findings fall into three main areas: those concerning the pressures and resiliences of the rhythms and realities of everyday life; those that reveal how people get along, or do not get along, in this context; and those relating to the narratives of responsibility regarding social cohesion. First, everyday realities are under pressure from the forces of individualisation, globalisation and post-industrialism in two main ways that connect with social cohesion. Social and economic transformations are experienced by everyone and have a strong impact on social cohesion in general because of the changes in work/life balance they bring about and by producing conflicting demands between family and work. Also these transformations produce winners and losers; and they have specific impacts in places where people do not see themselves benefiting from globalisation. In these places it is possible to chart varying responses to these pressures. Second, we found a de facto recognition that Britain today is multi-ethnic and multicultural and therefore social cohesion was not perceived as being about expecting consensus on values and priorities. The majority of long-term settled residents understood social cohesion to be about a willingness and ability to be able to negotiate a difficult line between commonality and separation. The dominant 'consensualist' sensibility informing social cohesion policies implies that immigration threatens a shared national identity. Its emphasis on identifying processes that can foster common-alities overlooks the way conflicts also underpin cohesive rhythms and realities of everyday life. Third, we did find differences, in particular these were about who was perceived as responsible for social cohesion and were rooted in the local and national narratives of history, immigration and belongings that characterise particular places and frame the under-standing of immigrants; these narratives are a key part of the complexity that underpins the relationship between migration and cohesion.

In this introduction we first examine what is meant by social cohe-sion and draw a distinction between social cohesion and the policy agenda of community cohesion. The following section focuses on a number of themes that are threaded throughout the book: the impact of macro socio-economic changes on the lives of the long-term settled and new immigrants alike; the specificity of place for determining the rhythms and realities of everyday life; the relationship between sustain-ing the welfare state and notions of entitlement; and the importance of an historical analysis of immigration and national belonging. Finally we discuss the main features of the research we undertook and describe the structure and organisation of the rest of the book.

What is social cohesion?

Perceptions of a crisis in social cohesion are hardly new. Pahl (1991: 346) logs the way in which arguments about individualism, mass society, and a central value system are constantly reappearing, old issues in new and fashionable clothing. At the most basic level social cohesion is about social order, what holds societies together and what sustains them (Jeannotte, 2003). Posed in this way it is clear that much social science, especially in sociology and anthropology, is concerned with social cohesion. From Durkheim onwards the analysis of order and disorder, that is, social integration, was the foundation of sociology as a subject. Social integration refers to 'the more or less orderly or conflicting relationships between actors of a society' whereas 'system integration refers to the more or less functional or contradictory relationships between its institutional subsystems' (Lockwood, 1992: 377). Solidarity based on shared values and beliefs is the aspect of social integration that is given greatest emphasis in Durkheimian and normative functionalist sociology. Durkheim believed that solidarity was the normal condition of society. He acknowledged that as society changes (for example, industrialisation) social cohesion becomes more complex. The complexity was rooted in the mutual interdependence produced by the division of labour in industrialised societies. The fact that industrialism also wrought turmoil and social change was largely understood within Durkheimian Sociology as amounting to insufficient normative regulation, resulting from individuals losing sight of their shared interests based on mutual dependence. The conflicting interests embedded in the economic system are completely obscured in this formulation. Durkheim's notion of 'mechanistic' solidarity is that individual members of society resemble each other because they cherish the same values and hold the same things sacred, and it is this that renders societies coherent (Fanning, 2011). This perspective is powerfully present in what we have termed the taken-for-granted relationship between migration and social cohesion that exists in most public debate. This bounded, homogenising characterisation of society is the predominant one and is strongly linked to a nation state container view of society.

Ulrich Beck a few years ago recognised that 'new realities are arising' and called for 'a new mapping of space and time' and for social science to be 're-established as a transnational science of the reality of de-nationalization, transnationalization and "re-ethnification" in a global age', because otherwise it runs the risk of 'becoming a museum of antiquated ideas' (Beck, 2002: 53–4). The dangers of methodological nationalism, that is the tendency to accept the nation state and its boundaries as a given in social analysis, are obvious but nevertheless, we argue, everything is not about denationalisation, transnationalisation and re-ethnification; it is about those processes *and* their relationship to countervailing processes and social forces. Brenner (2004: 45) points out in a reflection on globalisation debates that although 'previous rounds of deterritorialization and reterritorialization occurred largely within the geographical framework of national state territoriality' and the current round of socio-spatial restructuring has decentred the role of the national scale, nevertheless 'national states continue to operate as essential political and institutional sites for, and mediators of, the territorialisation of social, political and economic relations' (47). And nationalism has remained a key mechanism for ensuring citizen loyalty despite it running counter to neoliberalism's concern with market freedoms (Harvey, 2007).

Levitt and Glick-Schiller (2004) argue that we need a reformulation of the concept of society in order to rethink the boundaries of social life because of the complex interconnectedness of contemporary reality. From their perspective, integration for immigrants and enduring diasporic ties are neither incompatible nor binary opposites. Equally, we argue, for social scientists there is no contradiction, between simultaneous engagement with the national unit of analysis and a concerted endeavour to contribute to and interrogate wider theoretical and comparative horizons. This approach is also appropriate as a lens for the analysis of the long-term settled because as we outline below they are often in place because of previous immigrations, whether remembered or forgotten, and 'only a minority of people are born, live their lives and die in the same community or settlement' (King, 2002: 94). The seemingly most rooted of populations (for example, white British working-class people living on inner city estates) are also frequently embedded in transnational networks (Rogaly and Taylor, 2009).

Part of the appeal of cosmopolitanism has been its provision of a framework to understand these pluralisations. It offers new perspectives relevant to 'our culturally criss-crossed, media bombarded, information rich, capitalist dominated, politically plural times' (Vertovec and Cohen, 2002: 4). Cosmopolitanism assumes and legitimates plural loyalties and refers to a way of living based on 'openness to all forms of otherness' (Hiebert, 2002); but it also understands belonging. There is no inconsistency between affirming the cosmopolitan ideal and recognising the importance of particular attachments and the commitments they carry (Poole, 1999). For Hollinger (2002: 230) a new cosmopolitanism has developed that focuses on the universalist insight that even the least chauvinistic national project may inhibit any transnational interests of a wider human population. This is an insight that nationalists tend to deny. The new cosmopolitanism also focuses on a nationalist insight that a primal need for belonging is poorly satisfied by solidarities large enough to act effectively on challenges that are global in scope. And this he emphasises is an insight that universalists tend to deny.

Thus cosmopolitanism shares with universalism a suspicion of enclosures, but the cosmopolitan understands the necessity of enclosures in their capacity as contingent and provisionally bounded domains in which people can form intimate and sustaining relationships (Hollinger, 2002: 231). Vertovec and Cohen (2002) observe that there are few recipes for fostering cosmopolitanism. In this book we chart and analyse how forms of cosmopolitanism are embedded and generated in the social relations characterising some places compared with others.

This leaves us with the question of how to rethink society if we do not take national boundaries for granted as the definitive unit of analysis but we simultaneously register their importance. Or to paraphrase Ong (1999) if we recognise that national borders are both 'spaces of possibility' as well as spaces of control. We are already familiar with terms like 'the global city' (Sassen, 2001) and with thinking about the contemporary connectedness of societies as centring on flows of media, capital and people but although these notions capture the porosity of the nation state and the relative autonomy of certain urban spaces within them they do not offer a fully satisfactory way of locating the individual and her/his everyday activities and relationships within an understanding of how society operates. In an effort to neither privilege the national nor the transnational dimensions Levitt and Glick Schiller propose a view of society and social membership utilising Bourdieu's concept of social field.

> Bourdieu used the concept of social field to call attention to the ways in which social relationships are structured by power. The boundaries of a field are fluid and the field itself is created by the participants who are joined in struggle for social position. Society for Bourdieu is the intersection of various fields within a structure of politics.
> (Levitt and Glick Schiller, 2004: 1008)

They define a social field as a set of multiple interlocking networks of relationships through which ideas, practices and resources are unequally exchanged, organised, and transformed. Conceptualising society in this way entails tracing the dynamics of social cohesion within a social space, 'in essence, a macro-version of Bourdieu's fields' (Jeannotte, 2003: 46). Glick-Schiller (2009) defines transnational social fields as networks of networks that link individuals directly or indirectly to institutions located in more than one nation state as part of the power dynamics through which institutionalised social relations delineate social spaces. The term is used as a means of situating individual migrants within various unequal social relationships that connect them to various specific places and their socially organised relationships.

In order to account for the complexity of the political, spatial and socio-economic dimensions underpinning social cohesion the phenomenon needs to be distinguished from its discursive construction (i.e. the way social cohesion is represented and understood by policymakers, politicians, the media and some academics). This is a fundamental premise of our approach. The phenomenon of social cohesion is embedded within social relations that are perceived as positive by most individuals and groups living in a place defined by the unequal exchange of discourses, practices and material resources. The tension between the positive quality ascribed to social relations and the structural inequality of the exchange informing them points to the most defining aspect of social cohesion: its intrinsically dynamic and contested status. We will return to this key aspect later in this chapter, when we will attempt to formulate a definition of social cohesion. Right now, by emphasising the dynamic and contested status of social cohesion, we underline the way it is the product of competing forces, resources, and discourses.

We argue that the cohesiveness of social relations depends on the prevalence of a positive appreciation of their quality; cultural constructions of what positive social relations 'are about' play a pivotal role therefore in the unfolding of social cohesion. For instance, our analysis shows that local hierarchies of social entitlement and mobility, the acknowledgement of transnational affiliations, belongings and histories of diversity and/or homogeneity are all constitutive of social cohesion. The phenomenon of social cohesion needs to be distinguished from normative and functionalist models of social cohesion, which are embedded in pre-digested and essentialist understandings of what 'a good society' should be about. Rather than understanding the socio-economic dynamics according to which places experience the social relations underpinning them in either predominantly positive or negative terms, normative and functionalist approaches evaluate places as cohesive or not according to criteria and standards which are not drawn from the realities they examine. In doing so, they risk adding pre-digested notions of social cohesiveness/uncohesiveness to the many discursive dichotomies building new boundaries between places in contemporary neoliberal times. The governmental apparatus and rhetoric of community cohesion, is, as we will show, yet another embedding device for further polarisation between places on the basis of selective criteria of what constitutes cohesiveness and community.

There remains much research and policy formation about social cohesion that conforms broadly to normative functionalism. A considerable body of research focuses on the social cohesion of social groups or organisations and is minutely concerned with the relationships of individuals to groups. So one recent survey of this literature proffered the following definition of a cohesive group:

> Groups are cohesive when group-level conditions are producing positive membership attitudes and behaviors and when group members' interpersonal interactions are operating to maintain these group-level conditions.
> (Freidkin, 2004: 410)

Although our focus is on society rather than groups per se it will become apparent that much policymaking in this area is largely underpinned by the assumptions inherent in the above definition of what makes for a cohesive group. Social cohesion is construed as being about functioning, bounded systems in which it is possible to identify individual-level and group-level phenomena and their mutual impact and interaction.

The 'problems' of cohesion are also usually racialised, ethnicised, and classed. At the end of the twentieth century academics were pointing out that it was 'the problem of cities and particularly the problem of poor people in neighbourhoods in cities' (Forrest and Kearns, 2001: 2126) that were central to governmental concerns about social cohesion in the UK. A year into the new century these concerns about urban spaces had been refocused on south Asian communities and their claimed self-segregating tendencies, and the issue became the parlous state of relations between communities (Cantle, 2008). The community cohesion framework that resulted from the review of the 2001 civic disturbances (Cantle, 2001) adopted many tenets of existing debates and policies about cohesion. However, it inflated one particular aspect – that there could be tensions between socially cohesive neighbourhoods – into the most worrying cohesion problem because of parallel lives (Robinson, 2005). In this way social bonding within communities became stigmatised in certain contexts. By the late 2000s the issues had become 're-classed' and re-ethnicised in that a concern with the perceived insularity of traditional white, urban working-class communities came under the spotlight and this was centrally linked to the high profile of debates about immigration (Denham, 2010).

In these policy debates throughout the first decade of the twenty-first century cohesion concerns focused unremittingly on various categories of 'deprived populations', and one of their greatest deprivations was argued to lie in their lack of bridging social capital. Robert Putnam's (2000) theories about social capital have been extremely influential, strongly shaping government policy responses to perceived threats to social cohesion. According to Putnam the golden era of social cohesion predated mass television viewing and women's re-entry into the labour force, that is, the 1950s, the last moments of industrialism sustained by the crest of post-war reconstruction. This was a period he argued of higher levels of active associational membership and correspondingly higher levels of civic engagement. This theory was largely based on the idea that when people get together in an association's activities they are more likely to discuss civic or community matters. The growing strength of individualism since then, he argued, corroded community cohesion generating appetites for 'bowling alone' separate from the responsibilities and concerns of community association. In Putnam's conception voluntary communal association is consensual and to further cohesion across diversity a more capacious 'we' must be developed. Thus bridging social capital is seen as inclusive and capable of generating broader identities and reciprocity, while bonding social capital is deemed exclusive, inward looking and will reinforce exclusive identities and homogeneous groups (Hewstone et al., 2007). A key driver in the appeal of a focus on social capital is the notion that social cohesion at the societal level may be derived from the forms and quality of social interaction at the local level (Forrest and Kearns, 2001). In later research, Putman (2007) specifically states that the greater the diversity in a community, the fewer people vote, the less they volunteer, and the less they trust their neighbours. He paints a bleak picture of civic desolation, although not of heightened tension, in diverse communities.

Our findings challenge these widespread assumptions (see also Hewstone et al., 2007; Finney and Simpson, 2009; Dorling, 2011) and show that difference is acknowledged, and even accepted by most people. As we will show there is a strong suggestion in our interviews that many people have an understanding that pluralism necessarily entails conflict and that the goal sought is agreed means of resolving conflict rather than a mythical harmony based on common values. Social cohesion, in other words, is not about avoiding conflict; it is about resolving conflict. We want to argue against these erasures of conflict and to challenge predominant ways of conceptualising the threat that conflict poses. Drawing on Gilchrist (2004), we use social cohesion as a term not to denote the absence of conflict, but to signify *the ability within the individuals and groups informing a social field to manage the inequalities, differentiations and tensions intervening within and between them in terms that they perceive as positive and successful*. By conceptualising social cohesion as an individual and social ability to navigate or negotiate inequality and difference whose successfulness is contextual (i.e. meaningful within a social field) and processual (i.e. the outcome of a dynamic process), we accept, drawing on our findings, and on Mouffe (1996), the intrinsic pluralism and fluidity of social arrangements.

Mouffe (1996) advocates a pluralism that gives a positive status to difference and refuses the objectivity of unanimity and homogeneity, that is, where individuals are united by shared goals. This, she sees as unrealistic and always revealed as a fiction, or based on exclusion. She argues that liberal democracy is more than a form of government, it concerns the symbolic ordering of social relations. In her framework of plural or radical democracy pluralism is not just a 'fact' (as in much social commentary and indeed in the theories of other philosophers, for example, John Rawls) it is an axiological principle, it is of intrinsic value. Pluralism implies the permanence of conflict and antagonism and we must take these conflicts and confrontations as evidence that democracy is alive and inhabited by pluralism. In other words a degree of disorder, of conflict between centre and periphery, between capital and labour, between regions, even between communities (perhaps constituted around a specific essence for the purpose of a particular campaign) is necessary and desirable.

This means that we have to abandon the idea of a complete reabsorption of alterity into oneness and harmony and accept what pluralism inevitably entails. This is not new – modern societies are predicated on differences and multiplicities. We live within societies and economic systems that produce inequalities and differentiations and hence this leads to conflicts of interests and exploitations. By utilising the lens of difference, rather than of diversity, the focus is wider, it is not restricted to the cultural realm, and it detects hierarchies and power relations. Nevertheless, as we will show, the ability of people to 'rub along together' is a strong countervailing force because their expectations do not necessarily include sharing norms and goals with their neighbours or workmates; this helps to explain the sustainability of social relations.

Our approach is in direct contrast to the understanding of social cohesion that underpins the taken-for-granted relationship between migration, cohesion, and society which shapes most political and policy debates. As referred to earlier this largely stems from Durkheimian notions of solidarity. This Durkheimian model is translated in contemporary understandings of community cohesion into a problem of excessive bonding capital (mechanical solidarity) on the part of some communities and the absence of bridging capital (organic solidarity) towards other communities. However, the bonding of some groups, for example, the bankers who have recently wrought havoc on the financial system, is not considered problematic enough to give rise to a specific cohesion strategy to ensure they share bonds and values with the rest of society, instead 'we are all in it together' (Osbourne, 2009) in paying for their greed and mistakes. Whereas 'a tale of three cities' (Goodhart, 2011) is continually retold so that Bradford, Burnley and Oldham cannot escape the reputational damage of civic unrest in 2001, 'Muslims' or 'Pakistanis' (depending upon the narrator) cannot escape being seen as segregationist, the white working class cannot escape designation as pathological and much of northern England stagnates due to the massive impact of deindustrialisation.

The politics of migration, cohesion and society are highly contested. Our contribution to this debate is to demonstrate how bonding and bridging capital are interlinked and engaged in all social contexts. We present extensive empirical evidence of the impact of socio-economic change on the rhythms and realities of everyday life; and of the ongoing ways in which the agency of individuals and groups is or is not able to manage conflictual situations, based on inequalities, differentiations and tensions, successfully. Social cohesion, with all its achievements and disruptions, is a process that is intrinsic to the rhythms and realities of everyday life rather than a goal that can be definitively achieved. Both how people relate to each other and divisive inequalities and discriminations are framed and configured by the social, economic and political changes of particular eras. These processes are freighted with an array of local, national and transnational histories and it is this complexity that we explore.

Our approach and themes

Certain themes and areas of exploration occur across most or all of the chapters. They constitute the connecting threads of our analysis. Here we want to provide a brief rationale for their central importance in the arguments we develop about migration and social cohesion in the UK.

Structural processes: Neoliberal restructuring, individualism, post-industrialism, and globalization

Our approach stems from the perspective that global socio-economic transformations resulting from neoliberal restructuring and the transition to post-industrialism frame contemporary social relations. Neoliberalism can be defined as a series of projects of capital accumulation that from the 1970s on sought to reconstitute social relations of production, including the organisation of labour, space, state institutions, military power, governance, membership, and sovereignty (Glick-Schiller, 2009: 9). It is underpinned by a political-economic theory that 'human well-being can best be advanced by liberating individual entrepreneurial freedoms and skills within an institutional framework characterized by strong private property rights, free markets and free trade' and it emphasises that the role of government is 'to create a good business climate rather than to look to the needs and well-being of the population at large' (Harvey, 2007: 2, 48). Harvey argues that the aim of neoliberalism was to achieve the restoration of class power as the post-war settlement after 1945 had involved restraining the economic power of the upper classes and according a larger share of national wealth to labour. This had been tolerable during the 1950s and 1960s, an era of growth, but with the economic crisis and stagflation of the 1970s a different strategy was required for capital accumulation. Since then the share of national income in the hands of the top 1 per cent has increased exponentially in most developed countries (2007: 15–19).

Individualism refers to the everyday preoccupations of an individualist culture in which 'individuals must continually strive to be more efficient, faster, leaner, inventive and self-actualizing than they were previously' (Elliott and Lemart, 2006: 3). These pressures downgrade social connections other than those of the family and the market and as Margaret Thatcher famously stated 'there is no such thing as society'. For neoliberalism all forms of social solidarity were to be dissolved in favour of individualism, private property, personal responsibility, and family values (Harvey, 2007: 23). Even though today it is no longer politically viable to echo Margaret Thatcher's stance on society, the reality is that the neoliberal market-based populist culture of differentiated consumerism and individual libertarianism that has developed generates tensions and pressures that have a strong impact on cohesive social relations.

The term 'post-industrialism' is a contested one which has been disputed since its earliest formulation (Bell, 1973) although little disagreement currently exists on the changes initiated in the epoch of deindustrialisation that inspired Bell's periodisation. The oil crisis of 1973 led to a period of deindustrialisation, economic restructuring, massive unemployment in the North and debt crises in the South, and the gradual emergence and consolidation of the knowledge economy which subsumed a reduced manufacturing and industrial sector in advanced Western economies. We concur with the analysis of Pierson, (1998, 2001) that

> [t]hree profound transitions have been taking place as the advanced industrial economies become post-industrial ones: the slowdown in the growth of productivity (and consequently economic growth) associated with a massive shift from manufacturing to service employment; the gradual expansion, maturation and 'growth to limits' of governmental commitments; and the demographic shift to an older population. Each element of this 'triple transition' to post-industrialism represents a powerful and continuing source of pressure on the welfare state.
>
> (Pierson, 1998: 541)

By the 1990s, equally contested terms such as the risk society, the new economy, the knowledge economy competed to identify the redrawn formations of economy and society (Perrons et al., 2006). Consensus is far from being achieved in this later debate either, and although some have disregarded the term 'post-industrialism' entirely others continue to use it interchangeably with other conceptual indicators of the shift beyond the era of industrialism.

We have chosen to signal these shifts as post-industrialism. First, this is because the shift that it represents has been particularly profound in the UK because of the relative dominance of the manufacturing sector compared with its competitors prior to the 1970s. The UK's economic preeminence of the nineteenth century was built on early industrialisation. By the middle of that century over 40 per cent of employment in the UK was within the industrial sector (Germany did not reach this proportion until after the Second World War). UK employment in industrial manufacturing peaked in 1960 at over 45 per cent. This was a higher proportion than any of its rivals, Germany being fractionally less than this, the USA significantly less at barely 35 per cent and France and Italy on 37 and 38 per cent respectively. Since then there have been dramatic changes. In 2005 less than 20 per cent of UK employment was in the manufacturing sector; in Germany it was 27 per cent, the USA 17 per cent, France 21 per cent and in Italy 28 per cent. The scale of the shift from industrial employment to employment in the services sector is therefore far more pronounced in the UK than in its peer countries (Colquhoun, 2005). Second, we use the term 'post-industrialism' because it provides a reference point against which economic shifts and their impact on social life can be measured (that is from the period when industrial production commanded advanced economies). Third, it provides an overt connection to earlier imagined ways of belonging which are often invoked as emblematic of 'real cohesion' by those who see the spread of individualism and a more pluralised migration as throwing 'community' into crisis.

How have the changes rendered by post-industrialism impacted materially and discursively on contemporary formations of the social? The decline and restructuring of manufacture and the old heavy industries, the switch from a predominantly male, full-time, blue-collar workforce to a feminised flexible service sector workforce ushered in some of the most significant changes in the twentieth century (Ferree et al., 1999; Hutton, 1995). Simultaneously privatisation policies eroded the old post-war welfare state (Pierson, 2006). Finally, the reproduction on a global scale of the push-pull factors of capitalism created new migratory flows shaped by the competition for skilled and unskilled labour (Kofman et al., 2000; Anderson, 2000). These macroscopic social changes have impacted heavily on the rhythms and realities of the everyday lives of everyone and have made great demands on the fabric of social cohesion. The demands of the neoliberal, post-industrial order became apparent during the 1980s and 1990s and include flexible and mobile workforces, longer working weeks, dual income households, restructured welfare spending and curtailed community expenditure and the normalisation of structural worklessness. These changes to the social are challenging both at the level of lived relations and at the level of policy intervention and strategies of governance.

In globalised post-industrial societies the requirements for migrant labour are diverse and complex and this sits uneasily with constructions of the stranger as problematic and threatening. Fundamental changes in migration and mobility are a key feature of the transformations and adjustments of current processes of globalisation and their concomitant restructuring of European political, economic, social and cultural relations since the 1980s (Lazaridis and Williams, 2002). This has involved altered geographies of migration and also a wider range of contexts of and motivations for migration. The relationship between labour demand and supply is 'dynamic and mutually conditioning' and the persistent demand by employers in certain sectors for migrant labour can to a significant degree be explained by 'system effects' including the level of wages and conditions on offer for low-skilled work (Ruhs and Anderson, 2010: 16, 29). Ruhs and Anderson (2010) discuss how from a national policy perspective employer demand for migrant labour is treated as if it is a residual demand rather than structurally embedded in the system. This is an important distinction in our view because it in part explains the contradictory positionings about immigration adopted by politicians and policymakers ostensibly supporting the benefits of immigration for the British economy.

As a result of our research we identified the following three institutional sites as key when considering migration and social cohesion in this context of neoliberalism, individualism and post-industrialism: work and deprivation, family and housing and education; each is intimately interlocked with issues of the distribution of income and resources. We found that the changing nature of work, the configurations of work and worklessness, and labour markets and migrant settlement, could not be ignored in trying to understand the dynamics of social cohesion. There is a simultaneous demand for both low skilled and highly skilled migrant labour. And worklessness and working poverty exist alongside: the bonus culture of the financial sector, the wealth-generating knowledge economy and work-intensive cultures more generally. It is also necessary to understand the realities of refigured gender relations and their impact on the range and dynamics of family formation, demographic realignments and transformations of intimacy, place and belonging. The downgrading of the public socialisation role of schools as the market has been increasingly introduced into their operations is also a crucial issue given the dynamics of aspiration and social mixing that revolve around neighbourhood schools. All these combined to restructure the spaces of cultural and social encounter in the UK. These new spaces of work and non work, of home and work and of schooling, and transnational and global ways of working and living make many demands on the social solidarities enjoining the mosaic of everyday life in the UK.

Place

We wanted to tie together different levels of analysis in considering migration and social cohesion in the UK and so this forms part of the distinctiveness of our approach. A further connecting thread is that we operationalised place as a strategic vantage point from which to observe the emergence of harmonious and/or antagonistic social relations between long-term settled and newly arriving populations. Conceptualising the embedding of social relations within a specific spatial dimension allows us to address the increased significance of localised narratives, histories and socio-economic realities in the contemporary experiences of social cohesion. Exploring contemporary social cohesion dynamics in the UK means engaging with places, their rhythms and realities of everyday life and their politics of belonging. Place is and has always been important because most people live within a micro society of friends, family and informal relations and groups, even in an era of easy global communications, and it is all too possible to underestimate this (see Forrest and Kearns, 2001). The phenomenon of social cohesion is about the contested dynamics of getting by, getting on and getting along in everyday life. In this respect, places structurally do not pre-exist social relations, they are 'made of' them (Massey, 1994), which means that social cohesion is embedded within the complex of social relations informing 'places'. Moreover, places do not emerge historically in self-reflexive isolation, but are inherently open, 'porous' and constituted relationally as 'products of other places' (Massey, 1994: 59). In other words, social and individual experiences of place and belonging are the outcome of the interplay between several factors and layers, including 'the forces of production, the actions of groups, factors within knowledge, within ideology, within the domain of representations as well as the networks and pathways which facilitate the exchange of material things and information' (Lefebvre, 1991: 77). Thus, researching social cohesion means researching the complex of socio-economic relations which define a 'place'.

The structural complexity and interrelatedness of 'place' was deeply transformed by the combined forces of post-industrialism, globalisation and neoliberalism and their reconfiguration of pre-existing livelihoods, identities and social relations. Since the early 1970s, the coupling of the rise of the knowledge economy with the de-localisation of production renegotiated established places and the systems of socio-economic dynamics and relations underpinning them. In order to capture the extent and interconnectedness of these dimensions and transformations place needs to be conceptualised 'as a complex, tangled mosaic of superimposed and interpenetrating nodes, levels, scales, and morphologies' (Brenner, 2004: 66). The hegemony of neoliberal ideologies and policies restructured the welfare state and reduced the associated opportunities of social support and coincided with the transformation of existing ideologies of social solidarity and political participation.

What all of these dynamics point to is the renewed emergence of locality as a forum of contestation, 'de-politicised and privatised' (Bauman, 1999: 107) yet political. In fact, localist discourses subsume and express rhythms and realities of everyday life emerging at the intersection of locally strategic categories, such as class, education, gender, race, faith, ethnicity, and so on, and informing what it takes 'to be local' (Willis, 1977). Recent research on the UK confirms that age, class and where we live are more key to limiting or assisting our life chances than either ethnicity or religion (Thomas and Dorling, 2007). Place affects our access to jobs and public services (especially education), our access to shopping and culture, our level of personal security and the availability of medical services (Dreier et al., 2004). Thus economic segregation, age and place may impact more strongly on social cohesion than the existence of any 'ethnic clusters'. Within localist discourses and practices the entitlement to social and spatial mobility becomes implicitly re-politicised in new forms and therefore emerges as a key category of confrontation, as 'the poor have to put up with that from which others can move' and 'locatedness becomes a way of speaking class indirectly, but spatially, through geography and physicality' (Skeggs, 2004: 50). In the process, locality, mobility and cohesion emerge as key discourses expressing the intersection of race, ethnicity, gender, faith and class underpinning existing hierarchies of power and belonging.

The emphasis on place as a major theme is also important for another reason. As we will see in the analysis of social cohesion dynamics in, for example, deprived inner city estates, the representation of specific places as homogeneous, bounded and immobile is currently a way in which class-based distinctions are reproduced and invisibilised by being translated into a spatial metaphor. The advent of neoliberalism's de-regulationist ethos has therefore produced a fragmentation and polarisation of the social experiences of place and mobility. The study of social cohesion needs to address the extent to which the structural porosity, openness and connectedness of any 'place' are acknowledged publicly and privately by both long-term settled residents and new arrivals. This is in order to understand the way the recognition of the structural porosity and connectedness of place informs local politics of belonging and experiences of cohesion.

The welfare state: Sustainability and privileged entitlements

Debates about immigration and social cohesion are rarely separate from discussion about the principles of welfare provision and pressures on public services. In the current era competition for work between migrants and the long-term settled continues to receive attention, in the media and in the protests of some workers, but perhaps even more critically the basis of expressed antagonism also centres on competition between 'communities' for access to welfare support and public services, including education and housing. The basis of collective belongings in this era of rapid socio-economic transformations is frequently problematised in relation to the funding and delivery of public services. Racialised hostility and community divisions are seen as at least in part related to questions about perceptions of fairness and entitlements in the allocation of scarce resources within the welfare state (for example, Goodhart, 2004, Dench et al., 2006). Among service providers recent surveys (Pillai et al., 2007; Ford, 2007) showed that difficulties were rated highest in the provision of affordable housing, in schools (the turnover of children and the difficulties in teaching those with different languages and cultures were cited) and in health (due to increases in GP caseloads and in the expanded traffic through many A&E departments of hospitals). Paradoxically the reformation and expansion of provision of these services under the New Labour government was one of the processes that drove heightened requirements for migrant labour in the 2000s.

David Goodhart's (2004) argument that Britain is becoming too diverse achieved a lot of publicity in 2004 because he was focusing in particular on ethnic diversity and its undermining of an implicit national contract about the welfare state. The growing ethnic diversity of Britain was threatening to undermine its social cohesion and specifically for Goodhart the values of solidarity that underpin the welfare state whose distributive mechanism, he argued, depends on people agreeing to its operation on the basis that the people receiving benefits are 'like themselves'. He defines citizenship not as an abstract idea of rights and obligations but as something 'we' are born into arguing that when politicians refer to the British people they are talking about 'a group of people with a special commitment to one another'. This position is an articulation of the dominant paradigm about social cohesion where immigrants can retain their cultural distinctiveness but must abide by British norms and values, a form of communitarianism. Rutherford (2007) comments that to sustain this argument Goodhart has to ignore a whole history of prejudices and inequalities internal to the 'British people'; and ignores that economic inequality not ethnic differences is the main driver of social and cultural divisions.

Although massive cuts are now being implemented in the public sector in the UK and the Conservative-led coalition government is determined to cut the immigration of third-country nationals (those from outside the European Union) the safe prediction is that immigration will continue. Employers are worried about caps on skilled immigrants and, with an ageing population, demand for labour in sectors of the economy that are not popular, such as the care industry, are bound to increase. It is also clear that introducing measures for a cap on immigration or arguments about the economic need for a continuous supply of immigrants if Britain is to be 'open for business' will not have a placatory impact upon those sections of the public most exercised about immigration. These are often (former) Labour voters concerned about the reshaping of the welfare system and its emphasis on getting people off benefits and into work at a time when jobs are disappearing and immigrants are perceived as coming in and taking what jobs there are. This was the heart of the infamous exchange between the Prime Minister, Gordon Brown, and Mrs Gillian Duffy, a Labour supporter, during the 2010 General Election:

> **Brown**: But they shouldn't be doing that, there is no life for people on the dole anymore, if you're unemployed you've got to go back to work. At six months –
>
> **Duffy**: You can't say anything about the immigrants because you're saying you're – but all these eastern Europeans coming in, where are they flocking from?
>
> **Brown**: A million people come in from Europe, but a million British people have gone into Europe, you do know there's a lot of British people staying in Europe as well. So education, health and helping people, that's what I'm about.
>
> **Duffy**: I hope you keep to it.
>
> (*Timesonline*, 28 April 2010)

The exchange became infamous because Brown later referred to her as 'bigoted'. Perhaps his real mistake was not to listen carefully. She was correctly identifying immigrants from the European Union both as ones who could not be stopped by government and alluding to it being immigrants who had filled many of the low-skilled jobs available (see Balls, 2010 for a Labour *mea culpa* on the subject). Many people such as Mrs Duffy are concerned about local changes in their neighbourhoods, the erosion of service provision and the vagaries of the lower end of the labour market and they are aware that a cap on immigration does not deal with mobility within the EU. In this book we will discuss the scenarios which do appear to give rise to changes in peoples' understandings and responses to immigration locally.

Layered histories of immigration and contemporary multiculture

Another major theme of the book that assists us in identifying how people form their understandings about immigration is the focus on how previous immigrations are perceived/experienced and how this informs the contemporary moment of immigration and settlement and the dynamics of social cohesion in different places. We are particularly interested in the layered histories of migration, and historically constituted diaspora spaces, that is the spaces of multiculture encounter (Brah, 1996; Gilroy, 2004). This historical perspective we view as a vital lens of analysis for understanding migration, cohesion and society. Given the focus on the UK this involves our engaging with Britishness and belonging in an explicitly historical manner. Our approach is based on recognising the historical importance and contemporary reverberations of two projects in the formation of the nation state: the multinational state (the United Kingdom of Great Britain and Northern Ireland) and the British Empire. We argue that the formative influence of these two projects on Britishness and belonging, and their unravelling since the 1950s, is an important context for understanding the different positionalities and identifications of the long-term settled population. This approach also entails the consideration of the limitations and possibilities of other ethno-national identifications such as Englishness, Scottishness, Welshness, the specificity of being from Northern Ireland and a range of other ethno-national hyphenated identifications. Adopting this approach is a direct attempt to avoid representing what might appear as 'new' phenomena as isolated from historical processes. A historical perspective within the social sciences should have as one of its aims the explication of structures, processes and categories which are currently 'taken for granted'. We are therefore utilising the memories of our participants in the research in order to counter continual processes of 'forgetting'. Just as there are specific cultural memories of and about different groups, different immigrations and different places, so there are also proactive processes of 'forgetting' about specific groups, about past immigrations and about the history of particular places. In particular there appears to be an active process of forgetting emigration.

Migration in most people's minds equates with immigration but occasionally in recent years emigration has featured as part of a discourse about unwelcome changes:

> Over the past nine years, much of Britain has been transformed. At the heart of it has been Labour's decision to abandon our borders and encourage mass immigration from all over the world. ...
> Neighbourhoods have been transformed almost overnight. Longstanding residents, including – often especially – those from the settled immigrant communities, feel threatened. They become strangers in the place they grew up.
> They aren't racist ... They just didn't vote for this and weren't told it was going to happen ... Is it any wonder so many people are turning their backs on Britain? They are convinced Britain has turned its back on them.
> (Littlejohn, *Daily Mail*, 28 July 2006: 15)

The argument being advanced here is that emigration results from immigration; in this way a solid link is established between the 'loss of Britons' and the arrival of immigrants. To put these remarks in context, in the year Littlejohn was writing 398,000 people emigrated, 53 per cent of whom were British citizens; this rose to 427,000 emigrants in 2008 of whom 40 per cent were British. An estimated 368,000 people emigrated from the UK in 2009; the drop from 2008 was due to a decrease in the number of British and EU citizens leaving the UK for at least a year. An estimated 567,000 people arrived to live in the UK in 2009. This is not significantly different to the previous year (590,000 in 2008). Long-term immigration to the UK had been at similar levels for the previous five years. By the year ending June 2010 (the latest year for which data are available) an estimated 572,000 people had entered the UK on a long-term basis while 346,000 emigrated. The net migration figure has been increasing since December 2008 (when net migration was 163,000), caused in the main by declining emigration. The scale of these flows is significant in both directions. Emigration has historically been a major feature of UK migratory movements but rarely discussed in terms of social and economic transformations but rather it is linked to the negative effects of immigration.

For many people, therefore, migration is a key indicator, and often the scapegoat, of social change. In Britain it often occurs in periods of uncertainty involving economic expansion, reconstruction or re-structuring and with political transformations such as independence for former

British colonies and the 'end of empire'. We emphasise the importance of understanding social cohesion and the nation through the formation and (re)formulation of prevailing narratives of belonging, obligation and identity. These narratives inform the way social heterogeneity, resulting from social and geographical mobilities and the porousness of multiculture spaces of encounter, is managed in different places and at different levels, encompassing the global, the national and the local dimensions.

The research and methods

Our confidence in our findings and the conclusions we draw from them derives from the research methods we used and their scope. Using qualitative methods, but on a large scale, we aimed to draw out the specific and comparable realities of people living in contemporary, multi-layered communities in diverse geographically spread neighbourhoods encompassing relations of deprivation and affluence, cohesion and fragmented uncertainty. Narrative accounts and ethnographic evidence from these neighbourhoods have been gathered in order to describe and understand the realities of life through the textures and weaves of memories of past migrations and the localities in which immigrants settled, new migration flows and their impact on local experiences of social cohesion and civic association across the social demarcation lines of ethnicity, gender, class and social status. In this way we trace with and elucidate from participants their reflections over time that enable the contextualisation of the ways in which social and historical processes reproduce everyday practices of both solidarity but also of differentiation.

In order to operationalise research about social cohesion it is ostensibly much easier if the research is predicated to one degree or another on a normative functionalist approach. In other words it is more straightforward if the entity to be studied can be presented as bounded and subject to the production of typologies of the characteristics of cohesion, or the domains of cohesion, or the functioning prerequisites of cohesion. What these approaches obscure, except in their most sophisticated deployment, is the messiness and unboundedness of the rhythms and realities of everyday life. The process of disaggregation required to produce a typology stands in the way of reaching an understanding of how mutually constitutive are the disaggregated factors. The chief use of typologies is in creating the illusion that complex phenomena can be measured. We have departed from this approach and are using qualitative methods to convey the relationships between the rhythms and realities of everyday life and the dynamics of social cohesion. Pahl (1991) writing nearly 20 years ago argued that there was an urgent need for more sociological research and analysis on social cohesion not so as to come up with utopian policies but to make clear what are the unwarranted assumptions of the policies that are pursued. It is in that spirit that we engaged in this research although we also sought to establish 'what works'. Our findings therefore do provide pointers that are clearly of relevance for policymakers but few of them conform to the short-term requirements of most policy formulation, driven as it is, by the electoral cycle.

Our fieldwork took place between 2005 and 2007, in the final two years of one of the longest periods of economic growth in recent British history. So while the research was undertaken at one moment in time and writing in 2010–11 the global and national contexts and circumstances have changed, we are also confident that we have produced an analysis that is relevant to these transformed times. First, because we engaged with communities under strain during boom times and all the factors we discuss are still in play. Second, because the long histories of locality we gathered also show previous instances in which individuals and communities faced recession and successfully negotiated cohesive social relations.

Our investigation of different places in the UK gives strong indications of 'what can work' as well as 'what should be avoided' in any assessment of what it takes to live in proximity with 'difference' in times of socio-economic transformation. Also prominent in why the analysis has ongoing relevance is the likelihood that immigration and emigration will continue, due to the ageing demographics of most mature Western societies. However, the fundamental plank of our argument is that the crucial parameters of the social cohesion problematic are a constant feature of societies, and this involves response to conflict rather than avoiding conflict in understanding how people live together. In discussing cohesion, migration and social change we aim to bring together conversations about 'the good life' and about social changes and economic recession with conversations about multiculturalism, difference, and local, national and transnational identifications. We suggest the priorities to be kept in mind, and to be funded, in times of economic contraction in order to enable individuals and neighbourhoods to adapt and respond to change and engage productively in the on-going dynamics of social cohesion.

We aimed to understand how people are trying to make their lives work, negotiating the flows and contradictions of everyday life across borders, historical shifts, changing cultural languages, new economic circumstances and changing gender regimes. We wanted to capture the voices of new migrants and long-term residents, and the collective experiences of the neighbourhoods to which they belong. Our analysis is based on research in six places across England, Scotland and Northern Ireland – Leicester, Kilburn (north-west London), Downham (south-east London), and Peterborough in England, Dungannon in Northern Ireland and Glasgow in Scotland. In these places we explore the actual lived lives and practices of both new immigrants and the long-term settled population and through this lens consider both the dynamics of social cohesion and the relevance of community cohesion policies. In each place we established partnerships with local organisations, community groups or other non-governmental organisations, in order to implement the research. Our partner organisations assisted in contacting research participants or providing other contacts and in understanding the complexity of the histories and social dynamics of each research site. They were actively involved in the analysis and dissemination of the findings of the research.

Our combination of methods – ethnography, semi-structured key informant interviews, life narrative interviews – was designed to produce evidence-based policy recommendations grounded in our assessment of what works and when and how people do and don't get along in post-industrial society. In so doing we aimed to outline the contours of belonging and marginalisation, audit the transnational and national currencies of social capital and assess the social and human costs and benefits secured by migration. Accordingly we carried out ethnographic observation and 320 in-depth qualitative interviews across the six locations. We based our selection of interviewees on purposive sampling, trying to ensure that the broad demographics of the locality were represented. We shaped interviews that could mobilise historical memories and experiences in order to illuminate the variegated patterns of migration and the multiple rhythms of community and locality in the UK encompassing successful strategies of integration. In analysing our extensive data we addressed structural processes that need to be foregrounded when considering social cohesion (full details of the aims, sites and methods of the research are given in the appendix).

The study also assumed that in order to comprehend the relationship between social cohesion and immigration, research about new arrivals has to be integrated with understandings about those already here. To facilitate this we developed a set of descriptors for the population that enable us to avoid some of the pitfalls of other (usually) deployed terminology. The usefulness of the category 'long-term settled', already used in this introduction, rather than 'indigenous population' or 'host community', is that it encompasses all those not categorised as new immigrants and directs attention to the history and influence of different phases of immigration to the United Kingdom and the inherent heterogeneity of the 'British people'. The expression 'long-term settled' positions those who consider themselves 'the host' (but may of course be resident in the UK because of long-forgotten immigrations) equally with minority ethnic communities, who in the very use of that term or another widely used term, black and minority ethnic, are usually positioned in a subordinate role in the nation. The term 'long-term settled', therefore, attempts to give equal consideration to the different stakes and concerns within a national population characterised by a range of social divisions.

When we want to distinguish between different groups within the long-term settled we sub-divide the category into two and use the terms 'long-term settled majority ethnic' and 'long-term settled minority ethnic'. The long-term settled majority ethnic population refers to people who in other accounts might be referred to as 'the white community' or as 'the host community'. So, for example, by 'long-term settled majority ethnic' in England we mean people who the category 'White British' in the 2001 Census of England and Wales was meant to capture. We did not include in this term people who might self-identify as either 'White Irish' or 'White Other' (the other sub-divisions of the White category in the 2001 Census). The term 'long-term settled minority ethnic' refers to the people who all the other categories in the ethnic question in the 2001 Census apart from 'White British' were meant to capture (including 'White Irish' and 'White Other'). Many of these people are either those who immigrated as part of the large post-Second World War movements from the Caribbean, the Indian subcontinent and Ireland or are their children and grandchildren.

In Scotland, we use the term 'long-term settled majority ethnic' to refer to people who perceive themselves as part of the 'indigenous' population in Scotland or a foundational immigration from Ireland in the nineteenth century. The term 'long-term settled minority ethnic' is used to refer to all the long-term settled residents in Scotland who do not see themselves as part of these two groups. In Northern Ireland we were cognisant of the need to ensure that the term 'long-term settled' should encompass the Catholic/Nationalist and Protestant/Unionist/Loyalist populations and others who would not ascribe to any of these labels. Consequently we sometimes refer to 'long-term settled' meaning the person is not a new immigrant; sometimes we have specified the ethno-religious background of the person if relevant, for example, when discussing the data about belonging in the UK. We have made all these distinctions in our usage of the term 'long-term settled' to signal the deeprootedness of the heterogeneity of the UK's contemporary population.

Organisation of the book

The book is organised so that we can address the major themes discussed in this introductory chapter. Accordingly, the first chapter, 'Community Cohesion and the Backlash against Multiculturalism in the UK', revisits the common sense view about the relationship between migration, cohesion and society, especially as encapsulated in the community cohesion policies of the 2000s, examines how alternative approaches were sidelined and outlines the main critiques of community cohesion that have been advanced during the past decade. This first chapter also explores and critiques 'community' as a form of governmentality. It concludes by establishing the importance of a historical account of Britishness and belonging for understanding the relationship between migration and social cohesion in the UK; explores the possibilities and impossibilities of Britishness as a social glue and analyses New Labour's attempts to revitalise Britishness.

The second chapter, 'Social Cohesion in the New Economy', shifts focus in order to explore the cohesiveness (or otherwise) of working life from the narratives and experiences of our interviewees across the six places of our research. These narratives are shaped by different economic sectors, different labour markets and by jobs differently classified in terms of skill. In understanding the impact of work on social cohesion it is important to understand how the inequalities and polarisations brought about by neoliberalism undermine the ability of people to find agreed positive responses to the circumstances of the new economy. In our research we found an intricate response to the socio-economic challenges posed by the convergence of post-industrialism and neoliberalism. Next, in 'Place, Belonging and Social Cohesion', we explore how the post-industrial transition to a knowledge-led economy and the neoliberal re-organisation of production across the globe means that local contexts were disaggregated and reassembled in new ways. In the process, there was a fragmentation and polarisation of people's experiences of place and we explore how this has led to a different understanding of the spatial dimensions and narratives of locality and mobility. We argue that the key issue at stake in understanding dynamics of social cohesion is the degree to which the complexity of each social and cultural setting is acknowledged within predominant narratives and practices of local belonging, such as locality and convenience. People's pluralist or homogeneous experiences of belonging are resilient because they are deeply embedded in their individual and social identities. It is within this social and discursive context that new arrivals will be perceived and addressed as an opportunity or a threat.

The fourth chapter, 'Housing and the Family', investigates the complexity of the connections between the altered and altering terms of housing entitlement, belonging, conditions of settlement and rights to family life and how they mark out relations between people that are inevitably fraught and constitute challenges for social cohesion. The conditions of post-industrialism, the changing demands of work, the altering dynamics of housing markets and housing bubbles, the logics of mobility and transnational life as well as the demands of consumerism have produced many pressures on families and home making and the social connections that sustain them. However, we found that the privileging and valuing of family life was central in allowing people to navigate the post-industrial world of individualism. This was a value shared across different kinds of families and could be a resource enabling people to recognise and negotiate common conflicts and tensions structuring the places and communities they live in. In, 'Education and Social Cohesion', we focus on the role played by education settings, with particular reference to secondary schools and city academies, in the unfolding of social cohesion, by focusing on the social relations intervening between long-term resident and newly arriving people. These social relations are heavily influenced by local 'learner identities', which are rooted in the life trajectories and histories of new arrivals and long-term residents, as well as in the socio-economic realities they come from and live in. Education is deeply implicated both in the development of social cohesion and in the emergence of social tensions. There is an important interplay between education, social cohesion and local experiences of 'being young', which are informed by the local availability of opportunities and educational provision, as well as by globalised transformations of youth and discipline.

The penultimate chapter, 'Social Cohesion and the Politics of Belonging', explores experiences of belonging to Britain and understandings of social cohesion. The following questions inform this chapter: How do people express their sense of belonging in Britain? How does this impact on their experiences and understandings of social cohesion? In what ways is the arrival of new migrant groups implicated in this interplay? We argue that people's belonging to Britain and the resources they have available are structured by the parallel invisibility of Englishness and neoliberalism. This invisibility is embedded within the cultural logic of hegemony, which naturalises and produces further inequalities and differences out of diverse and already unequal places. The dissimulation of diversities and inequalities under naturalised hierarchies of Britishness and inclusion into the neoliberal knowledge economy makes it more difficult for people to be able to negotiate them in terms which they 'cohesively' deem successful and positive. The final chapter, 'Conclusions', draws the threads of our evidence and argument together.

1
Community Cohesion and the Backlash against Multiculturalism in the UK

Introduction

In this chapter we want to examine in some detail how the backlash against multiculturalism came to underpin policy formation in the UK in the first decade of the twenty-first century. Although part of a Europe-wide phenomenon there are specificities to the backlash in each national context. In the UK multiculturalism had emerged as part of the policy response to the 'riots' or 'uprisings' that punctuated the summer of 1981 in Bristol, London, Liverpool and other cities. These largely involved young people, in many instances both black and white, in street battles with the police and were first and foremost a protest against policing practices. At issue, for example, was the arbitrary reviving and use by the police of the 'Sus laws' to stop and search black youth on the street, based on the powers bequeathed to them to stop suspected persons by the Vagrancy Act of 1824. The subsequent development of multiculturalist policies, particularly in education, prompted critiques at the time especially from antiracists on the left, who argued that the policies colluded with institutionalised racism and promoted ethnic exoticism. Nevertheless in the two decades from 1981 until the civic disturbances in northern England in 2001 what developed in Britain was a model that enabled plural identities and 'helped Britain adjust to the presence of minority citizens whose difficult life experience could not ... be adequately contained under the heading "immigration"' (Gilroy, 2006: 3). Today with forms of global capitalism predominant, new ethnicities are fully commodified. 'Ethnic' food and fashion and popular cosmopolitanism are ready sites and sources of exploitation by creative industries. 'Difference' at one level has become 'good for business' but registering difference has uneven outcomes, for some a joyous inclusiveness, for some a destabilising contact with otherness, for some a reminder of the unavoidable materiality of their marginalisation (Jacobs and Fincher 1998: 13). And no amount of 'Asian chic', for example, necessarily dislodges hierarchies of racism (Huq, 2005) or of belonging.

Nevertheless in the late 1990s there was a spirit of optimism in part reflected in the election of a New Labour government in 1997 promising a 'modern Britain'. The new administration moved quickly to fulfill some key campaign pledges including establishing an inquiry into the murder of Stephen Lawrence, a black teenager killed at a bus stop in south-east London in 1993, and setting in process moves towards devolution for Scotland and Wales. The MacPherson Report about the murder of Lawrence was published in 1999 and, unlike the Scarman Report on the Brixton Riots of 1981, it identified institutionalised racism in the police force as a serious problem, one that had impeded the investigation of the teenager's killing; it recommended various measures for bringing the police under greater public control. In September 1997 referendums were held in both Scotland and Wales about devolved government in the United Kingdom; and in April 1998 the Good Friday Agreement was signed in Belfast promising the end of 30 years of 'The Troubles'. By 1998, the Scottish Parliament, National Assembly for Wales and Northern Ireland Assembly were all established by law to secure these developments. The Runnymede Trust felt it was a propitious moment to set up a commission on the Future of Multi-Cultural Britain; and although not a government initiative its deliberations were launched by the Home Secretary, Jack Straw, in 1998. On the face of it then it could come as some surprise to record that at a political level in the first decade of the twenty-first century multiculturalism came under attack in the UK as never before. This chapter sets out to explore the complexity of this conundrum.

A crucial site of the backlash against multiculturalism is 'community' and its relation to the nation. For the past 200 years national myths have shaped understandings of 'community' at a society-wide level (Anderson, 1991). These nationally imagined structures came under pressure both from the fluidity of global connections and the resurgence of the claims of the local (Brah, 2002). Bearing these influences and others discussed below in mind, this chapter addresses the development under the New Labour government of 1997–2010 of community cohesion policies as part of a backlash against multiculturalism. It explores critiques of this policy framework, takes a historical approach to investigating the relationship between migration and national and local belongings in the UK, and looks at the attempted revitalisation of Britishness under New Labour; and the continuance of this policy agenda under a new government.

The development of community cohesion policies

During the period of New Labour rule there were numerous reports that traversed and re-traversed the territory of immigration, integration and cohesion, many of them commissioned by government departments, others the product of NGO, think tank and academic endeavour. Two stand out, however, as landmarks in their very different ways: The Parekh Report (commissioned by the Runnymede Trust, 2000), and the Cantle Report (commissioned by the Home Office, 2001). The second of these, the Cantle Report became enormously influential in both central and local government discourses and practices, whereas the first, the Parekh Report, received a very hostile reception in the press and from the Home Secretary. Below we outline the main tenets of the Parekh and Cantle reports and consider why their fates were different in terms of reception by politicians and the media and what implications we draw from this.

The Parekh Report, *The Future of Multi-Ethnic Britain*, was the result of two years of deliberations by the Commission on the Future of Multi-Ethnic Britain. Its remit was to 'analyse the current state of multi-ethnic Britain and to propose ways of countering racial discrimination and disadvantage and making Britain a confident and vibrant multicultural society at ease with its rich diversity' (Parekh, 2000: viii). The Parekh Report argued that differences matter profoundly. But that differences are not necessarily polarising as many people live 'in between' or with more than one identity. The commission's aim was to generate a critical social imaginary that could move British society from *laissez faire* 'multicultural drift' to a 'purposeful process of change' (p. 11). The report observed that a politics of recognition had developed alongside the struggle for equality and racial justice because racism had not disappeared and thus assimilation had proved impossible. This was depicted as one aspect of the complex, multifaceted, postnational world in which national allegiance is now played out. The report concluded that the 'need for equality and difference, and the need to respect the rights of both individuals and communities, appear beyond the compass of existing political vocabularies' (p. 37). It suggested that a hyphenated Britishness was probably the best resolution for many to express their identity but that there was still the difficult obstacle that 'Britishness as much as Englishness, has systematic, largely unspoken racial connotations' (Parekh, 2000: 38) and unless deep-rooted antagonisms to racial and cultural difference can be defeated and written out of the national story then the idea of a multicultural post-nation would remain an empty promise.

The Parekh Report was a carefully calibrated document but nevertheless it caused a furore when published. Ostensibly this was because of the reference to the racial connotations inherent in Britishness. The media response to the report, led by the *Daily Telegraph* the day before it was published was highly charged: 'Straw Wants to Rewrite Our History: British is a Racist Word, says Report' (*Daily Telegraph*, 10 October 2000). McLaughlin and Neal (2007) observe that depending on government patronage, with the Home Secretary launching both the commission's work and its final report, proved a disastrous strategy as this was in tension with the commission's 'intellectual ambition to shift understandings of race and nation and the ways of being British' (p. 922). In suggesting a re-imagined multicultural Britain, that represented a post-national multiculturalism, based on 'a community of communities' the report was distinguishing itself from cruder versions of multiculturalism as extant in many local authority policies on 'ethnic minorities'. The reception of the Parekh Report showed that the public sphere is both racialised and patrolled by a powerful conservative press hostile to any problematising of national identity through the lens of race and ethnicity (McLaughlin and Neal, 2007: 924). The media response also 'reveals a version of British nationalism that imagines the nation as already inherently multicultural' (Fortier, 2005: 561). In fact claims of being a 'mongrel people', benefiting from the 'inter-breeding of different peoples and cultures', have frequently characterised statements about the strengths of the British/English; this goes back as far as David Hume's two-volume history of England published in the eighteenth century where, for example, this trait is explicitly contrasted with the barbarism of the Irish (Hickman, 1995). Charges of racism therefore cut to the heart of imaginings of Britishness.

While for some on the left the Parekh Report was viewed as a welcome progression, the dominance of the community cohesion paradigm during the subsequent decade can be seen as constituting a refutation of the approach it encapsulated. A key moment for the public diagnosis of multiculturalism as problematic and for the branding of cohesion policies as community cohesion was the publication of the Report of the Independent Review Team (IRT) on civic disturbances in Burnley, Bradford and Oldham in 2001 (Cantle Report, 2001).

The government had commissioned the report and it led to the use of a particular language for talking about 'diversity' that located the problems at the margins of the polity. This discourse had its origins in New Labour's policy reviews of the 1990s (Pitcher, 2009), and they in turn had a close relationship to the form of corporatism that had characterised the oppositional Heseltine wing of the Conservative party during the 1980s (Kellner, 1990). The specific terms of reference of the Cantle Report were to consult 'on the issues that need to be addressed in developing confident, active communities and social cohesion' (quoted in Pitcher, 2009: 87). The lessons drawn from the Report and the policy framework it proposed were rapidly absorbed by central government, local government and related agencies in a push to replace previous policies of multiculturalism (Worley, 2005).

Broadly the community cohesion framework rests on the following four assumptions:

- migration is a fact of life and greater diversity is inevitable;
- problems are posited in relations between differing, culturally based, homogeneous communities/groups;
- segregation is perceived as having a strong negative impact on inter-communal relations because lack of contact between communities leads to ignorance and irrational fears;
- mutual understanding and a shared set of values are much more likely to emerge from interchange based on shared experiences at all levels.

(Cantle 2008)

The contemporary challenge is therefore posed as being about making multi-faith, multi-ethnic and multicultural communities work. Inbuilt is a notion that they cannot necessarily work without intervention, especially in deprived areas. Cantle's analysis sees the 1950s and 1960s as a period of dramatic change that ensured that the 'immigration problem' was more than ever one of 'race'. He locates Britain as one of the 'white nation states' that were mono-cultural until 50 years ago, at which point they were transformed into 'white host communities'. Governments responded to the concerns of the 'host white community' in Britain by passing a series of Immigration Acts and to the evidence of discrimination and the demands of immigrant communities by passing a series of Race Relations Acts. In retrospect, it is argued, the problem lay in the very limited attempts to 'promote good race relations' by working with the white community to improve their understanding of black and minority ethnic communities, especially when compared with the efforts made to include ethnic minorities within the equalities agenda. Thus little attempt was made to influence the underlying attitudes and values upon which direct and indirect discrimination were based, once a law was passed to outlaw them in 1976, and little thought was given as to how the host community and the new minorities might relate to each other or how mutual respect and understanding might develop. Consequently, Cantle argues that what the country needs is a new paradigm to help conceptualise this change and to develop policy and practical responses to it (Cantle, 2008).

Community cohesion policies are therefore designed to plug this gap in social policy. Community cohesion is to be achieved by creating shared experiences and values which produce attitudinal change and assuage the 'fear of difference'. This approach is counter-posed in particular to multiculturalism seen as entrenching separation and reinforcing differences on the basis of the evidence of the disturbances in 2001 (Cantle, 2001). Achieving a consensus within a community cohesion framework depends on three factors: breaking down the separateness between minority and majority communities and between different minority communities; the creation of mutual trust and a common sense of belonging through constant interaction and shared experiences; and a clear political will to reach a consensus on what level of 'difference' is accepted and which differences are acceptable.

The idea of 'parallel lives' that the Cantle Report evoked was, however, widely taken up. Even though in other cities the report team visited – Birmingham, Leicester, Sheffield – they found a greater sense of cohesion, others still assumed that more thorough research 'would have shown only a marginal difference' in cohesion existed in these places compared with the three northern English towns (Salmon, 2002). In 2002 a formal definition of community cohesion was arrived at as a result of collaboration between the Local Government Association, the office of the Deputy Prime Minister, the Home Office and the Commission for Racial Equality and was issued as *Guidance on Community Cohesion* (2002). This definition states that a cohesive community is one where:

- There is a common vision and a sense of belonging for all communities;
- The diversity of people's backgrounds and circumstances are appreciated and positively valued;
- Those from different backgrounds have similar life opportunities;

- Strong and positive relationships are being developed between people from different backgrounds in the workplace, in schools and within neighbourhoods.

The *Guidance* became one of the most well-used source documents on community cohesion and was updated and republished in 2004 (Cantle, 2008). Commitment to community cohesion policies soon followed from bodies such as the Audit Commission and the British Council, and an injunction on schools to promote community cohesion was in place by 2007.

What was it about the Cantle Report that made it acceptable to government compared with the Parekh Report? It was commissioned by a government department to provide analysis and solutions of problems identified by government although that is not in and of itself a sufficient guarantee of impact. In our view the welcome it received lies in the set of assumptions about societal cohesiveness that underpins its predominant framing of issues about migration and cohesion in Britain. This set of assumptions underpins specific understandings of the nation, the polity and notions of community and as such underpin discussions about difference. The report's analysis and recommendations enabled the 'ringfencing' of perceived dysfunctional communities – inward looking minority ethnic enclaves, Muslims in general, deprived communities – through its deployment of a new language of diversity and individualism. Within New Labour discourse the realm of culture 'becomes the terrain upon which citizen-subjects will be managed and produced, inducing a form of citizenship that is essentially in harmony with the economy' (Finlayson, 2003: 155). Because in important areas the contemporary British state has rescinded its commitments to the post-war social contract, emphasis has shifted onto the orientations, obligations and duties of citizens to lend greater coherence to the social fabric of the nation (Pitcher, 2009: 46).

The Cantle Report was published in December 2001, so while the civic disturbances in Northern England took place in the spring and summer of that year the reception of the report was in a post-9/11 world. As the disturbances in northern England were largely seen to be the result of the cleavages in those towns between two settled populations – English and Asian – it fed into a degree of paranoia that existed in the aftermath of the attacks in the USA in September. Strong supporters of communitarianism were strategically placed in government departments and articulated fears about growing polarisation of the population into sharply defined groups. This is based on fears that instead of unifying under wide banners people now tended to commit themselves to groups that press for changes on behalf of their exclusive group interests. And this is held responsible for the erosion of the social fabric that holds people together (Tam, 2007). The extent of the Cantle Report's influence was confirmed by a rethink at the Commission for Racial Equality (CRE). The Director of Policy at the CRE reinforced that institution's rethink recently by arguing that in the past 'we' have emphasised what divides us over what unites us, and tolerance of diversity has led to the effective isolation of communities. The wish of the CRE as it became part of the new Commission on Equality and Human Rights (CEHR), was to create and sustain a Britain where diversity is celebrated but where difference does not have to mean division and therefore they advocate a strong integration policy based on core values rather than ancestral values (Johnson, 2007).

In July 2005 one of the responses to the bombings of three London tube trains was the setting up in June 2006 of the Commission on Integration and Cohesion (CIC) by the Department of Communities and Local Government. The then Secretary of State for Communities, Ruth Kelly, announced the commission saying its origins lay in a concern with the 'unease of white Britons'; and that the nation had moved on from a period of near consensus on the value of multiculturalism to one where a debate was required about the role multiculturalism had played in encouraging residential segregation along ethnic and religious lines. The remit the commission was given was to consider how local areas can make the most of the benefits delivered by increasing diversity – and also to consider how they can respond to the tensions it can sometimes cause. It was tasked with developing practical approaches to building communities' own capacity to prevent and manage tensions. The CIC report published the following year adopted a different approach to that of the Cantle Report. It argued that cohesion policy was relevant to every locality and not just those that had been the recipient of immigration and exhibited the characteristics of fractured communities. There is far less emphasis on the problems of segregation that were identified in Northern English towns in 2001.

The CIC set out proposals for building integration and cohesion at a local level based on four principles: a sense of shared futures which entails emphasising what binds communities together rather than what divides them; a new model of rights and responsibilities making clear a sense of citizenship at national and local level and the obligations that go along with membership; an ethics of hospitality that involves a new emphasis on mutual respect and civility; a commitment to equality that sits alongside the need to deliver visible social justice and prioritise transparency and fairness and build trust in institutions that arbitrate between groups. Their definition of an integrated and cohesive community when compared with the *Guidance* issued in 2002 lays greater stress on a 'bottom-up' approach to the construction of a shared vision for a neighbourhood or city and also emphasises the importance of recognising the contribution of individuals and communities to a locality. However, in other respects it summons up similar core ideas and aspirations with a stress on the need for 'people from different backgrounds' to have similar life opportunities and to have strong and positive relationships. The CIC report received a very positive response from government including a statement as to how each of its 65 recommendations were going to be implemented or progressed (Blears, 2008).

Fortier (2010) comments on the shift that the CIC report represents compared with the Cantle Report of six years earlier starting with the positioning of diversity:

> No longer an asset to be celebrated, as it was in earlier definitions of community cohesion, diversity is now more ambivalently recognized as inevitable, desirable and valuable, while it is also seen as disturbing sign of change and a potential threat to stability, peaceful cohabitation, cohesion or safe living ... diversity has shifted from an asset to a potential source of conflict and is the basis of a new identity crisis and question about what binds the nation together.
>
> (Fortier, 2010: 24)

The commission's own name paired together integration and cohesion and in so doing identified Britain's official policy; its report projected a future of shared belonging cast in an 'anti-multiculturalist, post-historical future where there is no "broad civic value in the ability to live with difference"' (Fortier, 2010: 24). It is this ability to live with difference that we set out to investigate as part of attempting to answer the questions: 'do people have to get on well together?' and 'how do people live together in times of economic and social transformation?' Based on our research we argue that shared values or a shared vision are not necessarily the key feature of social cohesion or the goal to which cohesion policies should be directed. Rather it is agreed means for resolving conflicts that are essential, not necessarily formal in arrangement but importantly capable of adaptation in changing circumstances. Fundamental to this distinction is our concern with social cohesion rather than community cohesion; we explore this further in the rest of this chapter.

The discussion of the three reports above point us towards two concerns that warrant further attention: 'community' and Britishness. First, we examine the former through various critiques of community cohesion as a policy framework with the aim of analysing its underlying assumptions and their implications. Critical commentaries on community cohesion policies in Britain fall into two main areas. One is that its diagnosis of what is failing or causing problems in Britain is incorrect. These misdiagnoses are usually identified as either the destablisations resulting from rapid social change under a neoliberal economic order or insufficient recognition of the impact of race and inequalities more generally. The other type of critique is that community cohesion constitutes a governmentality programme that institutionalises a hierarchical and divisive problematisation of specific communities and latterly a new sort of intervention to produce the right type of citizen by shaping how people feel about others. Second, we move on to establish the importance of an historical account of Britishness and belonging and explore the implications of the possibilities and limitations of Britishness as a social glue and New Labour's attempts to revitalise Britishness.

Critiquing community cohesion policies: An incorrect diagnosis

Destabilisations

The world is becoming a more unpredictable place as a result of a rapid advance in social pluralism resulting from economic, social, cultural and moral transformations (Parekh 2000). So ingrained is the acknowledgement of the destabilising effects of globalisation that few would query this assessment of the potential perils of social pluralism. Bauman (1999), for example, emphasises that the truly potent powers of today are essentially extraterritorial, while the sites of political action remain local and therefore there is a disconnect between the location of determinant social forces and decision-making from the places where the limits of sovereignty are drawn and the essential premises of political endeavours are decided. McKibbin (2001) and other commentators on the left accept that since the late 1970s traditional forms of cohesion have unquestionably eroded due to the social decay and 'ungovernability' of Britain. Society has become more 'democratic' and therefore people are less willing to perform traditional roles or obey traditional authorities; increasing family instability has surfaced which the British welfare state is not well equipped to deal with; and the strength of individualist ideology under New Labour has served to highlight that older forms of cohesion depended more than is now recognised on a large industrial working-class, a strong trade union movement and a broadly accepted hierarchy. McKibbin also cites a decline in the legitimacy of the British state as exemplified in the processes of devolution as destabilising. This critique emanating from the British left is broadly in line with Putnam's analysis of the United States, in that the third quarter of the twentieth century is identified as the period in which a form of recognisable cohesion still pertained, and since then transformations have produced instability.

Lynne Layton (2008) argues that in the past 30 years neoliberal economic policies have created enormous disparities between the rich and the poor; and that this situation of gross inequality together with neoconservative foreign policy and the experience of 11 September 2001, have created a traumatogenic environment (Hollander and Gutwill 2006). Writing about the USA she says government has increasingly retreated from providing any functions that might contain anxiety and trauma; on the contrary, in concert with the media and corporate policies government has done its best to keep people frightened. Fear has led to splitting and projective identification, and large segments of the population, traumatised in different ways depending on social location, have taken up polarised positions of 'us' versus 'them'. Instead of mourning the losses produced by government or corporate policies or challenging these policies most subjects have sought refuge in the narcissism of minor differences and/or an intensified individualism. It is no accident that the very decades marked by neoliberal policies have been those in which virulent backlash movements against women, immigrants, and racial and sexual minorities have arisen. This is neoliberal change as not only destabilising but also as polarising, and migration is frequently cited as at the heart of unwelcome changes.

Elements of Layton's type of analysis have also been applied in the UK. Rutherford (2007) has written of the way in which asylum seekers are reminders by their very presence of change and disruption. The loss of a previous way of life personified in the asylum seeker echoes 'our own experience of loss'. One impact of the process of individualisation characteristic of neoliberalism, he argues, is that the idea that 'we're all in this together' has been superseded by the belief that survival and getting on is down to 'me alone' and deprivation of a common life is the real lack; we live insecurely in the world to the degree that strangers create anxiety and hatred. Also the contradiction is that New Labour's

Britishness project, of which more below, represented an effort to promote a sense of social cohesion that was steadily eroded by the then government's own commitments to privatisation and welfare reform (Pitcher, 2009). In the current period, as we have already noted, part of the 2010 coalition government's message in support of their austerity programme is to strongly assert that the whole nation, 'our country', is in the effort together of reducing the debt produced by the 2008 financial crisis. This is a high-stakes gamble as various independent bodies, including the Institute for Fiscal Studies, have demonstrated how the June 2010 budget and subsequent cuts in benefits and public services will load the relative weight of contribution to clearing the debt on the least affluent. The deployment of a 'national' message here amply demonstrates the contradictory need of neoliberal policies to engage a collective message in order to gain the consent that will enable the restitution of the financial system and the permeation of market philosophies to every aspect of public life; the very forces that have produced a range of destablilisations and fears in everyday lives.

Racism and inequalities

The Cantle report has been critiqued as a return to the misplaced preoccupation with cultural difference that typified much policy formation in the 1960s–1980s. The case is that rather than attending to long-standing issues of racist exclusion from mainstream institutions, racial harassment and racial segregation, the Cantle Report prioritises assimilationist policies such as the 'statement of allegiance' and emphasises integrationist policies, interpersonal relations and inter-group activities between culturally defined groups (Ben Tovim, 2002). The analysis of what lay behind the civic unrest in Bradford, Burnley and Oldham in 2001 in Cantle's report (2001) has been strongly questioned and the case made that it should be understood, in a context of post-industrial decline, more as a demand for full inclusion as Britons rather than as a story of parallel lives (Amin, 2002; also Khundani, 2007). This critique of the Cantle Report resonates with a more general charge that the politics and practices of racism and discrimination are often underplayed in initiatives promoting bridging social capital. To the extent that community cohesion strategies address new immigrants they may ignore those whose experiences include discrimination, extreme poverty, oppressive living conditions, crime and lack of access to basic services (Hope Cheong et al., 2007: 33). Racism and threat perceptions may permeate the bridging relationships that are deemed to be important for building a cohesive society and this means that the view that social capital is reparative of fractured social cohesion created by ethnic diversity and immigration can be simplistic. Gilroy (2006) suggests that for Britain to develop durable and habitable multiculture still depends upon working through the legacies of departed empire. The chief obstacle to this is what he calls postcolonial melancholia, a condition that involves an inversion of victimhood amid 'the loss of a fantasy of omnipotence' (Gilroy 2004: 108), with post-colonial immigrants as constant reminders of an imperial past. Due to their neglect or downplaying of racism, community cohesion policies are criticised for their focus on the inadequacies of minority ethnic groups rather than on the need for wider social reform, and racism remains conceptualised as primarily the outcome of individual prejudice and ignorance (Alexander, 2007; see also Burnett, 2004).

Cantle (2008) has responded to many of these charges by arguing that community cohesion is not an attack on ethnic minorities but is concerned with segregation; further that the policy and the various reports that established it as government policy did not neglect structural issues and all noted the lack of equal opportunities for parts of the population and the poverty and disadvantages of many of the areas they were investigating. However, community cohesion policies do not sufficiently acknowledge the way in which 'race' is a deep part of everyday 'national' culture. The policies do not get to grips with the ways in which the ordinariness of the complexities and anxieties of 'race' are embedded in policies of tolerance and cohesion rather than being located solely on the extreme edges of hatred and intolerance (Lewis, 2004). The turn towards tolerance, inclusion and diversity which the community cohesion framework characterises itself as representing is exemplified in its disaffiliation from the more overt forms of racism and racial violence associated with the white working class BNP activist and in that process the latter is perceived as shameful. The consequence of the desire to eradicate this shame is to push the dissident or racist subject outside the national community but simultaneously it differentiates between citizens along racialised identities (Fortier, 2005). A key aspect of this process is that the very act of 'hailing' people as 'ethnic' which in Britain still suggests immigrant or 'non-white' also produces them as already suspected of dis-identification. An ideology of the visible is deployed which rests on the presumption that identities are visibly marked, so that those sharing physical resemblances will align themselves to the same community (Fortier, 2005). We would qualify this by noting that racialisation processes work in both directions, they also homogenise whiteness and in the process mask, invisibilise and underplay the hierarchies and discriminations that lie within an unethnicised whiteness. Our approach is designed to explore how layered histories of immigration inform the contemporary moment of immigration and settlement and the dynamics of social cohesion will help unpick these multiple (in)visibilisations.

Critiquing community cohesion policies: Governmentality and community

Although the term social cohesion is still regularly used, the policy framework, as we have noted, has been one of community cohesion. In this move the New Labour government eclipsed society as the focus of attention in order to target problematised groups: the marginalised poor within the majority ethnic and minority ethnic populations. Simultaneously in this move cohesion across class differences is sidelined (Forrest and Kearns, 2001) because the problematic is predominantly concerned with the alienated and impoverished 'white working class' and alienated and impoverished Pakistani and Bangladeshi 'communities' or Muslim 'communities' (especially young Asian Muslims). The wider society only hoves into view when a variety of events, for example, 'riots', or drug related killings or attempted bombings impact on and disrupt the safe and secure life the majority of the population feel they are either inhabiting or have some purchase upon. All of this is rather reminiscent of the theories of the Chicago School in the 1920s and 1930s, with its mapping of differences around supposedly stable and pregiven categories of distinction. The Chicago School's model of the city made specific assumptions about the social categories it mapped, according them measures of legitimacy, civility or authority, and in the process discursively constructing them within hierarchies of acceptability. Certain social groups were classified as 'problematic' and the spatial concentration of such groups served as an indicator of a dysfunctioning urban space (Jacobs and Fincher, 1998: 6).

An authoritative review of the literature on community sees the idea of community today as related to the search for belonging in an insecure world (Delanty, 2003). For example, the social theory of communitarianism has associated community with disadvantaged urban localities requiring government responses and civic voluntarism as in regeneration projects or health projects. What communitarianism allows is that community can be a basis of social integration, thus community is the basis for providing what neither society nor the state can provide, namely a normatively based kind of social integration rooted in associative principles of a commitment to collective good (Delanty, 2003: 192). The use of the term 'community' has therefore widened in recent years and it now embraces both a dominant notion of sociation such that we are all defined as members of communities based on places, relationships and identities, and it acts as a catch-all term for writing about problematised populations (see Clarke and Newman, 1997). What is generally defined as a cause for concern within problematic communities are the forms of sociation they entail and furthermore the structures of interaction between communities can also become problematised as they are in the Cantle report (McGhee, 2005).

What differs among the commentators on community cohesion policy is the degree to which they accept the implicit analysis of the crisis of social cohesion advanced by various government reports and agencies. For example, Khan (2007) argues that if the critics are right and multiculturalism has been encouraging separatism then we might expect more diverse areas to have high levels of bonding social capital but the evidence suggests that more diverse areas have low levels of bonding social capital as well as low levels of bridging capital (see Buonfino and Mulgan, 2006 for a similar argument). Khan argues that what matters is not simply the quantity of interactions we have with people of different backgrounds but the quality of these interactions (see also Hewstone et al., 2007). There is an implicit acceptance of a deficit model in this position that we question. McGhee (2003), on the other hand, describes building reciprocal relationships and a shared vision as unobtainable ideals, unobtainable but presumably desirable. We also find that Bauman's (2000) theories on 'liquid modernity' feed into a general framework of problematisation, by striking a note of inevitability about the negative impact of contemporary consumerism and globalism on sociality. Bauman quotes Manuel Castells's description of the split of urban populations into two polarised tiers. While the upper one is involved in the detaching experience of global flows, the lower remains territorially circumscribed. At the same time both groups lack to an equal extent the tools of sociality, necessary for dealing with the perpetual presence of strangers characterising urban life. A sociality based upon the notion of 'communities of similarity' is unable to deal with strangeness or difference, Bauman argues, and even avoids studying closer those that are considered 'same'. In time it breeds mixophobia, a reaction to difference that causes a self-perpetuating drive towards homogeneity and separation. Once it is accepted that a key requirement is to intervene to enhance community interaction or intercultural exchange the broad plane upon which community cohesion policies, for certain communities, are advanced is legitimised. Based on our UK-wide study we will outline the basis of our rejection of these various precepts.

Care has to be taken when considering not only the arguments but also the evidence presented by both community cohesion policymakers and social and political theorists. As Rogaly and Taylor (2009) suggest, the very idea of 'community' is a construction that does not necessarily reflect how people think about their relations with others in the neighbourhood where they live. 'Community identity' is constructed as much through external structural factors, government policies and institutional neglect, it is not a pre-existing, benign, natural alliance but is constructed as much by the state as by individuals (Alexander, 2007). One of the ironies of the community cohesion agenda is that it creates the idea of minority ethnic communities at the same time as it demands their disappearance and it fixes ethnic identity within these community boundaries while demanding that it should move outside them (Alexander, 2007). What we have in many ways witnessed in this first decade of the century is the development of new forms of government that underpin a new 'politics of behavior' that seek to recode citizens' values and sentiments as well as behaviour and in so doing seek to bring about cultural shifts in the population. McGhee agrees and sees all the various community cohesion programmes as doing a particular type of 'identity work' in and through social capital. They take what they define as narrow identities, perceived as reinforced by bonding social capital, and attempt to de-antagonise and broaden them out. He thinks this amounts to a reconfiguration of community from a territory of government to a means of government.

The attraction of community for government can be explained in how the concept carries with it a notion of civic obligations and moral commitments to society which produces the political effect of disburdening the state of responsibility and diluting social citizenship (Rogaly and Taylor, 2009; Delanty, 2003: 88). Community as a form of governmentality also entails strategies of social control (Pitcher, 2009). In effect community becomes a quasi-governmental discourse that facilitates new technologies of power and of social management (Rose, 1999). This is further explicated by O'Malley (cited in Gray, 2006) who argues that a particular attraction of the language of community in neoliberalism is that it locates rule in the everyday, voluntary interactions or commonalities of interest of private individuals. In this way communities are enlisted into governmental programmes to govern problems that cannot be left entirely to individuals. This gives an impression of the retreat of the state from governance and interference and in this way community formation can be an artifact of rule. Fortier (2010) argues that the project of community cohesion both relies on the 'affective subject' and seeks to shape 'affective citizens'. By this she means that an individual's personal membership of community is viewed as contingent on personal acts and feelings which are directed towards their shared, public, locally integrated lives. It is these acts and feelings which community cohesion policies seek to shape. This trajectory of public policy is therefore about achieving the conditions for the eradication of difference (and the isolation or removal of those who resist) and the suppression of conflict.

In summary, therefore, the focus on problematic communities eclipses society as the focus of attention, obscures the role of the state in constructing communities and shaping individuals' lives, and distracts attention from the inequalities resulting from deep-seated transformations driven by individualisation, post-industrialism, globalisation which shape the everyday life experiences of all the population. Singling out particular neighbourhoods as 'problem areas' or particular 'problem ethnic groups' can also perpetuate exclusion and distract attention from the causes of poverty (Rogaly and Taylor, 2009). Problematising communities also produces them and the social actors they are made of as singular, fixed, and static, which contradicts the intrinsic fluidity and porousness of people's individual and social identities. Such problematisation and blaming also diverts attention from the complex processes underway in which newly constituted communities are learning to get along within the changing realities of contemporary life, as we will demonstrate in this book.

Britishness/Englishness – national belonging and social cohesion

In the twenty-first century, right across the political spectrum, there is acknowledgement that Margaret Thatcher got it wrong when she declared there is no such thing as society, only individuals as economic units of consumption with the power of market forces and the fear of poverty holding society in a state of more or less equilibrium. The role the state is seen as playing in achieving cohesiveness is a critical factor. Some argue that the British state's ability to represent itself as the crucial factor in the maintenance of some perceived idea of social cohesion has contributed to its continuing existence (Black et al., 2001). Certainly at various times in British history the boundaries of the nation and of the imagined national community have been reconstructed, these reconfigurations may occur at times of war and other national crises, and it is notable that in the last century both migration and changes in national borders led to significant reformations of the representation of the nation and who belongs. In the 20th century the boundaries of the nation were re-inscribed in 1905, the 1920s and in the 1950/60s after respectively, the passage of the first immigration controls of the century, the granting of Irish independence and in the wake of considerable inward migration from the Caribbean, the Indian subcontinent and Ireland. After sustained new immigration from across the globe the twenty-first century has seen further attempts to reconfigure Britain and Britishness. A critical reexamination of this history helps explicate not only the continuing significance of two national projects – the multi-nation state and empire – for definitions of the limits of national belonging but also illuminates the ways in which community cohesion policies do not so much plug a gap in social policy as reconstitute for a new era ways of differentiating the population that are a historically constituted aspect of British nationalism.

The possibilities and impossibilities of Britishness as social glue

The issue of Britishness and what it represents, whether it is an identity that can continue to act as social glue, is resonant in all discussions about cohesion in the UK. The national identities of the constituent elements of the UK have a prominence in public discussion that was not apparent 50 years ago. The union of the multinational state is one of the two hegemonic projects of the British state. The other, the empire, disintegrated in the mid-twentieth century to remain semi-vivified in the Commonwealth. Now the second great project, if not at an end, is crumbling away. The impact of the waning of these two projects, both during periods of heavy immigration, cannot be underestimated in their impact on national identity. The UK has been both a multinational and multicultural state since 1707 when Scotland became formally joined to the kingdom of England and Wales (Wales had been incorporated in the sixteenth century) under the jurisdiction of the Westminster Parliament (see Kearney, 1989). In 1801 the United Kingdom of Great Britain and Ireland was declared after the more or less forced incorporation of Ireland; this was changed to the United Kingdom of Great Britain and Northern Ireland in 1927 after the secession of the Irish Free State. McKibbin recognises that this complex history of national formation and (re)formation has meant that British society is characterised by profound cultural differences, 'these differences, the absence of commonality, have historically been so wide as to make problematic historical assumptions about Britishness and the almost unique cohesion of British society' (McKibbin, 2001: ix). One of the problems for those determined on the functionality of Britishness as a social glue is Englishness, the latter is highly significant in prescribing the possibilities and impossibilities of Britishness.

The national project of empire was critical domestically both in terms of constituting and reinforcing cross-national alliances within the UK and for the formation of cross-class alliances within each nation. Sharing the spoils of empire was crucial for the social and political elites and especially with respect to Scotland. Scotland was allowed full trading access to England's colonies as a consequence of the 1707 Act of Union and the wealth brought back to Scotland during the eighteenth and nineteenth centuries transformed its economy (Maan, 1992). England shared these spoils confident that advantages of numbers, wealth and territory would ensure English dominance within the United Kingdom and the colonies (Crick, 1991). Ideas of race and hierarchy were a constant feature of much of the public discourse in the domestic arena in the nineteenth century as well as in various parts of the empire (Hall, 2000) and a myth of class monogenesis developed linked to the image of the 'freeborn Englishman' (Cohen, 1988). The franchise of the freeborn English man was gradually extended to an emergent working class as members of a superior island race invited to 'distance themselves from all those 'Others' who lacked such credentials' (Hickman, 1995: 37).

This briefest of excursions into the formation of the multi-nation state and the historical resonance of empire in the domestic arena is meant to give some indication of the complexity to which McKibbin refers. One of the consequences was that there was a complex interaction between forms of governance and the management of ethno-national relations which had a direct significance for developments in the metropolitan centre as the impact of the Indian National Uprising (1857), the Morant Bay rebellion in Jamaica (1865) and the Fenian rebellion in Ireland (1867), which included bombings in England, were to demonstrate. These events led to constitutional and institutional responses as well as intertwining elements of social subordination, cultural alienness and political threat in the framing of black Caribbeans, Indians and Irish Catholics. These histories and the understandings, discourses and contestations they gave rise to are not locked in a repository labelled 'past' but continue in circulation, sometimes more foregrounded than at other times. When in the twenty first century recourse is made to Britishness or 'being British' in anticipation of a route to social cohesion these histories and discourses need to be borne in mind, but this is not always the case.

One prominent supporter of multiculturalism, Tariq Modood (2005), argues that national identity should be the vehicle for common belonging in Britain. For him this means reimagining or reforming 'our national identity, our Britishness' so that everyone can be a part of it without having to deny or privatise other identities that are important to different Britons. Modood emphasises that liberal weddedness to a clear public/private split, with religion confined to the private sphere, masks its hegemonic dominance of the public domain and his critique of the impact of radical secularism is very well made. But he does not examine how an ostensibly plural, civic identity, Britishness masks the hegemonic dominance of Englishness. Or, it has until recently. When Modood is addressing Britain he is actually considering England. He differentiates Britain from the rest of Europe and believes because of its characteristics of tolerance multiculturalism in this one country is possible. The only problem for him lies when he acknowledges that 'English' is a closed ethnicity. It might be possible to be Asian-British but never Asian-English; therefore he has to put his faith in Britishness. Parekh (2007) broadly agrees with this view that puts being British centre stage. He sees being British as one of a range of a person's identities, hence Britishness must be open and loosely scripted, able to accommodate plurality and allow people to be British in their own ways.

Neither Modood or Parekh problematise communities; rather, from their own perspectives, they are suggesting different ways through which to make multiculturalism work. Nevertheless in advocating Britishness as a critical instrument for this task their arguments ignore the salience of the history of the UK and the uneasy union that has always existed as far as all the 'sub-nations' except England are concerned. Although we note that the Parekh Report (2000) did call for a re-thinking of the national story to include such questions as: 'how are the histories of England, Scotland and Wales understood by their people?' and 'what do the separate countries stand for, and what does Britain stand for?' In Scotland during the 1980s a partial answer had already been provided. Throughout that decade most people consistently voted against key policies of the Conservative government and eventually elicited devolved government as Westminster's response in order to maintain the Union. It is also important to bear in mind that the group of people for whom Britishness may have least resonance now, because of the unraveling of the two nation building projects, is the White British majority ethnic group in England, many of whom would far rather the category 'English' featured on the Census ethnic origin question as opposed to British (their wish was granted in 2011). Recent research conducted in southern England shows how many people in this group do not feel they belong to 'the British community' and most are sceptical that such a thing exists anymore (Clarke et al., 2007). Does this necessitate returning to Mann's (1970) observation that it is expedience rather than value consensus that holds things together or sustains societies in liberal democracies? He allowed that alongside pragmatism, manipulative socialisation, voluntary deference, nationalism and other elements of normative integration may play a role. In our consideration of the politics of belonging in the UK we will revisit these issues.

New Labour and the attempted revitalisation of Britishness

Tony Blair, in the final months of his premiership, articulated New Labour's stance that integration was not about culture or lifestyle but about values. In this way the then government argued that their policy did not represent assimilation because it was tolerant of different cultural traditions. The emphasis on values was justified because the prime task for the state is integrating citizens not people and thus the issue becomes – does everyone share British values? Core British values, Blair argued, consist of tolerance, solidarity and equality. Citizens have the right to differ from each other but have to express these differences in a manner that respects shared values and practices. Citizens have duties – such as obedience to the law and to live by democratic principles – and these duties take precedence over any culture or faith. Being British could be summed up, he concluded, as: 'the right to be different, the duty to be integrated' (Blair, 2006). Blair's definition of Britishness is in terms of universal liberal values rather than a re-telling of the national story. This position is broadly that also of Trevor Phillips, Chair of the Equalities and Human Rights Commission (Phillips, 2005), of the next prime minister, Gordon Brown (Brown, 2006) and indeed the subsequent one, David Cameron (Cameron, 2011). But is it enough to define Britishness in terms of these liberal values without re-examining the issues that these questions raise? Implicit in these formulations is a linking of the agenda on social cohesion and integration of immigrants with that of combating terrorism given that resulting speeches and policies often make specific demands on Muslim communities.

In the effort to reassure the long term settled that their localities are not being transformed out of all recognition citizenship measures have been introduced in order to accommodate newcomers to 'British' ways. But these are expressed in terms of liberal democracy and cannot be named in a particularistic manner. The irony being that these universalistic terms are not different 'here' (Britain) from 'there' (most other western states). The one exclusionary potential inherent in the civic-nationalist turn is to 'thicken' the liberal-democratic integration requirement and to make the liberal state one for liberal people only (Joppe, 2005). Hence Blair's statement: 'Our tolerance is part of what makes Britain Britain. Conform, or don't come here. We don't want hate-mongers, whatever their race, religion or creed' (quoted in Younge, 2006). These definitions of British norms and values in terms of those of liberal democracy – such as tolerance and equality – causes some to despair. Malik (2005) sees statements about British values, such as Blair's, as having reduced the meaning of Britishness to a minimum, to that of being tolerant, as the politics of identity fragments Britain. Others also see it as the way in which New Labour is sacrificing all to accommodate the 'fact' of multiculturalism and as a consequence of their 'open door' immigration policy. The declaration of liberal values is, however, a nationalist practice. Practices of tolerance are nationalist practices because those who are tolerant assume the power associated with imagining the nation as 'theirs' (Hage, 2003).

Tolerance is about the management of the threat represented by difference and it involves the simultaneous incorporation and maintenance of the otherness of the tolerated element (Brown, 2006: 28). As Brown (2006: 36) points out, liberal equality is based on sameness, it consists in our being regarded as the same or seen in terms of our sameness by the state and hence treated the same by the law. In contrast, tolerance is premised upon and pertains to difference. The incorporation of a language of tolerance into the contemporary ethos of cultural pluralism expresses a historical formation in which subjects are identified with and reduced to certain attributes or practices which in turn are held to be generative of certain beliefs and consciousness and these are presumed to issue from the essence or truth of the person or at a minimum from his or her culture, ethnicity etc. This process reifies and exaggerates the 'otherness' of a tolerated subject by construing it as a product of group identity representing a 'set of practices and beliefs different from ours'. The tolerated subject is not just disliked because it is different and different by virtue of its practices and beliefs; racialised being or, for example, sexual preference is treated as intrinsic and as generating certain beliefs and practices that are 'different' and therefore as producing an inherent permanent condition for which tolerance becomes the solution. Tolerance works as a disciplinary strategy of liberal individualism to the extent that it tacitly schematises the social order into the tolerated who are individuated through their deviance from social norms and whose truth is expressed in this individuation; and those doing the tolerating who are less individuated by these norms. Tolerance discourse, while posing as both a universal value and an impartial practice, designates certain beliefs and practices as civilised and others as barbaric, both at home and abroad (p. 7). Within secular liberal democratic states tolerance functions politically and socially to propagate understandings and practices regarding how people within a nation can and ought to cohabit (p. 11). The lens of difference, rather than diversity, is required in order to interrogate the basis of tolerance in the UK today.

There was an eventual acceptance (tolerance) that mid-century migrants were in Britain to stay. In the 1980s and 1990s the idea of multiculturalism was pivotal in national political debates/discourses so as to neutralise or contain the potential transformatory power at a political and cultural level of increasing reliance on shifting labour populations (Hickman, 2007; see also Gray, 2007). Even in this relatively constrained form multiculturalism is, post 11 September 2001, identified as part of the problem. Multicultural societies can only function now, it is argued, on the basis of some minimal convictions shared by all their members. In Britain this has led, as we have seen, to a renewed emphasis on the role of Britishness in achieving a workably diverse society. The nationalist practices of New Labour therefore were not so much expressed and mobilised by their rhetoric of commitment to uphold traditional British values of tolerance and equality, rather they were located in their act of syncopation. In their nationalist discourse the complexity of social cohesion was equated with community cohesion and this was syncopated with debates about immigration and minority ethnic groups and latent in all these representations is the spectra of 'suspect communities' that threaten the way of life of the tolerant British people.

Conclusion: Cohesion and difference

In this chapter we have set out the main precepts of the community cohesion agenda in the UK as it developed over the course of the first decade of the twenty-first century. We have analysed at length two of the main foci of discussion – 'community' and Britishness – in the course of which we outlined some of the main critiques which have been mounted against community cohesion policies as pursued by the New Labour government 1997–2010. Our interest has been to discuss ideas of community cohesion as they pertain to the perceived relationship between migration, cohesion and society, that is, community cohesion as a policy for managing diversity. We have not focused specifically on how ideas of community cohesion came to inflect the policy agenda on matters of security, crime and justice though we recognise their close interrelationship with our subject matter (see discussion in Fortier, 2010). Our concern has been to establish the broad parameters of government thinking on cohesion and explore why it became a dominant motif under New Labour as part of an attack on multiculturalism. We agree with Rutherford (2010) in locating this move in the contradictory tensions that existed between its adoption of Thatcherite neoliberalism and the legacies of its collectivist tradition. Our aim, however, has been to establish the modalities of a dominant understanding of social cohesion that exists within a strongly normative framework and is largely shared across the centre (right) ground of New Labour, the Liberal Democrats and Cameron's version of Toryism.

We explore in this book the extent to which this understanding of cohesion is largely out of tune with people's historically and economically constituted everyday lives and practices. We set these explorations within a historical context that takes account not only of the dominant narratives of the nation, of particular places, of 'elsewhere' in relation to 'here', but also of the historical narratives that are important to the new immigrants and long-term settled people we interviewed across the United Kingdom. For this reason we have considered here the historical context of national belonging in the UK and considered the contemporary efficacy of Britishness as a social glue.

2
Social Cohesion in the New Economy

Introduction

In this chapter we will analyse the cohesiveness (or otherwise) of working life from the narratives and experiences of our interviewees across the places of our research. These narratives were shaped by different economic sectors and different labour markets and by jobs differently classified in terms of skill. Our interviewees spoke from the perspectives of many work identities including those of knowledge worker, migrant worker, temporary worker, redundant worker, public/private sector worker, unemployed worker, inactive worker. These categories of work mapped onto and intersected with other components of identities such as gender, ethnicity, age and nationality that were also deployed in positioning people inside the spaces and relations of contemporary working life. National narratives of the economic realities of both contemporary and past economic eras also inform the working histories of our interviewees.

Particularly significant in these national narratives was a prevailing account of post-industrialism that identified the new knowledge economy as a distinctive and progressive economic formation that would deliver prosperity and stability. The term 'new economy' was coined by Tony Blair in a millennium address that laid down his endorsement of, and enthusiasm for, the promise and capacity of Britain's emergent and globally competitive knowledge economy.

> This new, knowledge driven economy is a major change. I believe it is the equivalent of the machine-driven economy of the industrial revolution. ... Knowledge and skills, creativity and innovation, adaptability and entrepreneurship are the ways by which the winners

will win in the new economy. We all have a responsibility to ensure that we are all equipped to succeed in it. That way we can all prosper. All our people. And all our businesses. For the benefit of Britain.
(Blair, *Guardian*, 7 March 2000).

The acclaimed universal embrace of the new economy to include 'all our people' signalled individual responsibility as the gatekeeper of inclusion. In this account participation in the new prosperity was non-exclusionary in that all individuals had a responsibility to equip themselves appropriately according to the requirements of the market. This rendition of neoliberal individualism was that individuals, in all their diversity, could participate equally through the acquisition of skill and entrepreneurialism. This version of economic egalitarianism however could only be sustained through complex exclusions. It excluded all those not part of the world of knowledge and skill and unable to access the world of education. It denied those made structurally redundant by deindustrialisation whose skills were no longer relevant and whose flexibility had been crushed by structural redundancy. And it completely eclipsed the economics of a workforce undertaking the substantial low-skilled jobs sustaining the day to day mechanics of the knowledge economy. The notion of 'all our people' violated the older constituency of 'our people' who, as manual working people, had been the traditional base of the Labour Party.

Under New Labour 'our people' were subsumed by the nationalistic appeal to 'all our people'. In this move Britishness was mobilised to define the knowledge economy and the categories of exclusion – low-skilled/unmodern/traditional – were repositioned in the national imaginary of modern Britain in a double move in which 'our people' became dubious contenders for inclusion as 'all our people'. The values of the new economy – equality and diversity – were advanced as consonant with the shared values of Britishness, the fair play, tolerance and egalitarianism that made Britain a modern cohesive society. This predigested notion of social cohesion was thus anchored in the harmonious and consensual values of equality and diversity that in Blair's vision of modern Britain progressively represented economic individualism and national prosperity.

The 'revolutionary' nature of the new economy meant significant change in working life and the relations that make it up. Researchers at the Work Foundation define the knowledge economy as a system in which 'the things we buy, and the methods we use to make them, rely more and more on knowledge and technology, and less on manual labour' (Levy, Sissons and Holloway, 2011). Manual labour however is far from eclipsed by knowledge production. A decade after Blair's speech in which the knowledge economy was consolidated, the audit on the inclusive prosperity it was held to deliver, was damning. At the end of New Labour's regime, the structural divisiveness of the new economy, as Wood points, out was clearly delineated.

> For the bulk of the population, low wages and flexibilization have increasingly become the norm, thanks to non-enforcement of the minimum wage and what Blair lauded as 'the most lightly regulated labour market of any leading economy in the world'. ... Inequalities of income are higher today than when Labour entered office: the top 20 per cent now earn more than seven times as much as the bottom 20 per cent.
>
> (Wood, 2010: 6)

Britain's knowledge economy includes a low wage sector that, at 21 per cent of the working population, has gained little from the considerable economic prosperity enjoyed by others (Sloane et al., 2005). However these low-skilled workers are denied by the celebration of the centrality of skilled workers to the knowledge economy. This celebration of skill eclipses from the new economy both settled workers and new arrivals who work in the low-waged sector.

Demand for skilled workers in advanced economies gave rise to globally competitive markets for skilled workers and initiated a governmental openness to migration and settlement. Nationally the demand for skilled labour led to policy regime changes that introduced equality and diversity programmes to facilitate access to labour sources without regard to the axes of difference – gender, ethnicity, age, disability – that had produced a specific distribution of labour in the industrial labour force (Kirton and Greene, 2010). Complementing this policy intervention, managed migration programmes to access skilled workers globally advanced the business case for migration and diversity. Skill as a category overrode and cancelled out the designation of migrant for many new arrivals who came to work in the knowledge economy.

Accessing labour migrants for the low-skilled sector was done with less policy flourish and political fan fare. As Ruhs and Anderson argue it was the absence of a range of policies shaping the domestic labour supply that created demand for migrant workers in many sectors. Moreover, the government's policy on low-skilled migration was effectively an incomes policy by default as labour migrants were competitive in what was an already a low-waged sector (Cruddas, 2010). These workers were identified not as skilled workers (although of course many of them were), but as *migrant workers*, a term that was to become synonymous with low skill, and therefore positioned as outside the cohesive values of equality and diversity celebrated by the government. As low-skilled workers these migrants, unlike their counterparts in the knowledge economy, were represented as peripheral and marginal to the new economy and as unfamiliar and unproven in their abilities to share in the official values of social cohesion.

Some settled workers were also marked as dubious participants in the new economy by other governmentalities that identified whole communities as deprived and without the skills to participate in the knowledge economy. The advocates of economic individualism identified the problems of failed community cohesion and deprivation in the unenterprising attitudes and behaviours of people making up those communities. Regeneration monies were distributed by successive Labour governments to foster entrepreneurialism and enterprise to alleviate this problem of attitude but delivered little by way of strategic interventions into the actual economic circumstances of deprived areas.

These discursive inclusions and exclusions that structured labour markets, working identities and the terms and conditions of both work and belonging, while making claims for the universal benefits of the knowledge economy produced a polarised workforce according to antagonistic categories of new economy/old economy, skilled/unskilled, British worker/migrant worker, permanent/casualised, high paid/low paid, economically active/inactive. Our data suggests that these categories and relationships and the exclusions they effected produced social relations and economic materialities that undermined social cohesion for many people working in Britain. These governmental determinants of work relations in the new economy limited many people's ability to resolve the tensions, disruptions and conflicts they encountered in their working lives. We also found however that for others the everyday world of work was successfully mediated by accessing solidarities beyond those of economic individualism. These solidarities were grounded in shared work histories and migrations, the dynamics of place and work, and the shared solutions to experiences of economic hardship.

In this chapter we will begin by mapping working life as represented in the experiences of our interviewees. Their working lives are framed by de-skilling, by sector and work hierarchies, by casualisation and by the locations of industries and the mobilities that make up workforces. They give a variegated and challenging account of social cohesion. From there we will consider the social relations that characterise niche migrant labour markets and how their economic formation in specific locations and in particular industries differently frame social cohesion. Finally we will consider areas marginalised by governmentality strategies of regeneration and the realities of in-work poverty that continue to integrate them in the new economy.

Changes in working lives and their consequences for social cohesion

Changes in working life have included radical changes in the social profile of the labour force. They also included continuities in discriminatory practices and growing insecurities in working life for settled workers and new arrivals. In the following quote a new arrival working as a skilled worker in Peterborough found his working life was compromised not by his status as a migrant worker but rather by the way his colleagues saw 'other' migrants as a threat to social cohesion.

> Even here sometimes when I'm writing up my notes and some English adviser comes in and says something like, 'oh, you know, another Lithuanian client ... trying to apply to benefits, and they think they can just come here ...'And I'll pretend I don't listen. I'm almost tempted to say ... think about the next time you go to Tescos and buy a bag of potatoes or a turkey. ... I used to work in a turkey factory for a minimum wage and this was two years ago.
>
> (New arrival, male, Peterborough)

This man had, like many skilled migrants, first experienced working in the UK by being deskilled in a 'migrant job' in the food industry, something we will discuss in a later section of the chapter. As a skilled worker he had to deal with the views of his co-workers that saw migrants not as people like him, a skilled worker, but as outsiders, people who came to scrounge off the welfare system. His colleagues were able to discuss this openly in his presence by participating in the dominant view that skilled workers had a different status to migrant workers in that they belonged to the new economic regime. In fact he understood this distinction well and felt invisibilised both as a migrant and as someone who had worked as a 'migrant worker'. The category of migrant worker represented to his colleagues a compounded alterity of a low-skilled, low-waged and benefit-dependent outsider claiming entitlements unfairly. These representations did not acknowledge the entitlements of migrant workers, their working contributions, their skills. They further denied that either he or his colleagues had any connections with migrancy because they classified themselves as skilled workers.

The exclusions perpetrated by the deskilling of new arrivals was seen differently by a long-term settled woman from Peterborough who worked as a manager and drew on the professional skills of one of her team even though this staff member was employed in a low-skilled job.

> One of my payroll team, a young lady who's got an MA in English, and is just, you know, she is so articulate. If I have a complex sentence or you know there is a word I can't spell I call her. Because her English is just so fantastic and so precise, it's just amazing. And she's on my payroll team. And she's also acting as a translator as well. I have to say, if I need anything translated I use her skills. But that's not why I recruited her.
> (Long-term settled, majority ethnic, woman, Peterborough)

The potential difficulties in the exploitative nature of these work relationships were overcome for the manager by her unstinting appreciation of the professionalism of her deskilled migrant employee. She also resolved the dilemma of this unfairness by criticising the recruitment procedures that employed migrant workers, something for which she did not feel responsible.

Other interviewees outlined different trajectories of effective deskilling in the new economy. In the following quote the registers of the old economy were experienced in the realities of racism that persisted in spite of the liberalisations entailed in values of equality and diversity. This was the experience of a young minority ethnic long-term settled man from Downham whose career was marked by this interplay between the old and the new in the skilled sector.

> I've got one foot in and one foot out. I am a visiting lecturer. You know, I literally survive on my wits, sort of thing. I am not affiliated to one particular place. There is no one particular place investing in my talent. You know, they are not saying come on this course or come and do this, do you know what I mean. So yes, I do feel out of it. In fact I feel today that racism is probably more prevalent today than it's ever been.
> (Long-term settled, minority ethnic, man, Downham)

His work history as a settled skilled worker in the educational heart of the knowledge economy was not shaped by the values of egalitarian diversity but rather by what labour market analysts have identified as the ethnic deficit or ethnic penalty that continues to differentiate workers in the skilled sector. A report comparing the labour market performance of ethnic minorities from 1991–2001 found that among second-generation minority ethnic workers with educational qualifications higher than their parents 'ethnic penalties have increased for second generation men: they are further behind their white peers than are ethnic minority men born overseas' (Simpson et al., 2006).

The working life of the man quoted above reflects the neoliberal casualization and flexibilisation of work, which fragments work patterns across a number of sectors. Here his ability to engage with and resolve the constraints of the ethnic deficit are dissipated by the forces of casualisation that deprived him of a base. While he stresses the problem of racism in his job, casualisation bears as heavy if not a heavier burden on his working life. Casualisation is transforming work for many into units of labour that don't constitute what used to be called 'a job', that is something that provides a place of work and a living wage for work over defined periods of time. All these elements of the new economy materially and discursively conspired to make his working life insecure and precarious, to limit his identity as a skilled worker and diminish his capacity to improve his predicament and make his working life viable and acceptable.

The 'old economy' had a complex presence in the work histories we collected. Memories of past migrations and earlier poor working conditions often illuminated the many ways in which the new economy eroded employment rights and working conditions. Some of these memories reflected on the impact of migration being used as a kind of wages policy to secure the lowest labour costs possible. This is captured by the account of a minority ethnic key informant in Kilburn, an inner city London borough with a long history of migration and settlement of workers supplying the low-skilled sectors that have served the London economy since the post-war period.

> Then you would have had a lot of working class men and women migrating from Ireland to the UK ... men went into work in construction and the women went into menial jobs like cleaning or catering. ... Then the Polish communities are coming here. They really remind me of the Irish community when they first came. And a lot of them are quite well educated as well. But what's

actually happening is they're kind of taking the jobs that we'll say the Irish traditionally had in the building. The women are also are doing all of that, cleaning. ... I know the Irish guys are angry at the moment because their work is drying up. ... Its causing tensions but that's because for financial reasons, it's not a dislike of culture. That is, your bread and butter.

(Key informant, Kilburn)

This quote layers the history of migration and low-skilled work in Kilburn through an account of labour market competition between new arrivals and settled people who are themselves migrants of long standing. The woman is not concerned that this situation will produce racism or xenophobia because Kilburn is a multicultural place grounded in the solidarities of migrancy and the shared histories of being positioned as cheap workers. The problem she identifies is the anger experienced by older migrants at losing their livelihoods. This anger is directed at the neoliberal logics of the new economy that displaces settled migrants and replaces them with cheaper new arrivals (EHRC Report, 2010). The disruptions to social cohesiveness for settled migrant workers, she suggests, are registered in their anger at the intractable realities of an at best, loosely regulated market and at worst an economy increasingly driven by reducing labour costs in the low-skilled sector (Wood, 2010).

This acceptance of new arrivals into the local economy of Kilburn was cited by another key informant as characteristic of the area. Commenting on the informal economy of the high street, this long-term settled majority ethnic Kilburn woman also made the point that the history of conviviality in the area sustained cohesiveness in the changing work environment of the high street economy.

Kilburn has a massive black market, even Kilburn High Road. You walk down Kilburn High Rd, it's quite funny because generally there is an Irish guy that is standing outside the pub selling rugs out of the back of a van ... in summer the Caribbeans sell jerk chicken out of drums ... then you have one particular bus stop where the Eastern Europeans sell fake cigarettes ... the South East Asian DVD sellers stand out on the streets with fake DVDs. ... And sell fake Gucci and Prada bags. ... The Somalis have opened up a lot of internet cafés and mobile phone shops. They tend to keep themselves out of the black market and set up business.

(Key informant, Kilburn)

This mixture of new arrivals and long-term settled sharing the particularly precarious area of work that bridges the formal and informal economies of Kilburn is worked through a prevailing acceptance of difference and a history of resolving conflicts through the shared experiences of working in the low-waged sector. As we shall see this acceptance is a key factor in the ability to negotiate the tensions and contradictions underpinning social cohesion.

We found other instances of settled workers appreciating the predicaments of new arrivals as evidenced in the quote below from a long-term settled man from Downham who worked in construction.

> I've worked with some [migrants], yes. They are only here to work, they are only here to earn money. ... Some of them do [the same jobs] yeah. I mean, I've worked with Lithuanians, Russians, Albanians, Polish. Erm, Italian. ... They are only here to earn money. If there was money in another country than England, if the money was worth more we'd probably go to that country the same as them. So you can't really – No, they are alright, they are just normal people.
>
> (Long-term settled, majority ethnic, man, Downham)

The empathy being expressed by this majority ethnic man towards his new arrival colleagues sidestepped the potentially divisive relations produced by new arrivals competing for jobs alongside local workers. Instead of seeing migrant workers as outsiders he chose to see them as 'normal', as workers like himself and therefore drawn, as he himself would be, to the most lucrative labour markets for their skills. He appreciates the overlay of global and local labour markets and that mobility is an option for all workers including settled people such as himself.

These examples illustrate people's ability to get along in the face of the disruptions of work. Other settled workers found the changes in working life, including the presence of new arrivals, more difficult to accept. This was particularly the case when these changes exacerbated their own vulnerabilities. Two examples of this are given below.

> I think it's quite a big issue. I am one of these lucky people to be in work. ... But there is a lot of people you speak to, you know, they are out of work ... they're got no money ... its bound to cause problems ... and the people that haven't get agitated by it, they want to go out and do it and therefore if they go out and mug someone they can go out and do it as well. ... It's a hard call but I think somewhere down

the line the government have got to draw the line and say I am ever so sorry but we cannot take anymore people into the country.'
(Long-term settled, majority ethnic, man, Downham)

The government are at fault to let them all, as much as they have, in. Cos everyone sees Britain as this brilliant place, the truth is it ain't that nice. As soon as they realise that they start messing about so ...
(Long-term settled, majority ethnic, man, Leicester)

Both these excerpts show, from different vantage points and localities, the potential difficulties that work creates for processes of social cohesion. Both centrally place the economy as the problem and in neither quote are new arrivals held responsible for introducing the difficulties, nor for bringing about failures of social cohesion. The dynamics of work have produced, as the man in Downham suggests, a situation in which many of the settled population are without work and are socio-economically marginalised. In his view, this had eventually to be addressed by a brake on ongoing immigration. This was said from the perspective of Downham where unemployment among the settled population is high and the social life of the area was diminished accordingly, particularly through crime. That the problems lay centrally in the nature of the economy was also signalled by the man from Leicester who knew from his own experiences that life at the bottom was 'not that great'. In his view, once new arrivals discovered the limiting realities of work in Britain they too would 'start messing about', because of the trials of in-work poverty and deprivation.

The identities and exclusions of working life that our interviewees recounted were multifaceted. Post-industrialism and neoliberalism have introduced disruptions and discontinuities within work that have altered its cohesive possibilities. Although many interviewees, especially, but not exclusively, settled people, were troubled by aspects of new migration, others found empathetic and convivial ways of working alongside new arrivals. In the following section we will consider niche migrant labour markets and the consequences for social cohesion of migrant workers being marginalised from settled workers.

Niche labour markets: The food industry and the care sector

We are addressing enclave work environments because they provide neither spaces for social integration nor means to easily participate socially, factors which impact on processes of social cohesion. Our two case studies are the niche migrant labour markets in the food industry and the care sector. They have emerged as a response to labour shortages in the new economy. These shortages were generated by expanding demands for goods and services that historically had been provided by the unwaged domestic work of women. As women re-entered waged work in ever increasing numbers, expanding demand for commodified domestic goods and personal services produced increasing demand for labour in the service sector. Much of this demand, in retail and care particularly, was met by settled women workers (Himmelweit and Land, 2008), but persisting gaps in labour supply were increasingly resolved by migrant labour (Mackay, 2009) Migrant workers in agricultural and industrial food production, distribution and retail, and in the care sector, came to represent a significant component of these workforces. Niche markets emerged as these sectors became reliant on the labour characteristics of migrants. Ruhs and Anderson (2010) in their analysis of these markets argue they are produced by the intersection of labour market policies or, in some instances the absence of policies and sectoral decisions not to offer higher wages in response to shortages but rather to resolve shortages by accessing migrant workers. In the logic of these sectors of the economy, migrants are seen as the best people for the job and below we explore the characteristics of 'the preferred migrant worker' and the employment practices that construct and sustain them. Our findings affirm the argument of Ruhs and Anderson that jobs in both the care sector and the food industry are created specifically for migrants because they effectively subsidise these industries.

In our research we interviewed new arrivals working in the food industry in Peterborough and Dungannon. We also interviewed new arrivals in Kilburn and Glasgow working in the care sector. What we found overall was that the prevailing discourse of 'the good migrant worker' that rationalised selective recruitment of migrant workers into these niche markets was indicative not of their ability to work well but of the way they matched an exacting profile that included high levels of flexibility around work schedules, low levels of understanding of labour regulation and work practices, limited knowledge of (or claim to) employment rights, and lower wage expectations than the settled population. While this profile has obvious benefits for these industries, the terms and conditions they presented to new arrivals were fraught with difficulties, which impacted on their abilities to negotiate the tensions and inequalities they met in positive terms.

The food industry: Peterborough and Dungannon

In Peterborough in the south east of England, and in Dungannon, our site in Northern Ireland, the agricultural sector and industrialised food production were significant dimensions of the local economy. In both localities labour agencies and gangmasters were key recruitment conduits of new arrivals although we found more extensive evidence of bad practice in Peterborough than in Dungannon. The agro-food sector in Peterborough included a central operational presence of the major national retailers, whose pressure on the local labour market played a key role in the proliferation of irregularities and bad practices (McKay and Winkelmann-Gleed, 2005). There were also many similarities between Dungannon and Peterborough although Dungannon was distinctive in terms of the recent history of 'The Troubles' in Northern Ireland. This history was marked by the heritage of a long standing ethno-national struggle, the effects of which continued to be felt in different ways in the patterns of outmigration, the impact of labour substitution by migrant workers and the patterns of belonging these new arrivals were offered.

Our interviewees in Peterborough recounted a wide range of bad practices among the gangmasters and agencies that delivered migrant workers to the different sectors of the food industry in Peterborough and the wider area. These practices of inadequate and illegal payment systems, non-payment, demanding work schedules, threats of deportation and gross misrepresentation of working conditions in the UK constituted enormous difficulties for new arrivals.

> I had Russian and Lithuanian clients going crazy because of their line of work. I had Brazilian clients that were abused and they wouldn't say anything. We're talking about really, really grueling things. People don't imagine, people sitting at home, English people, they sit at home, they don't know what's going on. You don't just work 14 hours a day from your own free will. But the thing is, even if you just do £3 or £4 an hour it's so much more money than back home.
> (Key informant, Peterborough)

This key informant pinpointed two central characteristics of niche migrant workers: their vulnerability to abusive practices and the invisibility of these work relations to the settled population. As reported to us by several key informants these conditions were acutely felt by new arrivals but they had little confidence either in their ability to challenge or resolve them or in the possibility of support agencies being able to defend their interests successfully. The contempt with which new arrivals were treated by agencies and gangmasters was often underwritten by threat and menace as conveyed by this minority ethnic man recently arrived in Peterborough.

> Sometimes people [working for an agency] have to phone every day and ask if there is work. So still they do not know they are working at seven o'clock or even six o'clock, yeah. And sometimes they are working for fifteen hours ... and that's all the time. ... And there are, they have been told that if they do not agree they would go back.
> (Recent arrival minority ethnic man, Peterborough)

The threat of being sent back enforced work schedules that casualised and flexibilised workers without any consideration for them as social beings with lives beyond work. These relations of denial embedded in work, limited the possibilities for workers to access relations of sociality beyond work. Moreover the effective segregation of niche markets ensured these workers are not able to learn about their rights from other workers, a situation that helps to sustain employment practices clearly in violation of UK employment law. Thus there were few restraints limiting the exploitative possibilities of utilising migrant workers and in this sense the economic benefits of niche markets were considerable.

> I had payslips after all the deductions, they've had zero on it. ... They charge something they call agenciamento, which is an amount of money. 'I know you're illegal, if you want to work for me, I have work for you but you have to pay to see, and the average is £150'. So ... they pay to work. ... But ... where does this lead us? They're obviously important for the economy, regional economy, and for overall British economy. You go to Asda you have things cheap, you go to Tesco's, you know, they're doing quite well.
> (Key informant, Peterborough)

Under these conditions of sustained vulnerability to exploitation in the context of these social relations of denial new arrivals had very limited chances to improve their predicament. This is true even though, as this key informant points out, new arrivals can be seen as key workers in several respects. They work for very low wages and thus keep supermarket food prices down (and profits up) and contribute to a key infrastructural industry that is reliant on their participation. New arrivals however cannot easily position themselves as making a good contribution through their work because they are invisibilised by the marginalising practices of the agencies and by widely accepted discursive accounts of migrants as people who come to Britain to exploit its economic possibilities rather than people whom British employers exploit as migrant workers. These circumstances offer little by way of positive resolution of such powerful odds.

A counterpoint to this situation in both Dungannon and Peterborough, was the involvement of NGOs and union organisations that intervened to support these workers. Many worked hard to inform workers of their rights, counteract their scepticism and generally provide access to the possibility of more usual ways of working in the UK. In several cases legal challenges led to closure of some of the worst of the agencies and in Peterborough the local council supported a designated support organisation, New Link, to help in re-positioning new arrivals in the working and community cultures of the settled population. These solidarities deflected some of the worst excesses of niche markets although many of the support agency workers felt that their capacities were inadequate compared to the power of the big supermarket chains that strategically utilised these working conditions and the gangmasters and recruitment agencies that exploited new arrivals through opportunistically capitalising on the many vulnerabilities of migrancy.

This opportunism was evident in the altering composition of new arrivals in Peterborough that gave rise to increased tensions and strains in inter-ethnic relations in the area. Conflicts that existed between Kurdish and Iraqi refugees and the Portuguese and East Timorese seasonal workers were overshadowed and ultimately displaced by the 2004 EU enlargement and Britain's acceptance of A8 citizens as having full EU citizenship rights of mobility. This allowed for direct agency recruitment of Polish and Lithuanian workers who were identified as 'good' and therefore 'preferred workers' because, in addition to matching the profile of the 'good migrant worker', they were also seen as conflict averse, with higher work standards than either local workers or the new arrivals who preceded them. These dynamics were mapped by a long-term settled, majority ethnic key informant woman from Peterborough.

> We did have an issue where migrant communities were fighting with asylum seeker communities because the asylum seekers were taking the work in the factories illegally, some failed asylum seekers were. Then the migrant communities started coming which meant that they – because they had the paperwork ... the agencies started just using the migrant workers. I think also possibly paying a lower rate initially so

the failed asylum seekers who were doing that work became unhappy and particularly the Kurdish workers, part of the Kurdish community and there was some – there was a bit of backlash over that.

(Key informant woman, Peterborough)

In this instance, agency constructions of the desired migrant worker were cast not against settled workers but undocumented workers, a comparator that allowed a further reduction in wage levels. This illustrates how misjudged are the arguments that new migrants take British jobs. These claims deny the reality that 'migrant jobs' violate the employment rights enjoyed by British workers and deliver wages calibrated against the composite vulnerabilities of new arrivals.

Well, the thing is an English person they is easy for them to get a better job. It's much more easy. Because they are treated a little bit different. ... Polish person is cheap person because they have to work hard, they have to work hard to survive, they have to work to pay for rent, for everything, for food, so they will work hard to not lose a job. And we are like people see us as cheap workers, cheap hard workers most of all.

(Recent arrival minority ethnic man, Peterborough)

Other constructions of the 'good' migrant attributed them with narrow work motives to make money and return home, an assumption that eclipsed the process of settlement and wider community involvement and further consolidated the social marginalisation of these workers. Against this, many of our interviewees said they hoped their families would join them and settle permanently in the area.

The concentration of national and ethnic groups in the area over time led to settlement strategies in spite of the impositions of working life. The complexity of the political, spatial and socio-economic dimensions of social cohesion in Peterborough effected by the incorporation of this niche labour market into the regional economy was challenging for both Peterborough and the new arrivals. Over time however new arrivals developed cultural spaces from which to better navigate the restrictions of working life. These, in conjunction with trade union organisations as well as designated migrant and general support agencies in the area, went some way to creating better prospects to living and working in the region. In this way, new arrivals were able to achieve a degree of resolution of the socially destabilising practices constituting the local niche labour market.

Similar patterns and flows of new arrivals made up the working population engaged in industrial food production in Dungannon but unlike Peterborough these demographic changes represented a different kind of shift in the social makeup of the community. In 2001 Portuguese and East Timorese were recruited by agencies in response to an acute labour shortage prompted by outward migration from the area. The new arrivals, delivered in the first instance by gang masters, effectively restored the economic prospects of the sector through its continuing use of agencies to supply a substitute workforce for the major food processing factories in the area. As one settled key informant noted:

> If you look at food processing, if it wasn't for inward migration, the factories would have closed. Everyone in them would have lost their jobs, most of the farmers on which the rural economy depends would also have lost their jobs ... which eventually will have a knock on effect in terms of public services. ... So the economic impact of inward migration has effectively been to save the rural economy and so safeguard it.
> (Key informant, Dungannon)

In what had been a homogeneous but divided community in which sectarianism constrained and limited conviviality and divided schools, shops and other amenities the change introduced by, in particular, the settlement of Polish, Lithuanian and Latvian workers in 2004 was both sudden and dramatic.

> You got up one morning and there seemed to be a significant group of people who had just arrived in the community and initially they were mistaken for tourists, people who might be passing through.
> (Long-term settled key informant man, Dungannon)

These arrivals followed the departure of many settled people from the area. This was significant in a town long demarcated by conflict, which produced relative depopulation. In workplaces as well the change in personnel was significant. It coincided with changes in the nature and tempo of the industrial output in the factories of the area. About these changes one settled worker commented:

> I left after 3 years ... I couldn't do it anymore, I didn't like it anymore ... it got worse in the place. The pressure was worse, they

wanted more work out of you, the pay wasn't really good. I had a good friend in there he left, so I worked with people, you couldn't talk to them anymore.

(Long-term settled majority ethnic man, Dungannon)

For this man work had become untenable. Language differences meant he could less easily collectively mediate the changing pace of work and this compounded the reduced conviviality of the workplace for him. He did not directly blame new arrivals for his predicament but they were in the same frame as other changes he objected to. Language differences were seen as an intractable problem introduced by outsiders rather than an issue that needed social support in view of the strategic importance of outside workers to maintaining local economic viability and stability.

In Dungannon a welcome characteristic of new arrivals was their often studied indifference to the deep histories of political conflict in Northern Ireland. This positive appreciation of the 'outsiderness' of new arrivals promised for some settled people different, less fraught ways of getting along with others and altering the dynamics of social cohesion in the area.

Now, you move that scenario to people that have started to make friends with Polish, Lithuanian, Portuguese guys, and suddenly their culture is beginning to expand. All of a sudden, it's much more important to have your friends than whether they are Catholic or Protestant.

(Key informant, Dungannon)

The dynamics of friendship with neutral others gave different permissions for social intercourse. It was the case however that some new arrivals were also caught up in the inheritances of years of conflict. However while many interviewees commented upon and valued the gains to the community arising from new arrivals in Dungannon, others were more circumspect and cautious and recognised that for social cohesion to be embedded in this new context, the economy of the region had to remain buoyant.

My sense is that our social cohesion is quite fragile. There are good examples of strong social cohesion as well as examples of bad practice and racism and poor practice. But even where we have got good examples of social cohesion, I sense that in quite a number of cases that could be quite fragile, and a change in the economy, how robust would that cohesion be in a changing economic environment. It's an interesting question and hopefully one we are not going to have to find the answer to.

(Key informant man, Dungannon)

It is something of a truism to say economic downturn exacerbates existing divisions and hierarchies and produces conflict. The point being made here is that even in conditions of economic buoyancy bad practices potentially undermine social cohesion by undermining people's ability to find a common understanding to reconcile the inequalities and conflicts shaping their social fields.

The low pay and unsecured rights of migrant workers in the agricultural and food industry are contributing factors to the sector's productivity and profitability but in their impact on people's lives both at work and in the communities in which they live these economic strategies present many intractabilities for social cohesion in places where niche markets are set up. Although, as in Peterborough, Dungannon provided a number of effective mediating agencies that supported migrant workers and social cohesion, it was also the case that the sectoral dynamics reduced the opportunities of working life for new arrivals. The competitiveness of an industry that was based on the different vulnerabilities of new arrivals and on subsidisation disregards life within and beyond the workplace (Ruhs and Anderson, 2010). However in spite of these circumstances dictated by unrestrained economic rationalisation new arrivals and settled people working in Dungannon and Peterborough managed with the help of social interventions from voluntary organisations, local councils and trades unions to build workable solutions to challenging economic circumstances both within and beyond the UK.

The care industry: Kilburn and Glasgow

Across the UK, the care industry was transformed by the postindustrial expansion of the service sector and the demographic shifts in declining fertility and increasing longevity. The industry is now a major employer of low-skilled labour and numbers a workforce, largely feminised, that is larger than that of the NHS (Moriarty et al., 2008). The workforce for the sector is delivered through intersecting and overlocking global, local and sectoral labour markets that utilise women locally and globally as an already constituted workforce of low-waged carers. Although recently upgraded, care work is positioned at the bottom end of the skills table and continues to be low waged. The

UK care workforce is composed of a small number of skilled workers and a large low-skilled group. The industry continues to be casualised and demands unsocial hours due to the 24/7 work regimes of care (Williams, 2011). It is labour intensive and unproductive and increasingly represents a fiscal challenge to welfare budgets and a challenge to profitability to business budgets (Dilnott, 2011). As in the food industry, migrant care workers are an important component of the care workforce where similarly their profile as migrant workers holds down costs and accommodates poor working conditions (Lutz, 2008; Himmelweit and Land, 2008).

Unlike the previous case study, in the care sector new arrivals are not segregated and they work together with settled workers in hierarchized relations that place some new arrivals in positions of authority over settled local workers. To gain accreditation highly skilled new arrivals work alongside settled women, many of whom are trapped by a skills deficit that forecloses their access to better jobs. This deficit contrasts significantly with the skill profile of new arrivals in the sector. These inequalities and tensions have the potential to antagonise workers and to impact negatively on processes of social cohesion at work and beyond.

The dynamics between skilled and low-skilled care workers played out differently in Glasgow and Kilburn, the two sites we focus on in this section. In Glasgow the migrations of the past decades were often discussed in the language of sectarianism rather than multiculture or assimilation. The increasingly diversified migrations of the twenty-first century were framed differently in Scotland compared with England. They were seen as an important counterpoint to Scotland's declining population. Nonetheless new arrivals prompted many issues around hierarchies of belonging and relations of cultural diversity both at work and beyond. These played out in the care sector according to ideas that because 'migrant workers' were seen as inherently low skilled, they were also seen as having less entitlements than settled workers in the hierarchies of both work and place. These resonances were picked up by a skilled worker from the Philippines who settled in Scotland with her family.

> Scotland is not a multicultural place ... they don't know how to deal with foreigners and sometimes they are very, they get insecure if they see that you are higher up in education. For instance, in our country a Bachelor of Science in Nursing is four years, and sometimes it's even five years for those who have the new curriculum, so then when they start to know you are knowledgeable more than them,

that's where the tricks come, they try to – they are being intimidated. Because they will always say oh, I know you are a nurse we are only a carer, but blahblah this is our country, we know where we are, we know where we stand.

(New arrival, Filipino, woman, Glasgow)

Her experience captures the fraught relations present in the sector that are grounded in 'the tricks' of ethnonational identifications, of being 'from here', that defensively attempt to mitigate the compounded threat to these privileged belongings represented by work hierarchies that place new arrivals as more skilled and therefore 'superior' to long-term settled workers. This diminishing of the currency of whiteness (Hage, 1998) produces what we have called a 'settled backlash' (see following chapter) from those dispossessed by post-industrialism who perceive themselves displaced by new arrivals. For settled care workers the hierarchies of class become more conflictful when overlaid by differences of migrancy and ethnicity, and convivial work relations are accordingly more difficult to achieve.

At work many skilled new arrivals laid claim to their professional status as a way of dealing with accusations of not being 'from here'. They used this strategy to protect themselves from negative comments about being migrants. This was less easily done outside work however where their professional standing was less clearly marked. A highly skilled new arrival said the following.

What I have seen is that the general public don't understand the basics of the immigration system in this country. So when they see a foreign person sometimes they think you are an asylum seeker or an illegal immigrant ... because you are foreign ... you don't feel the same way you feel like if people knew that you are a professional in this country. You've got a job, you are here for a purpose. You are someone who knows what they are doing. You are not seeking asylum. You won't feel the same if people look at you and see you in a different way.

(New arrival, Zimbabwean, male, Glasgow)

This man objected to the complex racialisations marginalising him as black, a foreigner, and therefore an asylum seeker. In the first identification he is seen as someone who does not belong in Scotland and in the second he is seen as someone who, as an 'asylum seeker' is 'bludging off the system'. His reality as a migrating professional recruited into a skilled labour market is doubly eclipsed by being seen as a workless and illegitimate outsider making demands on Scottish resources. Migration, race, ethnicity and skill intersect to position this professional as a non-person within the care sector and in the wider public world. This interviewee felt he could make few claims on his right to belong in such a resistant and inhospitable cultural environment that invisibilised his working identity.

Both the workers quoted above were members of the Overseas Nurses Network, an organisation set up to respond to the needs of migrant workers working in the health and care sectors. The network represented a remarkable resource for new arrivals and provided a social space for people to discuss these kinds of problems in a shared and sympathetic environment. The network was set up by three women who were themselves long-term settled migrants. It worked through regular open meetings that provided a convivial space and a meal, as well as making available speakers and information packages to help new arrivals with the business of settlement both in work and their wider life in Scotland. It was supported by union but its motivations came more from the experiences of past migrations than the attentiveness of the union to defend migrant workers. This resource did much to alleviate the strains on social cohesion encountered by new arrivals, by providing them with support, information and advice, enabling them to negotiate the conflicts and inequalities they met at work and beyond.

In Kilburn we found evidence of past migrations feeding into and supporting new arrivals. There were women who entered the care sector in the 1970s who had little support apart from the church to help them in their working life. The following quote is from an interview with a Filipino female worker who migrated as a nurse. She was later repositioned by her employment agency as a live in domestic. She tells of the strategies of resilience she and her fellow live-in domestics devised to navigate their new working lives.

> And what happens is sometimes we buy one portion [of food] like and we have half for my friend and for me. If it's fish and chips, half fish and half the chips. That's all we eat because we only got little money ... but I said why are we here, you know, sitting in Golders Green ... why don't we find a flat, you know in order for us to have somewhere to stay, you know. So it's six of us friends. So we went around and we found a flat in Finchley Road.
> (Long-term settled, minority ethnic, woman, Kilburn)

Social life for these workers was limited to one day off work spent in public spaces that allowed few creature comforts to her or her fellow workers. The solution of collectively renting a flat transformed their lives. It delivered a shared space for domestic conviviality denied them by their work and continues to be used as a shared space. This woman subsequently worked as a live-in cleaner for luxury serviced apartments and helped other live-in workers to escape tyrannical employees by taking refuge in her basement flat. She herself went on to have a successful career and owned several houses. The deskilling initially imposed by the agency she later subverted by undertaking a Business Management and Law degree which allowed her to finish her working life managing a law firm. In conjunction with her fellow migrants her negotiation of the migrancy deficit – the discriminations, conflicts, constraints and deskilling of low-waged care work – was converted into social capital that provided new arrivals with both collective knowledge and a communal space with which to mediate obstacles to their own strategies of work and settlement.

Alongside this history of care workers in Kilburn we found new arrivals working in the sector to support either their studying or project to learn English.

> I did part time care work and then I was studying at the same time. It was really lovely to work as a carer because I had so much fun learning from old people, I improved my English as well and I learned so many things.'
>
> (New arrival, woman, Kilburn)

This interviewee went on to talk about the migrant histories of those she cared for and her appreciation of the depth of the multicultural character of life in Kilburn. Older care workers testified to this. They had been able to access the Catholic Church in Kilburn whose history was intricately entwined with the different trajectories of Irish migrations into the area and which facilitated the settlement of the many other groups into the area. This environment and the resilience of the long-term minority ethnic settled migrants was clearly shaped by and contributed to the easy acceptance of others that prevailed in Kilburn.

Like the food industry, the care sector also had a history of incorporating migrant workers into the sector in ways that made settlement and belonging far more difficult than they needed to be. The tensions and contradictions that positioned new arrivals were severe.

However, these care workers were able to access other solidarities to ease the harshness of their working lives. In both Glasgow and Kilburn working lives were underpinned by the embedded resiliences of past migrations. These made social cohesion more possible by providing people with narrative resources to negotiate in their own terms injustices and divisions.

Conclusion

In understanding the impact of work on social cohesion it is important to understand how the inequalities and polarisations brought about by neoliberalism undermine the ability of people to find agreed positive responses to the circumstances of the new economy. In our research we found an intricate response to the socio-economic challenges posed by the convergence of post-industrialism and neoliberalism. This included informal work, in-work poverty from casualised and low-waged work, different narratives of migration and settlement and different resources that were collectively and separately mobilised in the struggle against neoliberalism. Settled people and new arrivals alike were all too familiar with the very polarising nature of the new economy and its deep similarity to the inequalities of the old one.

Migration is at the heart of 'the new economy' because globalised competition for skilled labour makes the business case for migration an economic necessity for the Government and employers. The expanding number of low-skilled jobs that are as necessary as skilled jobs to the knowledge economy is less acknowledged in public debates, because of the marginalised settled populations made increasingly redundant by structural unemployment. New arrivals undertaking low-skilled jobs, for example in the food and the care sector, lowered existing wage bars thus increasing profitability in sectors structurally resistant to productivity. Britain continues to have one of the largest low-skilled workforces of any advanced economy, which suggests a wide-ranging commitment to hold down wages as a counterpoint to productivity. Niche migrant labour markets have emerged to draw on vulnerable globalised workers who can afford and need to migrate, which means they will accept poorer working conditions and lower wages.

Far from these new arrivals dislodging the social solidarities of Britain they contribute economically alongside some of the marginalised settled population. The transformation of work in the new economy had potentially divisive effects on working lives for both long-term settled and new arrivals. The potential to undermine workers' cohesive ability to reconcile divisions between them and thus navigate social cohesion, was countered by the role of local histories of migration, solidarity and heterogeneity at work. It was also countered by the work of third-sector organisations, providing new arrivals with the support, information and advice enabling them to negotiate the conflicts and inequalities they met at work and beyond.

3
Place, Belonging and Social Cohesion

Introduction: Placing belonging

The contemporary historical phase of late modernity is characterised by the technological compression of the spatial distance between places (Harvey, 1991) and by the increase in the global mobility of people, goods and cultural products (Appadurai, 2001). In addition to these transformations, the post-industrial transition to a knowledge-led economy and the neoliberal re-organisation of production across the globe means that local contexts were disaggregated and reassembled in new ways, according to 'place specific forms and combinations' (Brenner and Theodore, 2001: 28). In the process, there was a fragmentation and polarisation of people's experiences of place. In the previous chapter we discussed the effects of these processes on working life. In this chapter we will consider how the fragmentation and polarisation of place lead to a different understanding of the spatial dimensions and narratives of locality and mobility and gave renewed significance to people's understanding of themselves as 'being from here' as this increasingly became a way of defining one's place in the world (Back, 1996).

Late modernity is also characterised by the hegemony of neoliberal ideologies that have transformed previous ideologies and practices of social solidarity and participation. In particular people's access to welfare support and employment was restructured through new and old social divisions and boundaries that marginalised places from the late modern neoliberal economy (Balibar, 2004). For those who were able to achieve the skills to navigate the new economy, late modernity can be a space of increased opportunities. However, those who are left behind experienced further limitations to their social and economic participation.

This significance of place and mobility has also changed as social identities have been transformed by anti-racist and egalitarian legislative interventions that have instituted equality and diversity as the hegemonic paradigm. As a consequence of the progressive anti-racist and egalitarian movements of the 1960s, racialised discourses ceased to be socially and politically acceptable ways to exclude people from social protection and economic participation. Increasingly, racialised, gendered and other markers of identity were subsumed into the categories of locality and mobility. The resurgence of locality and mobility as markers of belonging and identity is the product of neoliberal depoliticisations of the public sphere and of public discourses that legitimise the spatial remapping of social divisions (Brennen and Theodore, 2002: 63). Discourses of 'being from here' and 'being mobile' reproduce, through the geography and physicality they designate, the late modern parameters of distinction and exclusion (Skeggs, 2004: 50).

We found evidence of the use of narratives of 'being from here' and 'being mobile' in the socio-economic inclusions and exclusions operating in all the localities we researched. In order to explain the renewed relevance of these narratives and practices in post-industrial and neoliberal times, we elaborate on the concept of 'white backlash' (Hewitt, 2005). This term refers to a reaction, common in the USA, Australia and UK against the ideologies of racial equality of the 1960s and more specifically against 'the possibility of whites having to compete with blacks on legal, occupational, educational and/or residential grounds where white advantage would be diminished if not nullified' (Hewitt, 2005: 5). The concept of the 'white backlash' is useful in understanding the way in which race became the main discourse and reference point of a 'white' form of governmentality in post-war and post-imperial Britain (Hesse, 1997).

In order to account for the renewed resonance of the local in people's understanding of their place in the world we introduce the more comprehensive concept of 'settled backlash'. This concept acknowledges the persisting dynamics of race and ethnicity in discourses of 'being from here'. By underlining the 'settled' rather that the 'white' character of this backlash, we do not underestimate the enduring role of race or ethnicity within social relations. We underline that, against neoliberal depoliticisations, race and ethnicity remain central to social divisions, alongside class, religion, gender, age and sexuality, whose intersections shape the social hierarchies of place. The term 'intersection' originates from the theory of intersectionality, referring to the way in which different social and cultural categories and dimensions overlap and interact within social relations and processes to legitimise specific social hierarchies and inequalities (Crenshaw, 2003).

The socio-economic transformations introduced above call for a renewed engagement with place in relation to the current renegotiated spatial and social co-ordinates. As we have anticipated in the introductory chapter, exploring contemporary social cohesion in the UK means engaging with places that are increasingly open, 'porous' and constituted relationally as 'products of other places' (Massey, 1995: 59). At a spatial level, this means addressing social cohesion as it unfolds between macro (national, regional and urban) scales and dynamics and more localised 'thirdspaces' of resistance and domination (Soja, 1999: 276) emerging between and within neighbourhoods. At a social level, engaging with the renewed relevance of the local dimension means focusing on the individual and social narratives of 'being from here' or 'being mobile' constituting local experiences of living and belonging in a place. These may mark the experiences of a few households and families or those of entire areas or cities. It also means addressing the extent to which the structural porousness, openness and connectedness of any 'place' are acknowledged publicly and privately by both long-term settled residents and new arrivals.

Before moving on to the analyses of contemporary experiences of place in Britain, it is important to explain the way we understand the interplay between individual identities and representations of the local. Drawing on both symbolic interactionism (i.e. Jenkins, 1996) and post-structuralism (Hall and Du Gay, 1996), we understand personal and social identities as forms of self-representation which are socially constructed through the constant interaction and dialogue with the material and narrative worlds people live in. Self-representations and self-identities, for both individuals and localities, result from the complex interplay between hegemonic representations and their internalisation, mediation or rejection. This interplay characterises localised experiences of social cohesion, as hegemonic self-representations reproduce social divisions and categories enhancing or constraining the ability to resolve conflicts in ways which are perceived positively by the individuals and groups involved. The evidence we analyse in this chapter goes against an *á la Cantle* (2001) reductive understanding of social cohesion as being about absence of conflict or about people and communities leading 'parallel lives'. On the contrary, we found that most people valued as cohesive the ability and possibility to negotiate both what is separate and what is shared in the communities and places they lived in. The self-representation of communities and places as plural and mobile or as segregated and deprived is deeply implicated in the unfolding of social cohesion. It enhances or hinders, respectively, the cohesive ability of individuals and the communities they live in to straddle the inequalities and divisions constituting their places in ways which are deemed positive by the majority.

Drawing on our research findings, we will show that in de-politicised and 'politically correct' neoliberal times, locality and the convenience of place become new discursive fields of political struggle for social groups and individuals, who strategically include or exclude other groups or individuals as unwelcome 'newcomers' or desirable fellow 'long-term settled residents'. We will examine the way in which local experiences of living and belonging in a specific place are influenced by socio-economic transformations that impact on long-term residents' reactions to the arrival of new groups of immigrants. In order to understand the interplay between social relations and narratives and experience of belonging characterising places, we will first address the main common discourses and categories involved, locality and convenience. We will then analyse the way this interplay and these main discourses and categories underpin contrasting experiences of satisfaction and dissatisfaction with local areas, as well as 'positive' and 'negative' outcomes of the encounters between long-term settled residents and new immigrants. The comparative analysis of these different outcomes will highlight the specific role of social interventions and the relevance of public spaces and events in improving negative social trends and promoting social cohesion, which will be the subjects of the last two sections, respectively.

Locality and convenience: Prevailing self-representations of belonging to place

At a neighbourhood level, *locality* prevails over ethnicity/race/class as the main 'official' discourse defining the right to and experience of belonging. This does not mean that race, ethnicity or class play no part in the emergence of local structures of belonging, but that the main discourse through which they are expressed and indeed made socially viable is the one of locality, in other words, an ideology of 'being from here'. The narratives and ethnographic observations show that friendships and enmities are often extremely localised, with structures of belonging and attachment usually being limited to a road or to the end of a road. As it emerges from the two quotations which follow, affinities between different ethnic groups are sometimes traced in localised family systems and (extended) family structures and in 'being from' a specific road or estate, rather than in more abstract characteristics such as race, faith or ethnicity.

> I mean, I am Asian, I am Pakistani but erm, what I like about Braunstone is the extended family element. So on our street you've got mother, grandparents if you like living in one house, their children and grandchildren maybe not living far away and it's – although they don't live in one house, they do live very close to each other and that – so family social interaction if you like is much greater than in the rest of the city.
>
> (Long-term settled, minority ethnic, man, Braunstone – Leicester)

> In Dungannon, we grew up in a very nice neighbourhood. There was none of this carry on Catholics and Protestants, none of it was mentioned in them days, we all played together and we went from one house to the other. But there was a great house in the street, the McBride's, they are all dead and gone now, but it was the main house, they were shoemakers. Everyone gathered in that house.
>
> (Long-term settled, Protestant, man, Dungannon)

Both excerpts illustrate the relevance of the neoliberal resurgence of locality as a discourse framing local belonging against potentially divisive, but salient, dimensions of social differentiation. The interviewee from Braunston highlights shared patterns of 'family social interaction' being a defining aspect of local belonging in 'our street'. The older man from Northern Ireland singles out localised patterns of cohesion from a general context marked by religion-based antagonism and political conflict. Although both interviewees present themselves as belonging to and integrated within localised and 'socially cohesive' settings, the places they come from have been represented and experienced as marked by ongoing conflicts and polarisations. These antagonisms emerge at the intersections between race, ethnicity and class, in Braunstone (Leicester), a neighbourhood which until the early 2000s was (self)represented and experienced as 'white working class', and between faith and ethnicity in Dungannon, a town in Northern Ireland which was marked by a particularly antagonistic relation between the Catholic and the Protestant populations. In both interviews, accounts of 'cohesion' at a very immediate neighbourhood level resist prevailing self-representations and experiences of place in terms of conflict.

The prevalence of localised discourses framing antagonism or cohesion must be analysed in relation to the macro transformations encompassing and shaping locality and to the specific micro politics of belonging 'taking place' locally. For example, both of the 'locally positive' narratives of belonging and cohesion presented above are informed by local intersections of class, ethnicity and faith defining local criteria of 'being from here'. The Pakistani Braunstonian man is almost an embodied oxymoron given the historical connotation of the neighbourhood as white English. In the excerpt from his interview, he can be seen as referring to shared cultural traits – the extended family – as a strategy of self-incorporation and positioning into a 'local way of life' and into a social milieu which might have been exclusionary from an ethnic point of view. In turn, the Protestant Northern Irish narrative can be seen as invisibilising an antagonism which might not have been apparent to him during his childhood, but also from the vantage point of his hegemonic positioning within local society. In both cases, nostalgia and the discourse of 'the loss of community' (Rogaly and Taylor, 2011: 12) also might serve to gloss over elements of structural and heightened antagonism that were marking the localities they 'were from'.

Another 'localised' key discourse deployed by both new arrival and long-term settled interviewees frames *convenience* as a key positive category when defining a good place to live and feelings of belonging to their area of settlement. However, as in the case of 'localist' discourses of 'being from here', individual understandings of what is convenient or inconvenient are formed in relation to personal priorities and perceptions. These emerge at the intersection of race, ethnicity, class and gender and in relation to established hierarchies of belonging to place. It is this power laden local intersection that shapes prevailing as well as more individually specific understandings of 'locality', 'convenience' and acceptable public and private behaviour. The following quote, from the interview with a female East African Indian minority ethnic long-term settled resident living in a multicultural area of Leicester (Highfields) shows the relevance, but also the relativity of convenience in people's satisfaction with the place of living.

> It's quite a friendly atmosphere round here. Because, well I come from Africa but sometimes, I've been to India as well, and this area sometimes reminds me of Indian people you know? Because people are always standing outside, little groups are talking. ... I used to live on Moat Road before when the children was small, the school was

just like one, you just cross the road and the school was just there. But then when they grew up you know you need rooms for the boys and girls so we had to move down there. But I didn't want to go very far, because there's a shopping area and you can go walking you know? Post office is there, school is there, so even if you haven't got a car you can go and do your things.
>
> (Long-term settled, minority ethnic, woman, Leicester)

For this interviewee, specific forms of outdoor sociality can be seen as 'convenient' and positive aspects of social relations, as it reminds them of home. People forming groups and talking in the street are valued positively and play an active role in the perception of place in positive terms. At the same time, this minority ethnic long-term settled woman shows how cultural constructions and experiences of convenience are informed by specific intersections of ethnicity and class, which underpin localised community relations characterising social groups and the areas they inhabit.

However, experiences and discourses of convenience need to be read in the light of individual circumstances and narratives of local belonging. Some settings are characterised by social groups and relations producing dissonant rhythms and realities of everyday life. In these situations 'street conviviality' can be seen as breaching established patterns of neighbourly behaviour, as the following interview with a white male South African new arrival living in Peterborough shows.

> I like the area because it's very close to work, takes me 5 minutes to get to work and I'm happy with the accommodation in itself. The only thing that would impinge on that is the noise coming from across the road. Those people (new arrivals from Eastern Europe) often play loud music and stand outside fiddling with their cars or do you know what I mean and so there's sort of loud music and the drinking that goes on. ... But you know when I walk out of my front door, yeah, those two factors are kind of, they impact upon the previous positives, but the positives definitely outweigh.
>
> (New arrival, South Africa, white, man, Peterborough)

The arrival of individuals and groups with differing lifestyles and socialities can be seen as compromising the convenience and the positive appeal of the locality. As the last quote shows, these perceptions of convenience are not exclusive to long-term settled residents in relation to new arrivals, but inform transversal and shared strategies of positioning within specific localities and their established belongings and priorities.

In this first subsection we have analysed the way narratives of locality and convenience shape people's belonging to place. We have also underlined that people's appreciation of convenience is embedded in the interplay between their individual self-representations and circumstances and wider narratives and politics of belonging. The analysis of prevailing discourses and categories framing the relationship between place and belonging highlights the relevance of localised cultural constructions and social experiences of locality and convenience. These cultural constructions are informed by locally meaningful intersections of strategic dimensions of social differentiation such as class, gender, ethnicity, etc. The examples we give highlight the local meaningfulness of these intersections. They reveal the location and role of power, which lies in the control over the definition of local criteria of belonging and convenience. In other words, prevailing understandings of what it takes to be 'from here' and what is 'convenient' or 'inconvenient' mirror the power relations underpinning places and their social relations. Power is located in the possibility of defining hegemonic definitions of 'locality' and 'convenience', which become naturalised and invisibilised (Skeggs, 2004: 4).

The politics of convenience and locality we examine here play a strategic role in the unfolding of social cohesion, which we defined as the ability of the individuals and groups informing a social field to manage the inequalities, differentiations and tensions intervening within and between them in terms that they perceive as positive and successful. Cultural constructions of convenience and locality underpin the perceptions of places and the social relations informing them in positive and successful terms. At the same time, they are the expression of the power relations informing locally prevailing intersections between categories of differentiation. Analysing these power relations is key when understanding the interplay between migration, society and social cohesion, which cannot be abstracted from, but de facto coincides with and mirrors society, its conflicts and its complexity. The next two subsections will analyse the ways in which local understandings of convenience and locality inform the prevalence of experiences of satisfaction or dissatisfaction with place. These dynamics play a key role in the unfolding of social cohesion, as satisfaction with place is both a result of people's ability to negotiate local inequalities and a pre-condition for people's positive engagement in social cohesion.

Criteria and experiences of satisfaction and dissatisfaction with place

Localised narratives, resources and practices play a key role in the unfolding of social cohesion, which is the ability of individuals and groups inhabiting a place to negotiate its inequalities and diversities in terms they deem to be satisfactory. The power dimensions informing local definitions of 'being from here' and of convenience underpinning people's perception of satisfaction can be better explained by comparing places characterised by specific and different experiences. We found that people who were most satisfied about the place of settlement were those living in areas whose rhythms and realities of everyday life matched their expectations regarding

- safety, referring to different understandings of what constitutes a safe environment and the interactions and activities one should feel safe about;
- neighbourliness and civility, referring to different understandings of what constitutes the 'right' balance between closeness and distance as well as that between courtesy and intrusion in neighbourhood and wider social relations within the area of settlement; and
- social mobility, referring to the way individuals or groups can move upwards or downwards from one status or class position;
- lifestyles (individualised, family oriented, community based, work/money oriented, etc.).

Against this, interviewees whose expectations of social mobility, lifestyles and their understandings of convenience and security were very different from those they encountered in their lived realities of everyday life were the most dissatisfied with their place of living.

Strategic understandings and requirements of convenience and locality shape feelings of satisfaction/dissatisfaction with the place of settlement. The following interview with a long-term settled woman from Kilburn shows exactly how culturally and socially situated these perceptions are. For this young Irish woman, who converted to Islam, the increased in the number of mosques and in the availability of Halal food within a traditionally Irish area is a very positive development, which prompts a positive sense of satisfaction regarding the convenience of the area she lives in.

> It's changing. When I came here first there was a few different shops. Hamdullah there is lots of mosques going up and there's lots of

Muslim food you can get now whereas before we really had to search for food. ASDA is around the corner. You've got the tube station just around the corner, the shops are just around the corner. So I am right in the middle of everything. Now I know my way round it I don't want to move from here.
(Long-term settled, minority ethnic, woman, Kilburn)

However, in a different place and from a different (majority ethnic, other minority ethnic, etc.) point of view, the arrival of new groups of Muslim people and the spread of mosques and shops providing Halal food can be experienced as a 'Muslim takeover' of places. For instance, the following excerpt from Leicester refers to a situation of 'concealed white flight' from a culturally pluralist and relatively deprived locality (Highfields) to a more homogeneous and affluent neighbourhood.

We moved near Leicester Forest East because my husband couldn't park outside the house. That was 3 years ago. And we find that, I loved my house ... I was there 27 years, I mean I loved it round there and I loved the people. And we'd got Muslims, Hindu and there was quite a few different people around near us. Neighbours were lovely. I find when I go round there now it's a bit overwhelming, you know, because it's so, it's more Muslim orientated. Maybe I shouldn't say that. We find that a lot of them have moved into, a lot of them have moved into the housing. I think there's only 2 white couples now on the street.
(Long-term settled, majority ethnic, woman, Leicester).

The interplay between gender, religion and ethnicity in defining individual constructions and experiences of convenience is particularly powerful in this quote. While appreciating the quality of neighbourly relations in the culturally pluralist place she used to live in, the interviewee, a white English woman, also expresses her concern for the fact that, in becoming more 'Muslim oriented', it has become less diverse. At the same time, she underlines how the decision to move was informed by a gendered priority, her husband's inability to park outside the house. In the process the convenience of parking becomes invested with intersectional qualities, articulating gender with ethnicity and class.

Specific aspects such as the presence of Halal food in shops, the availability of mosques and the possibility to park easily inform perceptions of convenience reflecting wider cultural constructions and experiences of the entitlement to belonging and social mobility. These perceptions and constructions are informed by the social positioning of different groups and individuals. For instance, the Irish Muslim long-term settled woman from Kilburn 'maps' her neighbourhood and assesses its convenience according to priorities emerging at the intersection between gender and faith. The majority ethnic English long-term settled woman from Highfields (Leicester) quoted above hints at the unspoken assumptions about which individuals and groups are expected to park (i.e. reside) in a local setting for it to be seen as a convenient and desirable place to live.

When analysed together, the narratives and considerations we present here point to the way discourses of 'being from here' and convenience act as 'socially acceptable' embedding devices through which locally meaningful intersections of social categories such as class, faith, gender, age or race are expressed. The specific composition, in terms of the categories of social differentiations, of these local intersections mirrors the power relations intervening between the different social groups living in a place and influences whether people are satisfied with the places they live in, or not. Social cohesion is deeply influenced by these dynamics, as satisfaction with place is both a result of people's ability to negotiate local inequalities and a pre-condition for people's positive engagement in social cohesion. In order to capture the local specificity of this strategic interplay, the following subsections will compare the social dynamics and socio-economic resources at work in places characterised by different experiences of prevailing satisfaction or dissatisfaction with their rhythms and realities of everyday life.

Inner city multicultural areas

Inner city areas characterised by cheaper housing and by a long history of visible and acknowledged ethno-cultural diversity and migrancy are particularly strategic settings for the study of social cohesion. In these places, people can negotiate a fine line between their specific and shared values and practices, a possibility which, as we will explain in more detail in Chapter 6, we found to be one of the main aspects of social cohesion. Recent migrants and long-term settled minority ethnic groups living in such areas, particularly if they identify as Muslim, thought that overall they lived in a place which was convenient for their needs and priorities because they are safer from violence and marginalisation and they facilitate the expression of their ethno-cultural identities more fully. These interviews with a minority ethnic (Pakistani) long-term settled woman living in Glasgow and a new arrival man living in Highfields (Leicester) show the different ways in which culturally pluralist areas cater for the needs of different groups and individuals and their priorities in terms of safety and identity.

> So we fortunately did get housed in Pollokshields which was like worlds apart, totally worlds apart, it was great. Erm, the neighbours, the neighbours were, there was a Pakistani community and you felt so much safer. ... It was like different from Drumoyne. Because Drumoyne it was, there wasn't any other Asian families and it was just horrible. So I thought about moving to a house with a garden so that took me about a year and a half to actually find somewhere. And now I have been here three years and I love it, it's just great. Every day is like a Sunday.
> (Long-term settled, minority ethnic Pakistani, woman, Glasgow)

> Yes, I like living in it. The neighbourhood is very important since we all got to interact, especially children and then if you don't want them to get any bad habits from the children around you best way is to keep them away from bad habits. That's why we, I actually helped the Turkish community to set up a community centre in Leicester. Outside school hours and during weekends, we send our children there so they socialise and learn good things there so that they don't get any bad habits.
> (New arrival, Turkish, man, Highfields – Leicester)

These interviews highlight how the interplay between ethnicity, religion, relations between groups and lifestyles influences the development of individual and social identities and of cultural constructions of convenience in relation to settlement. They also show how these constructions reflect wider understandings and experiences of the entitlement to belonging and social mobility, which are informed by locally meaningful intersections and positioning. In the first quote, the interviewee's desire to have a house with a garden and her experience of social antagonism prompt her to re-settle in a multicultural neighbourhood where there are other Asian families, which makes her feel safer. The new arrival interviewee appreciates the possibility for his children to socialise with other children from different groups as well as to stay with other Turkish children, something he sees as important to steer them away from 'bad habits' which are not associated with fellow-Turkish (and Muslim) people.

The appreciation of the possibility to enjoy living in a pluralist environment was also openly expressed by some majority ethnic long-term settled residents living in an inner city multicultural area. A majority ethnic English man talks about his attachment to and enjoyment of the neighbourhood he lives in, Highfields in Leicester, where he sometimes feels like a 'minority in his own community', which encompasses a majority of Muslim long-term settled residents and new arrivals.

> I love living here, and sometimes I just wonder how I fit in as well, when I look at the neighbourhood round here we know that a very significant majority of the people are from a much more traditional Muslim culture. So in a sense I'm a stranger in my own community. Having said that, within this little microcosm of a community within which I live, all I have to do to move out of it is get on me bike and cycle and 5 minutes I'm in the city centre.
>
> (Long-term settled, majority ethnic, man, Highfields – Leicester)

The interviews we presented here show the intricate and contradictory interweaving of commonality and separatedness characterising people's experience of place. What this majority ethnic English man seems to enjoy most about living in a multicultural inner city area is the possibility of both 'being a stranger' in 'his own community', which he characterises as being 'traditionally Muslim' and of getting on the bike and accessing more pluralist and diverse places, such as the city centre. Altogether, the quotes show that living in a culturally homogeneous place does not necessarily mean living 'separate lives', which Cantle (2010) sees as leading to social fragmentation and segregation. What is particularly valued in a place is the possibility of opting out of or into the predicaments and opportunities offered by sameness and difference, by commonality and separatedness. As we will explain in more detail in Chapter 6, we found that this possibility is one of the main aspects of social cohesion, as it helps people negotiate the inequalities and diversities defining their places in terms that they deem successful and positive. Although social cohesion mirrors the intrinsically contested and dynamic nature of social relations, the cohesiveness of such relations depends on a positive appreciation of their qualities. In turn, this positive appreciation is informed by the possibility of appropriately negotiating the fine line between cultural specificity (and individual autonomy) and the participation in more collective forms of belonging.

Cultural and social diversity can be an attraction and positive aspect by itself for both majority and minority ethnic people, who are drawn and choose to live in culturally pluralist places in order to enjoy the everyday experience of their sociocultural diversity. Against apocalyptic and simplifying understanding of separatedness as inherently antagonising (Cantle, 2010), these observations highlight the overall viability of multiculturalism in contemporary Britain. In fact, as we will explain in more detail in Chapter 6, the majority of long-term settled resident and newly arriving interviewees appreciated the multicultural nature of the places they lived in and/or the fact that Britain is an increasingly diverse society. In this subsection we limit ourselves to underlining the plurality of trajectories and priorities of long-term settled residents and new arrivals who decide to live in multicultural inner city areas. For new arrivals and minority ethnic long-term residents these are primarily places where they feel safer and more able to give their children the opportunity to engage in their 'ethnic' culture. For majority ethnic long-term settled residents, these areas tend to provide the opposite opportunity to experience different cultures and customs and where they can enjoy the feeling of being 'a stranger in my own community'. For all residents, and this is a finding that emerges from all settings, a positive aspect of place is the possibility of negotiating, safely, their belonging to both separate and shared identities, values and practices in ways that correspond to the complexity of their belonging to Britain.

'Leafy Suburbs'

Relatively affluent areas characterised by dynamics of upward social mobility were also very strategic places from which to observe the unfolding of dynamics of social cohesion. These settings highlight the relevance of cultural constructions of the entitlement to social mobility, that is, to move up the social ladder, in shaping perceptions of convenience regarding settlement. Long-term settled majority and minority ethnic people living in affluent suburban areas which they saw as conforming to their expectations/hopes of social mobility were very likely to show appreciation for the areas they were living in. In general, people were very satisfied about having moved up in relation to their understanding of where they and everyone else should be in the social ladder.

However, sometimes the satisfaction with the process and area of settlement set in after an initial phase of adaptation from the previous place of residence. For instance, in the following excerpt, the same majority ethnic English woman quoted earlier, who felt they (as a couple) had to move away from multicultural Highfields because of the pressure on parking spaces from the 'increasingly Muslim' population, talks about the difficulty they experienced while adjusting to the new less diverse and quieter area.

> We are comfortable now ... but it took me a while because I wasn't used to quiet, and it's a bit more open because you're not in a terraced house. It took me a long while to get used to it because I was used to the people around me on my road. It doesn't matter what race, my friends were Asian as well as ... I mean my neighbour was African-Caribbean, we'd got friends there, you know.
> (Long-term settled, majority ethnic, woman, Leicester)

By underlining the feeling of loss of sociality and belonging she experienced individually and the comfort they experience as a couple, this majority ethnic English woman further highlights the gendered dimension of the decision to move out of Highfield, which seems to have been her husband's idea more than hers. In doing so, she also shows how moving up the social ladder can be experienced both in terms of satisfaction with one's social repositioning, but also in terms of loss of previous forms of social participation within more 'convenient' neighbourhoods.

The process of adjustment to a more 'convenient' place can be particularly difficult when minority ethnic people, including long-term settled residents, move from more deprived and ethnically diverse settings to more affluent neighbourhoods, inhabited by a greater proportion of majority ethnic long-term settled residents. In the words of this minority ethnic long-term settled man, the arrival of his affluent Asian family in a leafy neighbourhood in Leicestershire was resisted at first by local majority ethnic English long-term settled residents, although this upward social mobility pattern later came to be more accepted.

> Because I have success I can afford to buy a house in an affluent area, because I can send my daughters to a private school. It was interesting when I first moved to Leicester and saw a house. I made an offer and invested money to value it, and the owners undervalued it and had the legal work completed quickly because they didn't want to sell to an Asian. I think generally the Asian people are now seen as an asset. If you go to a middle class area they know you will keep the house, expand the house, you will invest in garden you will invest in so and so.
> (Long-term settled, minority ethnic, man, Leicester)

The decision of an 'Asian' family to move up the social ladder is actively resisted by owners, who can be seen as operating according to a localised cultural construction of belonging, convenience and of the entitlement to social mobility. The narrative frames the resistance to minority ethnic people's access to the higher strata of the housing market as something of the past.

Minority ethnic long-term settled residents can still be subject to a process of re-racialisation as undesirable 'asylum seekers', when they move to suburban areas characterised by a self-perception in terms of majority ethnic English homogeneity. A Councillor in Peterborough talks about his work of mediation between 'indigenous' people, that is, people who believe they are 'from here' and newcomers, which are stigmatised as asylum seekers in the meanwhile.

> When they do move out of their traditional areas, you've got the indigenous population saying oh, asylum seekers! And I have to say I do break confidentiality sometimes and say 'that person was born here and so were his two kids'. I had one in my village, and you can imagine it's even worse in a village. Had to go tell the whole pub! Once they knew, it wasn't a problem.
>
> (Key informant, Peterborough)

This councillor from Peterborough explains in his own words the way the category of migrancy can be implicated in the emergence of powerful new stereotypes and forms of social exclusion, which subsume the intersection of ethnicity/race and new 'settled' categories and hierarchies of local belonging.

In both of the cases presented above, the stigmatisation of and resistance to mobility, both social and geographical, happens whenever newly arriving groups are seen by majority ethnic long-term settled residents as 'transgressing' implicit social and economic hierarchies. As we have explained earlier in the chapter, discourses of locality and convenience act as embedding devices for power dynamics and intersectional hierarchies enforcing the differential entitlement to social as well as spatial mobility of social groups within and between places. These processes frame social cohesion. They underpin local criteria of convenience and of satisfaction with the place of living according to which social relations and inequalities are negotiated in terms deemed positive by those involved.

Inner city estates

Places and communities which were marginalised by the New Economy were named and classified as deprived early in the first New Labour administration through major investment programmes. These aimed to reintegrate marginalised places into the mainstream economy. The policy strategy was to renew infrastructural resources and regenerate local economies to counter the consequences of deindustrialisation: structural unemployment, poverty and poor neighbourhood and housing resources. However, the identification of particular areas as deprived instituted a form of governmentality that positioned specific communities and their places as themselves the source of the problem rather than the processes of economic restructuring that had marginalised them from the new economy (Rose, 1999). Regeneration monies were allocated with the expectation that the investment in enterprises and in individual skilling through education would increase marginalised people's employment rate and decrease their reliance on welfare. This New Labour synthesis of a social democratic public spending programme with a neoliberal enthusiasm for modernisation through enterprise and individualisation was remarkably unsuccessful in generating any real degree of economic integration. From 2004 successive years have measured a widening gap between the socio-economic parameters of marginalised areas and the mainstream (Parekh et al., 2010). These areas continued to be seen as sites of failed community cohesion by persisting identifications as deprived places. This avoided the need to engage with the failures of these policy interventions and to acknowledge the structural marginalisations and exclusions produced by the New Economy.

In this section of the chapter we will look at people's experiences in South Kilburn and Downham in London, Braunstone in Leicester and Glasgow. In our research we found no immediate correlation between deprivation and failed social cohesion in response to new arrivals. This was significant insofar as new arrivals coming to live in these areas were often seen as additional low-waged workers with limited resources constituting further pressure on scarce employment opportunities. The four areas under discussion were highly rated in the deprivation index, which measures the population density of people deemed economically vulnerable: the over 50s, people with disabilities, single parents, minority ethnic groups, young people and unemployed people. The realities of sustained and concentrated economic marginalisation placed considerable strain on the lives of people still navigating the consequences of deindustrialisation. These circumstances are made clear in the following quotes from long-term settled minority ethnic men from Braunstone and South Kilburn.

> You actually died younger if you lived in Braunstone. The death rate for men was something like ten years less than the national

average ... there was one doctor's surgery over here where there was one doctor, all the others had basically fled.
(Long-term settled, minority ethnic, man, Leicester)

Where I live now in West London, it's like – the area is too much. There is so many things going on. There is police every day in my estate. Everything is just – people are everywhere. ... Everyone are not really doing much with their lives ... just selling drugs and same old, same old.
(Long-term settled, minority ethnic, young man, Kilburn)

The realities of living with almost non-existent resources was ingrained in the reduced life expectancy in Braunstone The assessment of everyday life in South Kilburn suggests that the chaotic nature of social relations arose from many people living in the estate supplying the London night time economy with recreational drugs. This, in addition to the other demographic of the estate – a high concentration of problem families – prompted the local priest to submit a dossier to the District Coroner on the 22 murders in the recent history of the estate and its impact on families already suffering vulnerability (Hales, 2005). The historical and socially intersecting layers of sustained poverty, unemployment, casualised and informal work that shaped estate life constituted, in his view, challenges that made social relations unnavigable in any positive way. However the unfolding of social relations in the South Kilburn Estate did not follow the indicative measure prescribed by government of undermined community cohesion resulting in inter-ethnic violence and racism and segregated communities. Rather social deprivation was a registered in a desire of many to leave the estate but because of poverty only.

And it's a very deprived area, there are a lot of problems, you know ... but you don't ever feel it's around racial tensions or cultural tensions ... there is very high unemployment, there is a fairly low skills base in the workforce, there is poor housing, poor statutory resources in the area. ... And so, you know, I think the population here encounters some challenges but I feel that they deal quite admirably with those. And they generally rub fairly well together considering the challenges they face.
(Key informant, Kilburn)

This key informant, herself a long-term settled resident of the area was clear that deprivation could not easily be equated with preconceived ideas of failed social cohesion. She describes people living in the estate as able to deal positively with the potentially antagonising challenges, conflicts and tensions they meet in their everyday life. This cohesive ability, as we explain more fully later in this chapter and in the Chapter 6 on Politics of Belonging, is rooted in Kilburn's history of migration and multiculturalism, which was sustained in its integration into the unskilled labour markets produced by the old and the new economies.

Deprived inner city estates are the places that were most, but not uniquely, associated with feelings of dissatisfaction, on the part of both long-term settled residents and new arrivals. Most people felt that they should be 'somewhere else' in relation to their expected social positioning and trajectory of social mobility. Places characterised by the prevalence of feelings of dissatisfaction were also marked by a higher occurrence of antagonism and (sometimes) conflict over scarce resources such as subsidised housing, income support, and jobs. Our findings confirm what was evidenced by existing research (Rogaly and Taylor, 2011), that inner city estates are characterised by a variety of socio-economic profiles and trajectories. However, we also found that inner city estates tended to be places characterised by the prevalence of dissatisfaction, in which long-term settled residents, both majority and minority ethnic, feel betrayed by the state, the transformation of the local labour market and economy and by the allocation of scarce resources to new arrivals, who sometimes get priority of allocation because of the severity of their socio-economic and family situation. These two interviews with key informants from the social services in Kilburn and from a refugee organisation in Downham and show this complex interplay at work.

> Amongst refugee communities again you're beginning to see a kind of predominance within council accommodation and there is some evidence that that's beginning to cause some tensions with more established communities, and I don't just mean the white community. Because you're seeing, for example, black Caribbean households who are feeling themselves pushed out by black African households who have sometimes come as refugees, not always.
>
> (Key informant, Kilburn)

> Downham is a place where. ... I can call it a place where white working class people tend to live. Refugees have been offered accommodations there and after two weeks, three weeks they will come here complaining about racism and they phoned the police and the police actually recommended that they should be moved.
>
> (Key informant, Downham)

The interviews presented above show the combined impact of the structural unavailability of subsidised housing and the arrival of socio-economically vulnerable groups in deprived settings. This impact can antagonise local social relations as the needs and priorities of long-term settled and newly arriving vulnerable groups are forced to compete for key scarce resources, whose unavailability is likely to be further undermined by the implementation of neoliberal policies. The two key informants from Kilburn and Downham also show that as a result of the juxtaposition of long standing and new socio-economic vulnerabilities, new arrivals (particularly refugees and asylum seekers) experience violence and stigmatisation.

As is corroborated by existing research (Robinson et al., 2007), the allocation of council housing to asylum seekers/refugees and other new arrivals within or around deprived estates was the single circumstance most associated with cases of racially motivated violence. In the process, culturally constructed hierarchies of local belonging are mobilised in order to claim priority access to social support. As it emerges from the interview material we present here, these culturally constructed hierarchies can antagonise the relations between long-term settled residents, both minority and majority ethnic, and new arrivals. The case of Sighthill (Glasgow) is emblematic in this respect. After an initial resistance against the relocation of refugee families long-term settled residents formed an alliance with them which resulted in the allocation of shared resources. The example of Sighthill illustrates that the arrivals of new group in a deprived area does not necessarily coincide only with an increase in social antagonism. On the contrary, the challenge posed by the arrival of new groups reactivated local political cultures of social equality which transformed antagonism in cohesion, as existing inequalities were dealt with in terms which were deemed positive by most of the people living in a place. Dormant sociocultural resources such as political cultures of social equality are very important in the viability of everyday life in inner city estates, which are characterised by specific, as well as shared, forms of belonging and community when compared with other social settings.

Although long-term settled residents from inner city estates were among the most dissatisfied with their place of settlement, they also showed a particularly pronounced attachment to their areas and local communities. When prompted to explain what these feelings were related to most interviewees indicate the close knit network of social relations that they can (still) enjoy there, the stigma they (sometimes) face when they leave their area and their lack of self-confidence originating from the long-term experience of deprivation. These two majority ethnic long-term settled resident men from Braunston (Leicester) and Sighthill (Glasgow) illustrate the interplay between close-knit belonging, stigmatisation and community at work.

> There's a lot of like community spirit around the estate, like there's a little kid who died a couple of year back, and everyone chipped in for the headstone, everyone on the estate chipped in. So it's like if something like, if someone needs something they'll be happy to like lend you some sugar or something like that. ... But because of where I'm from people will like, if I'm going around another estate or something, people will automatically think I'm a thug or something. So it's just like a stereotypical view of the estate.
> (Long-term settled, majority ethnic, man, Braunstone)

> I like living here. The neighbourhood I'm in was one of the first kinds of council estates in Glasgow and was a successful estate. It's got a good community kind of feel about it ... there's a good feel about the place.
> (Long-term settled, majority ethnic, man, Glasgow)

These two interviewees from Braunstone and Sightill explain that many people living in inner city estates appreciate the feeling of belonging to a relatively close community, and this is a counter-weight to the stigma attached to the estate and to people living in it. As in most other social settings, solidarity and proximity are expressed more in moments of particular distress for the community around a specific issue or need. On the one hand these relations of solidarity and proximity and the strong feelings of attachment and belonging to the neighbourhood mentioned above are very important resources, as they counter the stigma associated with living in deprived inner city estates. These feeling of belonging are key to the development of social cohesion as they can form the basis to create or reactivate the ability to negotiate the inequalities of places in terms which are shared by its inhabitants. On the other hand, these very same resources can be mobilised against new arrivals, when they are perceived as further undermining long-term settled residents' already marginalised position. It is this complex politics of belonging that needs to be de-coded when trying to understand the relations between new arrivals and the long-term settled residents living in deprived inner city estates.

We found no direct relation between deprivation and negative social reactions to the arrival of new groups. Moreover, different groups of people show different levels and criteria of satisfaction about living in inner city estates, according to their individual socio-economic and cultural trajectories and their expectations (Rogaly and Taylor, 2011). The onset of post-industrialisation and neoliberalism coincided with processes of individualisation and diversification of people's expectations and priorities, which become increasingly important in mobilising feelings of satisfaction in relation to the place of living. The following two interviews with a young woman and a young man from Downham show the way in which a marginalised place can be a positive place of belonging, because 'it's down to earth' and become more pluralist as a consequence of the arrival of new groups and the onset of a more accepting mentality in the new generations. When compared, the two excerpts also show the way in which individual trajectories and histories, and particularly the intersection of ethnicity, gender, class and faith, shape feelings and experiences of belonging to place.

> Yeah, I grew up here. I love it to pieces. I couldn't move out of here. It's where you know everyone, it's just social, it's been alright around here. Different people live here, different cultures, all different age groups, there is a lot of different age groups around here. It's just like a community around here. You've got parts that are far away but everyone still comes together. It's really good. I wouldn't know different to be honest, I wouldn't know different. But when I see my mates that live in posh areas, I'd rather live here. Because it's down to earth and I know where everything is, I know where to get to everywhere. It's nice living here, I suppose.
>
> (Long-term settled, majority ethnic, young woman, Downham)

> At the moment the main problem is getting a job, a full-time job. Because no matter where you look all the jobs have gone. Don't get me wrong, I am not a racist person or anything else but they are all going to the immigrants. You look on the building sites then the immigrants have got it, because they are cheaper labour. It just seems to me that everything has gone downhill. It's like even the housing. My name has been on the housing list since I was fourteen. And I still now, 23, I haven't heard anything. But then you have all these people coming over and they get handed cars, they get handed houses, jobs, do you know what I mean. It's just like, it does wind a lot of people up because it's like well, you can't look after your own

but then you are willing to let anyone else in and give it to them on a place. Do you know what I mean?
>
> (Long-term settled, majority ethnic, young man, Downham).

For the white majority ethnic English teenager from a family which used to be working class but is currently better off, the sets of social relations, opportunities and expectations available in contemporary (relatively) ethno-culturally diverse Downham are satisfactory. For the white working class majority ethnic English young man coming from a poor and broken family, growing up in Downham is very different. Since he could not benefit from the opportunities of social support and employment available in this context, he deploys the 'settled backlash' discourse to argue that his needs, him being 'from here', should have priority over those of newcomers. Besides their specificities, both quotes highlight the existence of very dissonant experiences of isolation and connectedness within deprived inner city estates, as well as their increasing socio-economic and ethno-cultural differentiation.

Overall, available opportunities and resources, local politics and narratives of belonging and the related hierarchies of entitlement to social mobility are key factors informing people's satisfaction with the place of settlement. In other words, people's satisfaction with the place they live in results from the interplay between where they feel they should 'be at' and where they are 'actually' at in relation to their self-representation, their perceived social positioning and their understanding of 'who should be where'. The outcomes of these interactions will be seen as largely positive or negative by people inhabiting a specific place depending on how well individual/group expectations see themselves as matching, and actually match, the actual possibilities encountered locally. The interplay between all of these dimensions influences not only people's satisfaction with their places, but also impacts on local dynamics of social cohesion, as they influence the terms in which local inequalities can be resolved by people sharing a specific place in terms they deem to be positive and successful. Given the significance of these processes for social cohesion, we now more on to discuss the relation the complex local significance of place and its prevailing framing of cultural diversity and social pluralism.

The politics of place and the arrival of new groups

Having identified and discussed the main discursive sets – locality ('being from here') and convenience – informing people's positive and negative affiliations to place and analysed how they are implicated in dynamics of social cohesion, in this subsection we will focus more specifically on the way the arrival of new migrant group is implicated in this complex interplay. The study of social cohesion in contemporary social settings in the UK highlights very different experiences of the encounter between long-term settled and newly arriving groups. More specifically, in some places, such as Belgrave and Highfields (Leicester) and Kilburn (except the South Kilburn Estate) the arrival of new social groups was mainly accepted as a 'positive' or necessary (for humanitarian/economic/demographic reasons) contribution to local society or ignored as a matter of normal everyday life (particularly in Kilburn). In others, such as Braunstone (Leicester), Downham, and in Sighthill (Glasgow), Peterborough and Dungannon (Northern Ireland), it was consistent with the initial prevalence of 'negative' feelings of resentment, social antagonism and racially motivated attacks. All places, at different times in their histories, witnessed the onset of what we defined as the 'settled backlash' phenomenon, referring to the emergence of ideologies and narratives of localism (being from here) as new political strategies to reinforce or challenge existing social hierarchies. However, in all places, the initial mobilisation of feelings of resentment between long-term settled residents, majority ethnic people and newly arriving groups, was followed, to a different extent, by an improvement of these relations as a consequence of social intervention. Kilburn was an exception to these trends because its more historically established acceptance of cultural and social diversity meant that we did not find instances of settled backlash there. At the same time, the extent of disaffection and marginalisation we encountered in the South Kilburn estate meant that this specific situation was not successfully addressed by social interventions.

The history of place and migration are key in determining the local availability of the resources needed for a positive resolution of the conflicts underpinning social cohesion. Places such as Kilburn and Leicester, where people tend to view the arrival of new groups ether positively or neutrally, are not 'better' than places such as Downham, where the arrival of new groups coincided with social unrest. Kilburn and the city of Leicester, were places in which migrancy – that is 'not being from here' and the necessity to accept and mediate between a complex range of social and cultural diverse individuals and groups came to be accepted as part of everyday life in a more historical perspective. Because of their long history of positive resolution of migration-related inequalities and their very diverse populations, they simply had more opportunities to recognise, understand and accept, overall, the process of pluralisation of their social fields. On the contrary, places such as Downham had a more limited historical experience of pluralisation, mainly referring to the displacement to 'a place in the country' of people working in the Bermondsey docks in the early 1920s, which is when the estate was built as a project of social reformation of the deprived working classes. Until the early 2000s, the main reference to cultural and social diversity in Downham was informed by the hierarchies of Britishness, or unrecognised non-Britishness in the case of the Irish population, characterising the diverse population of 1920s Bermondsey, which still operated in the local history of place. Because of the lack of recognition of its social and cultural diversity and the relatively smaller and more recent impact of international migration places such as Downham are still self-representing themselves as homogeneous, which means that the arrival of new groups tends to be seen as an exception, rather than the norm. In order to capture the impact of the arrival of new groups on local experiences of local cohesion, in the next subsection we will focus comparatively on situations in which the arrival of new groups coincided with negative social tensions or were positively accepted as part of the social dynamics of everyday life.

Negative and positive reactions to the arrival of new migrant groups

Conflicts (and cohesions) emerged in relation to access to key (scarce) resources such as work, education, peer acknowledgement, recreational spaces, (subsidised) housing, income support, and proximity (the possibility of living close to family/friends). Negative dynamics of antagonism tended to happen in places marked by marginalisation from the post-industrial and neoliberal restructuring of the economy and/or perceived (by insiders and outsiders) as culturally homogeneous, whether these were deprived or not. As was the case with 'leafy suburbs', dynamics of exclusion and marginalisastion of newcomers can happen also in affluent places, where 'people from here' can try and maintain their socio-economic hegemony by preventing newcomers from entering 'their' places. Our findings show that the recurrence of social tensions in relation to the arrival of new groups was strongly influenced by the convergence between several of factors, which we summarise in the lists that follow, for the sake of clarity. Places which tended to respond negatively to the arrival of new groups tended to be characterised by:

- the feeling of declining (cultural, economic, spatial) predominance, in the present or in the future, of a demographically predominant group representing itself as 'from here';
- a prevailing social and cultural heritage referring to a 'close knit' social environment and translating into specific codes of convenience and neighbourly behaviour;
- a strain on strategic resources (employment, income benefits, subsidised housing, good education facilities);
- a lack of information about the arrival of new groups in their immediate setting, their background and their right to access shared (scarce) resources.

In these places, people who feel they represent the predominant 'declining' majority:

- Interpreted minimalist or different (culturally, urban/rural, etc.) notions of convenience and neighbourliness as lack of interest/respect and/or hostility.
- Expressed feelings of resentment for their subjection to prolonged deprivation/marginalisation and lack of access to social mobility, by blaming newcomers for structural (or potential) shortages in social provision (subsidised housing, non-exploitative low-skilled jobs, economic support, education).
- Produced dynamics of acute social antagonism (racist attacks, harassment, bullying, exclusion) against newcomers.

The opposite 'positive' case is that of places marked by:

- A significant demographic, economic and cultural presence of diverse migrant populations,
- The common (by long-term settled residents and by new arrivals) acknowledgement of the area's social and cultural heritage as mixed,
- The common acceptance of a plurality of understandings of convenience and of styles of neighbourliness,
- The common acknowledgement of the coinciding of socio-economic growth/stability and the arrival of new migrant or minority ethnic groups,

- The positive connection of a significant part of the local population with neoliberal and post-industrial capitalism because of the arrival of new groups.

In these contexts, the critical characteristic is that no specific ethnic, faith or racialised identity is able to claim a privileged entitlement to belonging to place. When this plurality of belonging is combined with the perception that the socio-economic security of place is reinforced by the arrival of new groups it makes it easier for the majority of residents to:

- Accept or ignore different (culturally, urban/rural, etc.) notions of convenience and neighbourliness as part of a predominant acceptance of cultural pluralism;
- Express feelings of appreciation for the cultural diversity of the area, which is seen as a positive asset of local identity;
- Produce adequate institutional responses of acceptance and solidarity towards newcomers;
- Experience the arrival of new groups as in line with the history and everyday experience of place and as a resource for the economic wellbeing of place.

Our definition of social cohesion is the ability within individuals and groups living in a place to manage the inequalities and tensions intervening between them in terms that they perceive as positive and successful. The analysis of the factors underpinning social cohesion shows that there is a relation between social cohesion, long-term local histories of migrant diversity, and the ability to survive post-industrialism and neoliberalism through the support of new migrant groups. We will examine this claim more thoroughly in Chapter 6, when we will focus more closely on the cultural constructions and experiences of social cohesion across the UK. Here, we need to underline that in multicultural settings, such as Kilburn and Leicester, which remained or became relatively more sustainable throughout post-industrialism and neoliberalism because of the arrival of new groups, the very ethnic diversity of place became a positive social and cultural asset.

The positive evaluation of ethnic difference should not be seen as a given, but as an outcome of an ability and willingness to resolve positively the inequalities and opportunities posed by the convergence of deep socio-economic transformations and the arrival of new migrant groups, together with their needs, skills and resources. In the case of Leicester, the council played a key role in measuring the opportunities posed by the arrival of an entrepreneurial class of Gujarati refugees from East Africa, who regenerated the declining hosiery industry, against the possibilities of social antagonism presented by the riots of the 1980s. In the space of about 10 years, the council passed from actively dissuading East African refugees from coming to Leicester by publishing ads on local newspapers in Uganda, to actively promoting the pacific coexistence of different ethnic groups through the funding of a capillary network of grass root ethnic organisations. This pragmatic turnaround is the epitome of the socially cohesive ability to resolve social inequalities in locally positive terms. The heritage of the 1980s social investment in multicultural governance which followed the 1970s attempt to prevent refugees from coming to Leicester is still the backbone of Leicester's exemplary record in achieving and maintaining social cohesion.

In other cases, a culturally pluralist stance was established more from below than from above. Kilburn, a historical hub of Irish migration in the heart of London, shows a more complex and contradictory picture of strategic alliances between different groups of both long-term settled residents and new arrivals. In Kilburn, the shared experiences of discrimination and migration of African Caribbean long-term settled residents and their Irish counterparts were cited by interviewees from both groups as the source of the ease with which these two groups were able to live together. This young minority ethnic Irish long-term settled man in Kilburn, explains how shared historical experiences of migrancy and discrimination formed the emergence of a pluralist mode of belonging in Kilburn.

> It's Irish and Caribbean youngsters, and they do plot together round here. Whereas in Hackney or somewhere like that or New Cross in Lewisham or whatever, there is big Irish communities and Caribbeans that live next to each other but they don't mix. But here for some reason they mix. ... I sort of know why, it's you know, back ages and ages ago when everyone come over some Irish people would buy up and then let Caribbeans stay. And then some Caribbeans would buy up and let Irish stay. So it's a sort of mutual respect thing. From Ladbroke Grove it started up and just moved up towards here like.
>
> *Do you think it is because they were both discriminated against?*
> Yeah. No dogs, No Blacks, No Irish. I even wrote a tune about that.
>   (Long-term settled, minority ethnic Irish, young man, Kilburn)

The shared history of belonging and discrimination of the African-Caribbean and Irish communities in Kilburn can be seen as having produced shared feelings of belonging that were also supported by a common experience of British colonialism, including a British-inspired education system and the establishment of English as a dominant language. The involvement in similar processes of resistance to discrimination and marginalisation in the context of migration to Britain and in relation to the British (post)colonial experience created a positive footprint that was to make Kilburn a place of constructive relations between different migrant and long-term settled individuals and communities to the present day.

What the cases of the city of Leicester and the area of Kilburn in North London have in common is a social and cultural context where, because of the acknowledged mixed heritage of each place, nobody can claim to have a predominant right to belong and benefit from shared resources. The shared perception of the arrival of new groups as an asset for the prosperity of one's place is indeed a key factor promoting the desire and willingness to accommodate and accept the reality of multiculture. Another key factor is the possibility for local places to benefit from the transformation of work and the shift to flexible livelihoods fostered by the convergence between post-industrialism and neoliberalism. For instance, Kilburn's proximity to the centre of London and to informal labour markets (roadside pickups for the construction industry, etc.) meant that it continued being a very strategic hub for migrants who were able and willing to tap into a transforming economy and thus to contribute to the socio-economic sustainability of place. As we mentioned, the fact that East African Gujarati refugees revitalised a local declining industrial sector made Leicester council aware of the asset represented by migration, which led to the elaboration of a model of multicultural governance that is still being praised as exemplary.

On the contrary, Downham's social history coincided with the 'ecological' project of social reformation of the working class and with the clearance of the London dock areas in early twentieth century, as well as with the labour needs of a manufacturing based and Fordist economy, which held until the late 1950s. In the years that followed, as most people could not translate their skills according to the requirements of the knowledge-based economy, the area fell into economic decline and was revitalised only partially and recently by the arrival of new groups of British, EU and third country people, which triggered resentment and animosity. Our findings are in line with recent research, highlighting that it is socio-economic exclusion, rather than the arrival of immigrants, which underpins the support for xenophobic discourses as those adopted by the BNP (IPPR, 2010). These observations are corroborated by the electoral results in Dagenham and Barking, where protectionist and localist parties such as UKIP and the BNP were defeated at the political elections in 2010, after having obtained a relatively good result at the European elections in 2009. We found that xenophobic trends and dynamics were not irreversible. In all of our sites, except Kilburn where we could not find instances of 'settled backlash', the acknowledgement of the intrinsic diversity of places and of the positive contribution of newly arriving migrant groups to the common well-being were promoted by social interventions which addressed positively issues which could destabilise local prosperity and harmony. As far as Downham is concerned, after a modest surge in consensus in 2009, the BNP did not even contest the area in 2010, while most of our interviews tended to see the migration-related antagonisms of the early 2000s as a matter of the recent past.

The case of Glasgow is paradigmatic in relation to the interplay between economic contributions of new group to the well-being of place and the acceptance of new migrant groups. The decision to extend the resources initially reserved to asylum seekers and refugees to the rest of the deprived population among whom they were dispersed played a key role in transforming an initial attitude of resistance and hostility to one of solidarity and acceptance. The lack of the presence within local histories of tangible examples of the positive contribution of migrants to the socio-economic sustainability of place is a pivotal aspect in the unfolding of social cohesion. When migrants are seen by long-term settled residents as further eroding already scarce vital resources, they tend to be seen as a disadvantage and refused, particularly when local communities tend to see themselves as 'from here'. On the contrary, when migrants are seen as and indeed bring new resources with them, they tend to be accepted, even in context of deprivation, and particularly where there are local histories of migrancy and struggle for social justice.

In order to understand the relationship between place, social relations and social cohesion, it is important to contextualise it within the socio-economic transformation of place promoted by post-industrialism and neoliberalism. The strategic role played by narratives of convenience and locality in framing local experiences of social cohesion and antagonism between deprived long-term settled residents and newly arrived individuals highlights the polarisation of places introduced by neoliberalism. The transformation of work according to the needs of an increasingly knowledge-based economy, the increasing polarisation between the rich and the poor and the proliferation of geopolitical conflict coinciding with the neoliberal order produced and concentrated new 'wasted lives' (2004) into localised and marginalised places, such as inner city estates. In the context of the onset of the 'settled backlash', marginalised groups and places can feel encouraged to align themselves with specific identifications as 'being from here' which are marked by and re-inscribe into place isolation, inferiority and boundedness. At the same time, places whose existing resources, including those brought about by migrant groups, allow them to reap the benefits of, or at least survive, post-industrial and neoliberal socio-economic transformations, produce narratives of multiple and pluralist belonging, which enable them to negotiate locally inequalities in terms which they deem satisfactory.

The fluidity of the contradictory histories of pluralism and homogeneity of the places we investigated allows us to underline how the outcome of the interplay between local inflections of post-industrial neoliberalism and of the 'settled backlash' phenomenon is not necessary or unchangeable. The cases of the city of Leicester and of the area of Sighthill (Glasgow) show that exclusionary local discourses and practices can be successfully countered by the existence of shared local histories of migration and the acknowledgement of the positive contribution made by migrants. Projects of social intervention can play an important role in maintaining or actually improving relations between new arrivals and long-term settled residents. This positive role was particularly evident in Dungannon, Glasgow and Peterborough, where the co-operation between the Council and non-governmental organisations improved mutual relations and perceptions. In Peterborough, where the settlement of new arrivals coincided with the rapid economic and demographic expansion of the city, the arrival of different groups since 2001 ignited different kinds of social alarms for differently established groups. Similarly, according to Police Service of Northern Ireland data (PSNI 2006–7), the arrival of A8 Eastern Europeans in Dungannon was consistent with a 48 per cent increase in the number of local racist incidents (including those between minority ethnic individuals) from 2004 to 2006 and by a negative press campaign.

In both Dungannon and Peterborough, a number of initiatives of social intervention (promoted and delivered by our partners New Link, in Peterborough and STEPS in Dungannon in particular) have risen to the occasion and actually produced good examples of mediation services between long-term settled residents and new arrivals, which impacted positively on their relations. The networking of different targeted services enabled the delivery of efficient social interventions catering for the complex of issues, mostly related to different understandings of convenience and neighbourliness, emerging from the encounter of long-term settled residents and new arrival groups. In both contexts, which were characterised by the unawareness of the extent of the largely positive economic contribution made by the arrival of migrants on the local economy, the ability to work across and with different communities of long-term settled residents and new arrivals, as well as to link existing and new projects and initiatives was key for the improvement of social relations. In this respect, initiatives of social intervention negotiating local inequalities and conflicts in terms which are seen as positive by the people involved are not only a key aspect, but actually an expression of the fundamental ability defining social cohesion.

Conclusion

All the places we investigated, with the exception of Kilburn, were involved in the 'white backlash' of the 1980s and/or in the 'settled backlash' of the 1990s and 2000s. This process took place according to different understandings and experiences of local belongings, which emerged out of different local intersections of class, race, ethnicity, religion and gender. Of our six sites, in Kilburn and Leicester (except in the context of inner city council estates), the awareness of the fact that migration was a key economic asset for as well as an integral part of place coincided with local narratives of belonging based on the acceptance of diversity. At the same time, both places were able to capitalise on the socio-economic transformations fostered by post-industrialism and neoliberalism, while local administration and civil society had adequate economic and cultural resources to identify and address timely issues of potential concern. In other words, in Kilburn and Leicester, migrants were both seen and actually were a key economic asset for local society.

In other places, like Downham, Dungannon, and Braunstone (Leicester) the interplay between prevailing self representations in terms of homogeneity and closeness and the long-term exclusion of long-term settled residents from the post-industrial flexibilised and knowledge-based economy were the background for hostile reactions to the arrival of new groups. Moreover, the arising tensions were addressed with a considerable delay, although in all of these settings measures were eventually put in place that improved the situation. In the process, popular discourses emerged framing newcomers as people who would exert a further strain on scarce resources, rather than as people who could contribute to the socio-economic improvement of the area.

The key issue at stake in understanding dynamics of social cohesion is the degree to which the complexity of each social and cultural setting is acknowledged within predominant narratives and practices of local belonging, such as locality and convenience. People's pluralist or homogeneous experiences of belonging are resilient because they are deeply embedded in their individual and social identities. It is within this social and discursive context that new arrivals will be perceived and addressed as an opportunity or a threat. This wider context is what social interventions need to address through cultural mediation and support that address both long-term settled residents and new arrivals. These remarks point to the conclusion that local feelings of belonging can be encouraged towards a positive acceptance of social and cultural pluralism and towards the cohesive ability to positively address local conflicts and inequalities through the improvement of the overall shared rhythms and realities of everyday life. This can be achieved through the delivery of services targeting the specific needs of new arrivals together with the long-standing needs of long-term settled residents, such as lack of employment and training/education and the associated lack of self-confidence. In this way, new arrivals become (and are perceived by the long-term settled as) an opportunity for rather than a strain on local resources. The experience of Glasgow, where the decision to extend the assistance given to asylum seekers to the long-term settled residents living in deprived areas was at the basis of a turnaround of an initial position of hostility to one of support and empathy, is an encouraging example of good practice in this respect.

4
Housing and the Family

Together, housing and the family make up the spaces of home structuring the day-to-day places and relations in which people live their lives. Housing accommodates family and personal life and spatially situates domestic familial relations. Housing and personal life are also framed by the wider dynamics of place that identify where people live and texture the social relations of how they live communally, locally and interpersonally. The common expression 'an English man's home is his castle' suggests that home also contains the spaces of national belonging through identifications of 'the family' best suited to reproduce the national population. 'The trope of the family is widespread in the figuring of national narratives – homeland, motherland, daughters and sons of the nation' (Walter, 1995: 37; McClintock, 1993). The domestic space – home and hearth – that reproduces the family is constructed through welfare and gender regimes that privilege, ethnonationally, the kinds of women and families that properly reproduce the nation (Yuval Davis, 1993; Gedalof, 2007).

The social infrastructures of family and housing, like those of work and place, are marked by the transformations of post-industrialism and the neoliberal recodifications of entitlements to both homes and families. Family relations have been transformed by one of the signatures of post-industrialism, the reincorporation of women into the waged workforce (Crompton, 2006) representing a partial return to an earlier period of industrialism in which the power of liberal economic individualism disaggregated families and created workforces of children as well as women and men. Post-industrialism is also characterised by declining fertility and increasing longevity within families, by the fluid and varied forms of families, and by the altering work/life balances that integrate families with working life (Perrons et al., 2006). These family dynamics motivated global migrations responding to labour demands previously met by the unwaged work of women and supported by welfare regimes that placed housing and family as central to their remit of social provision (Gluckmans, 2006; Williams, 2011). Housing was transformed not only by the altering patterns of personal living arrangements but also by neoliberal welfare strategies that introduced a partial privatisation of social housing in the subsidised right to buy provision that increased home ownership through the sale of council houses. Altered entitlements to social housing based on need further changed the experiences of housing for many. They generated one of the flashpoints of social cohesion in restricting access to social housing in a context characterised by increasing levels of migration (Hills, 2007; Rutter and Latorre, 2009). Ideas of national belonging, of for whom the country constitutes a home, became confused in the mix of diminished commitment to social provision and increasing support for migration, producing a real confusion for many about the instabilities of housing and family life in Britain.

In our research we found the problems of family life and the difficulties of affordable housing were sorely felt by many of our interviewees. The changes of post-industrialism had produced instabilities, conflict, tensions and contestations in everyday life that demanded resolution for the long-term settled as well as for new arrivals. Of these challenges to the daily routines of personal life perhaps the most critical were the changes in housing availability. The increased demand for affordable housing from the settled population arising from the changed patterns of personal life occurred at a time when public sector housing provision dramatically contracted. Affordable housing was restricted by the right to buy legislation and the curtailment of local authority housing expenditure that ushered in the neoliberal welfarism of the Thatcher government. This reduction of, and brake on the provision of affordable housing was not reversed by subsequent Labour governments until the latter years of the third term of office and the sustained impact of these policies across successive Conservative and Labour governments produced an acute housing shortage. At the time of our research, housing and family life were contextualised by an orchestrated housing bubble that seemingly ineluctably foreclosed the possibility of home ownership for increasing numbers of people.

In this chapter we will consider the impact of these discursive, political and structural changes on social cohesion. In the first section we will analyse the memories and narratives of interviewees about earlier disruptions to family and home life that shaped previous migrations and belongings. These histories deflect claims that new arrivals created the problems of housing scarcity by reflecting on previous overcrowding and segregations and the constraints on family life they represented as the lot of new arrivals. In the following section we will analyse how the strategies deployed by new arrivals in accessing affordable housing – including the use of networks, recruitment agencies and the intervention of support agencies – can both alleviate and exacerbate cohesiveness. The final section analyses people's accounts of the strategic and emotional as well as local and transnational dynamics of home making at the outset of the second decade of the twenty-first century.

Housing scarcity and entitlement

Many housing experts argue that housing shortage in Britain is both acute and structural. Structural due to years of non investment in affordable housing and acute because even if funding was made available the situation could not be reversed in the immediate term. The intractability of this situation and the possibilities for its resolution are denied by claims that pressure on housing from new arrivals explains the difficulties of the sector. The logic of this claim – reduce migration – both fails to deal with the ongoing economic demand for migrant labour and to address the actual problem of housing shortage (Hills, 2009). Many older interviewees knew from experience how disruptive housing shortages could be for family life. Others understood how blaming strategies could demonise migrants, who endured harsher living circumstances than did the long-term settled. In the following quotes from two long-term settled residents of Kilburn, one of whom used to be a migrant, we can see how their past experiences contextualise their current understandings of the impact of migration on housing.

> I had four children in one room and we were in the other. And we struggled and struggled. By the time we were given a place they were all grown-up. My eldest one was 21 by the time we were given a place. ... I don't agree with all this migration. ... Where are the houses? You can't build up and up. You've got to have – and it's going to be like it was when we got married, all you had was two rooms ... there was people living upstairs in two rooms and they had six children. And there is going to be people living like that again if they keep getting people into this country. There is not enough housing stock. And some of them are going to be overcrowded. And overcrowding leads to disease.
> (Long-term settled, majority ethnic woman, Kilburn)

This English woman participates in a discourse that blames migration for housing shortages, although her primary concern is to avoid a return, for anyone, to the overcrowding she experienced in the past. Her understanding of the impact of immigration on housing is qualified by her acknowledgement that 'there is not enough housing stock', meaning that Britain has limited capacity to accommodate newcomers.

Housing scarcity in the post-war period was also very problematic for migrants. It generated rental revenue at the expense of migrants being able to share the ordinary living conditions of the settled population, as this man explains:

> We certainly was not welcomed into the community. And we did get such names are 'Dirty Irish pigs' ... and my friends and everything else who was getting married, they couldn't get accommodation around here. ... This was all rented accommodation, private, we didn't, you didn't get it from the local authorities, these were private landlords, very scarce and very much in demand. ... So the housing crisis was terrific ... rooms that's only fit maybe for say two or maybe three people there could be camp beds, six, eight beds in that. This is the time they were going on about the Irish boozing and drinking. These lads had nowhere else to go. The only social place that they had or knew would be into the pub.
>
> (Long-term settled, minority ethnic man, Kilburn)

For this man, even the option of having overcrowded family housing was an improvement compared with the housing realities of migrant workers. The most frequent housing options for migrants, such as living in bed and breakfast accommodation or hostels, foreclosed any possibility of family life. Drawing on his previous experience of migration and settlement, this man explains that immigration does not necessarily produce a substantial pressure on housing availability because of the nature of the overcrowded types of housing of which they have to avail themselves. His understanding of how particular markets, in this case the market for single workers, could structure availability and determine future settlement patterns of new arrivals left him with little sympathy for the claim that new arrivals alone distorted housing provision. These accounts of overcrowding framed by settlement and migrancy respectively produce different inflections on contemporary housing problems. These considerations highlight the role played by memories of migration and settlement and by narratives of place in shaping understandings of the relationship between migration, cohesion and society. In this case, the direct experience of migration provides this Irish man with the resources to understand tensions and conflicts in terms that do not antagonise the relation between new arrivals and the long-term settled.

The disruptions and instabilities caused by the contraction of affordable social and private housing and the changing makeup of housing providers continue to impact on people's chances to settle and have families. They also generate conflicts around entitlement and accessibility. The following quotes from long-term settled majority ethnic key informants in Peterborough and Glasgow illustrate some of the altering dynamics in the UK.

> It's a nightmare. ... We've got I think it's 8000 on the waiting list at the moment. So yeah, it's not great at all. There is housing being built but there's talk that that is not going to meet the needs of the growing migrant communities. So people are finding there is some overcrowding going on.
>
> (Key informant, Peterborough)

> Glasgow doesn't have any public housing anymore. It's all Glasgow Housing Association. And they are struggling to deal with what they've got. The only people building new housing are housing associations and a lot of that is, you know, half of, more than half of that is to buy and the other bits are for rented. So there is a real dearth of good quality housing in Glasgow ... a lot of the property down here has been bought up for housing but it's all private accommodation and it's all gone into luxury flats – and I suspect Glasgow is no different from everywhere else in the country ... I wouldn't want to be entering in the housing market in Glasgow now, I couldn't afford it. They are building houses that people are going to struggle to afford, I think.
>
> (Key informant, Glasgow)

The problem of impossibly long waiting lists for social housing and limited capacity of the construction industry in the private sector to keep up with demand was identified as a problem in Peterborough that was seen as inevitably producing overcrowding as the population expanded to meet local labour market demands. This produced a 'nightmare' scenario of housing provision simply not being able to match the economic expansion of the area. In Glasgow by contrast the restructuring of housing providers in conjunction with the boom in luxury housing had created a different kind of scenario that nonetheless had the same effect of failing to adequately meet changing housing need. Whereas in Peterborough migrants are identified as part of the mix of housing difficulties, in Glasgow new arrivals are framed differently in part because of the declining population creating housing capacity and because new arrivals in the context of Scottish demographics are seen more as a resource than a drain on resources.

Entitlement to social housing was seen by many as something long-term residents could lay claim to against the needs of new arrivals. For the vast majority of immigrants routes into housing are limited to the private rented sector until the designated period of settlement allows for the right to go on the long waiting lists like everyone else. However this was not well understood by many of our interviewees. The perception that the composite figure of the 'migrant/asylum seeker' had greater claims to housing than existing residents was widely held and deeply resented. The following quote is from the interview with a minority ethnic young man from Kilburn.

> At first when I went from my hostel, I tried to go down the Irish route, I am a minority. [Laughs] They weren't having a part of it. No way. No, no, sorry, son, you have to go into a hostel like the rest of them. And when I went in there, there was loads of heroin addicts ... I did two and a half years, three years. I think it was three in the end. ... But erm, I had to deal with it all when I was in the hostel system. Like you know, like I just remember foreigners coming in and getting places straightaway. I had around five, six sets of neighbours while I was living there and I stayed there, you know. I used to, me and my housing officer used to have mental rows because I was getting to the point where I couldn't see the light at the end of the tunnel. And I was like why am I rotting away here and everyone else is moving in and up. But you can't say immigrants are moving, getting shit and moving out again. But if they knew the true story, you know. My family come in so we were immigrants at one point. Do you know what I mean. But we never come here and just expected – My family never ponced a day in their lives, they always worked. They come here and built the country for them. I am not trying to say that I'm entitled to something but more than these people, I am. Yeah, definitely.
>
> (Long-term resident, minority ethnic, man, Kilburn)

This quote combines a strong sense of entitlement to housing based on settlement with a sense of earned entitlement as a second-generation migrant who can moreover lay claim to his family having 'built the country'. He also, in his desperation to get housing, claimed the entitlement attached to being a minority ethnic person of Irish descent, which in his view potentially gave him a claim to special pleading on a par with that enjoyed by the 'migrant/asylum seeker'. His entitlements were abused by a system that humiliated and marginalised him as a single man whose need for housing was deemed less privileged than that of many co-residents. He wanted to get married and have a family, but when he was finally allocated a flat it was a studio. So although his endurance had achieved its goal it was the least best option for his plans to marry and have a family. He experienced this as a further marginalisation and felt that his housing allocation in the end identified him as someone who wasn't entitled to have a family.

The relation between housing need, affordable housing, immigration and social cohesion is grounded in the memories and outcomes of past housing and migration histories. The heritage of previous housing policies is a structural shortage of affordable housing which underpins the conflicts at work in the social fields across which social cohesion operates. In some cases the convergence of the shortage of affordable housing and of narratives blaming this on new arrivals can antagonise their relations with the long-term settled. Discourses blaming new arrivals have negative implications for social cohesion. By failing to engage with the actual circumstances of housing provision blaming strategies potentially disrupt processes of settlement and foreclose on the ability to negotiate possible resolutions to this situation. The memories and experiences of previous migrations however, can also be strategic resources potentially enabling new arrivals and long-term settled people to negotiate the conflict emerging around housing in terms that they deem positive.

Accessing housing and neighbourhood relations

For new arrivals accessing housing is a challenge made more difficult by the complex and fraught nature of housing provision throughout the UK. Their entry points to housing included: recruitment agencies, landlords geared exclusively to migrant accommodation, live-in domestic and hospitality work, accommodation tied to labour contracts, and rental obligation incorporated into job packages. They also utilise their own transnational networks as well as the more conventional route of directly or virtually accessing the private rental market. We encountered examples of all of these routes into housing, which reveal processes of social cohesion often embodying remarkable levels of resilience. In the next two sub-sections we focus on Peterborough and Dungannon, where a composite of these entry points and networks were very much in evidence.

Accessing housing through landlords and agencies

In Dungannon and Peterborough we found many instances of employment agencies incorporating accommodation into the labour contract package. The high rents demanded as a result produced overcrowding as a way of dealing with rent levels. In turn, high rents prompted many new arrivals to tap into migrant networks as a way of finding more affordable housing in the mainstream rental sector. In Peterborough resentment already existed among the settled majority ethnic population towards landlords – particularly Asian landlords. This was because on the one hand the buy-to-let market boosted house prices and disadvantaged first time buyers, and on the other hand the high rents they demanded produced overcrowding, which brought down the value of adjacent properties.

> If you can buy a house, if you buy on a mortgage and you can get five people in there, £350 a week coming in, thank you very much, that's a nice little earner isn't it.
> (Long-term settled majority ethnic key informant woman, Peterborough).

> Yeah. And they are getting huge amounts of money, you know. Because as one gets out – one will do night work and one will do day work and there is quite a few people complaining about that, you know, that they've bought a nice house and then there is [sic] thirty people in this one house, you know. They are all doing this constant, yeah, changeover, yeah, so there has been sort of some complaints about that.
> (Long-term majority ethnic settled man, Peterborough)

Many new arrivals were thus unwittingly dropped into this confrontation between housing for profit and housing for young families. This introduced new arrivals into a context that was already fraught with the problems of the buy-to-let market and its undermining of the first time buyer market. The resentment against Asian landlords arose because they themselves had moved to the 'leafy suburbs' and did not have to deal with changes in neighbourhoods that included their buy-to-let properties and the levels of rent they set led to hotbedding and the various disruptions produced by 24/7 households in areas still rather more governed by 9–5 time regimes.

In Dungannon too there was a recognition that high rents imposed by landlords were the main driver of overcrowding. Here however neighbourly relations between the settled community and recent arrivals were shaped by the rather precipitous arrival of new migrants as much as developments within the housing market to accommodate them. The two quotes below from long-term settled women from Dungannon outline the difficulties of dealing with dramatic change.

> People do say hi to them, but I am aware of the fact that when they are not there that the conversations, people are not very keen on them being there. I think the reason they are not so keen on the being here is like, it's alright if you have one or two, but all of a sudden you have literally thousands and it's been a huge change. It hasn't been gradual change, it has been almost instantaneous, and that's very hard on both communities.
> (Long-term settled, woman, Dungannon)

> Well, up until about 4 years ago you might have seen Chinese, that's about the height of it. … Then, and you are not allowed to use the word influx anymore, the migrant workers starting coming up to 2 or 3 years ago. It was serious there for a while, the landlords came in and bought the properties up and started renting them out.
> (Long-term settled, woman, Dungannon)

As in Peterborough, landlords were held responsible by many of the settled population for the overcrowded conditions in which many new arrivals lived. In Dungannon the private rental sector also included agency housing that was attached to jobs. This housing was particularly lucrative for the agencies because they controlled the shift patterns in the factories and could therefore double tier occupancy to fit with the shift regimes. In Dungannon hotbedding featured as did multi-occupancy rental arrangements – both practices producing conditions of unacceptable overcrowding and placing considerable strain on neighbourly relations.

Neighbourhood relations

In Dungannon, as elsewhere, failures of neighbourhood relations pre-dated new arrivals. Despite social relations in Dungannon being framed by 'The Troubles' in Northern Ireland we found that the possibilities of cohesiveness between new arrivals and settled people could be anticipated either positively or negatively. New arrivals were sometimes polarised according to pre existing divisions based on religion and antipathy to outsiders. Several interviews mentioned that in some Protestant estates long standing sectarian hostilities were easily converted into racism against all new arrivals.

> Well, people will tell me secretly or privately, and what people will admit to in public is completely different, but there is quite a bit of antagonism towards migrant workers. Housing is one of the issues ... there have been a lot of cars burnt, paint thrown at houses, people put out of various communities. A community leader in one of the Protestant communities told me privately that they had a community meeting and that any migrant workers who came into their community would be put out, and they have been put out. ... There is also another very large Protestant enclave in Dungannon where no migrant workers can go.
>
> (Key informant, Dungannon)

One example of 'putting out' involved seven houses being attacked with bricks thrown through windows in an attempt to dispatch recent arrivals from an estate that had a paramilitary presence. A key informant assessed this situation thus:

> Well in terms of orchestrated attacks, yes, the attacks are orchestrated and the loyalist paramilitary infra-structure may well have a role in them. Clearly, it may not be all loyalist groups, but I haven't seen any evidence of republican paramilitary involvement in racist attacks at all, that's not something we have seen any evidence of.
>
> (Key informant, Dungannon)

Such attacks were not limited to Protestant areas however although in Catholic areas they were framed differently. According to a long-term settled English woman living in Dungannon and quoted below, a gang of Catholic youths attacked a Lithuanian family and 'put them out', which she attributed to the misuse of drugs and alcohol by young people in the area.

> But we got trouble in the estate. There was migrant workers, Lithuanians I think, and the hoods put them out in the middle of

the night. The local hoods, they take drugs and drink. They just put them out in the middle of the night. Not only is it migrant workers but it's also that I have been threatened on a number of occasions with my life. ... I don't know why they done it, but this gang just threw them out of the houses, and it was an awful sight to see, you know, women running with their small children, and we felt helpless. ... 90% of the people in the area are good people, but they have got a fear of the hoods. They intimidate people, they would be into crime, drugs, intimidation. ... Then, maybe it was the drugs, I don't know, but they have just destroyed the estate.

(Long-term settled, minority ethnic English, woman, Dungannon)

This woman had lived on the estate for 15 years and had been involved in community projects and associations. In her view the estate, which had been predominantly republican had fallen into lawlessness after the war had ended largely she argued because the IRA had insisted the police were kept out of the estate. In this instance the conflict between new arrivals and settled residents was experienced and understood as a continuation of poor and traumatised community relations and a diminished way of being. The community had felt 'helpless' to protect the new arrivals and themselves from the gangs. Feeling vulnerable was an experience shared by the long-term settled and new arrivals alike.

Although Dungannon was described by one key informant as one of the 'most divided places in Northern Ireland' it was nonetheless also capable of providing real support for, and appreciation of, new arrivals.

But it's not; the factor isn't religion, or community. Some of the best work being done, the people in to the Old Warren estate in Lisburn which is very, very strong loyalist community, but again it has a good community infrastructure, that grouping in there is doing very much the same work that we are doing here, and creating a whole positive environment which is actually helping their own community to move forward. ... Working to integrate and negotiate and manage the difficulties, and that's a Protestant community and organisation working in the realities of their existence and therefore working closely with existing organisations like the Boys' Brigade, to incorporate young lads into sports and things that are happening. The local soccer clubs like the local GAA clubs are very active in encouraging the young men, now not necessarily all altruistic, they play better football, so gain the wee parochial place like this, to get a couple of players that maybe played for a half decent team somewhere.

The quote shows that it is not necessarily the sectarian divide that is determinant of how migrants are treated. In different places, Protestant and Catholics, are both hostile to, or supportive of, migrants. Some relations between new arrivals and settled people were amicable and ordinary. Others were ordinary in a more troubled way. An elderly long-term settled woman who lived with her son and was generally very welcoming of new arrivals recounted how she had had such a difficult time with extremely disruptive Portuguese neighbours:

> Men, women and children at all hours of the day and the music was shocking, barbeques, put their figures up to you or put their tongue out. Only for my neighbour I don't know what I would have done. I rang the police, a policeman and woman came down ... but then when they left they turned the music right up and that went to 2 o'clock in the morning.
> (Long-term settled, majority ethnic, woman, Dungannon)

This household had caused such distress that another elderly local man, who was recovering from an illness, had left the area altogether. The couple who eventually replaced the disruptive tenants were also Portuguese but were ideal neighbours who were polite, friendly and attended the local Catholic Church. The absence of support had exacerbated the experience and created a sense that either one had to personally intervene or remain in some sense a prisoner in one's own home.

In Peterborough the heritage of place was less fraught than that of Dungannon. The relative equanimity of Peterborough was nonetheless marked by disturbances between asylum seekers and labour migrants in 2003, prompting the local council to fund a support group to manage and help in the business of cohesiveness and settlement. The work of this group – New Link – was exemplary in assisting people to understand and mediate the new circumstances of Peterborough life.

> Not knowing who your neighbours are is an important problem, you don't feel safe if you don't know that. Also, if people speak different languages, it is impossible to ask them for a neighbourly favour. In addition, because the houses are overcrowded some problems arise from that.
> (Long-term settled, majority ethnic, woman, Peterborough)

They tend to move next door to somebody who's been there for 40 years and one case I had a lady that's been in her house for 2 years and daren't go out because she's got two either side of her full of she doesn't know who, but she daren't go out. And I think that's ridiculous but she doesn't feel safe in going out. And certainly Peterborough's face is changing.

(Key informant, Peterborough)

New arrivals were sometimes experienced as imposing insurmountable problems particularly in relation to language difficulties that represented a real obstacles to people getting to know one another thereby reducing, (according to both the long-term settled majority ethnic woman and key informant woman quoted below) the resilience of the neighbourhood.

The disruption to neighbourly relations this introduced was considerable and further dislocations occurred as large households of new arrivals introduced different cultures of neighbourhood belonging that revolved around the particularistic ways in which people occupied the outside of their houses.

Added to this was the issue of conventions of communal behaviour in maintaining standards of upkeep and presentation. Many long-term settled majority ethnic residents blamed the problems of the housing market on the Asian landlords, particularly the problem of overcrowding. They also held the new arrivals themselves responsible for not understanding how things were done in Peterborough. The public street culture of rubbish storage and collection and car parking and maintenance became one of dissonance in parts of Peterborough. The fractiousness this introduced into everyday relations of street life was considerable and improved neighbourly relations were achieved following strategic interventions by a migrant support agency set up by the local council. This can be seen in the following quote from a key informant from Peterborough:

Because our cohesion problems in the town, since the riots we had 2–3 years ago, have been more around what do you put in this dustbin, and we have printed what you put, we've got a three bin system. And we printed them in ten different languages 15 different languages, because one of the things we found that the indigenous population do not like is basically the different lifestyles. If you put the wrong thing in the wrong bin, it stays outside, stays on the street, just builds up around it, makes their whole area look a mess.

And we're working, we've got this thing called New Look, working with New Link to try and get round the residents associations and organisations that the indigenous population are in to give advice and assurance. And then from that, we do home visits to new arrivals to try and say look, this is what you put in the bin, please put some curtains up, please cut the grass, please don't drive that car without a licence. All the things that I'm sure you know are at.

(Key informant. Peterborough)

These mediating agencies while delivering support for both new arrivals and the settled population were also unambiguous in their analysis of the nature of the dynamics of neighbourly relations. New arrivals were expected to learn the conventions of household and neighbourhood ways, to learn how to behave as proper members of the community. While his offered chances to enhance relations between settled people and new arrivals, it gave greater weight to the conformity of new arrivals than to their contributions. This amounted to another job new arrivals were expected to undertake – the job of social cohesion. In both Peterborough and Dungannon the social relations of everyday life contextualised new arrivals in different ways but in both places the presumption was made that the work of getting along was the responsibility of the newcomers not the settled community that was dependent on their contributions as migrant workers.

Making homes

The transition of deindustrialisation that included the demise of the family wage and prompted the re-entry of women into the workforce transformed family and personal life. Women's economic activity now more closely follow that of men, although many women work part-time to accommodate their continuing unwaged caring responsibilities. State support for families is increasingly delivered through the pay packet of parents rather than through welfare subsidies for particular kinds of families (Esping-Anderson, 2009; Williams, 2004). The work of care within the home has also changed from predominant care of the young to care of the elderly as well as of children. For transnational families these changing care dynamics within families involve many new arrivals in complex caring strategies that straddle continents and diasporic kinship networks. These connect families across different countries of migration and settlement making the work of care a very complex enterprise (Lutz, 2008).

Our interviewees navigated these new circumstances of home making from, in the main, rather different perspectives than those embedded in ethno-national presumptions about the right kind of family. Many migrants found their ambitions for family reunification thwarted by immigration policies that persistently eroded rights of settlement. Some settled families experienced sustained economic marginalisation that frustrated ambitions for creating a better life for their children. These varied and altered circumstances of making homes posed many issues for social cohesiveness and our data showed people both retreating from and embracing the realities they faced. A troubled account of life in Britain is presented by a minority ethnic long-settled man recently arrived in Leicester.

> There is no moral code of conduct in British families. This is first. This is the first thing I notice. The second thing is that parents look after their children when they are young but when children are eighteen they leave the home more or less, or twenty, twenty five, doesn't matter. And they don't care about their parents, what they do, where they live. And most of the parents have a miserable elderly life. Either they will be living in their own home alone without anybody visiting them or they will be living in an elderly care home without anybody visiting them. So I think both parents and children are having very miserable life. They may call it independence but ehm ... what sort of independence I just wonder.
> (Long-term settled, minority ethnic, man, Leicester)

This view of British family life was somewhat anxiously held by many new arrivals, who feared for the well being of their own families coming under the influence of these trends. Some new arrivals such as the one quoted below from Glasgow even found the family protection of young children as wanting. A Ghanaian nurse and father of two spoke of his despair at encountering a 12-year old Glaswegian boy collapsed in the gutter drunk. The man's despair came not just from the state of the boy, but from his insistence that everything was alright.

> The other day I saw a boy about twelve who was totally drunk lying in the street, in the road, and people were just gathering around and even I thought he was dead, I thought he has just been knocked down by a car, but he was drunk. When he was helped to stand up he said 'Phh come on' and off he went. But I ask you when young boys see this as an acceptable part of the culture, I say to myself probably I don't want to stay, it's not good enough.
> (New arrival, man, Glasgow)

The perception by new arrivals of British families besieged by forces that undermine parental authority and family discipline was one which focussed on issues of respect, with many taking the view that mutual respect between parents and children was corrupted by wider social forces and moreover that these problems were not properly addressed by society. Although excessive drinking by young people is acknowledged as 'a problem', it is not necessarily seen as a problem of social cohesion. For this recent arrival the public display of failure of both family life and community values he witnessed suggested a lack of cohesiveness. When swept along by these processes of change families of new arrivals were themselves uncertain how to engage with them, particularly when they were divergent from communal patterns of family relations that many of them had left behind.

Many of these concerns were echoed by long-term settled interviewees. If not 'British family life', family life *in* Britain was considered by many to be under pressure from the demands of work, the pace of life, the altering terms of parental authority, and of an increasingly consumerist society in which children are targeted as active consumers. The changing demands on families were seen as impacting on both community and family life insofar as children and communities are deprived of adults who had adequate available time to support them.

> In terms of parents or parenting now, you know, when I was a kid my mother was at home, my father was at work. Now you couldn't afford to do that. Mother is out as well. And I think that breaks down the family community as well. You know, there is no interaction, or there is not as much interaction. You know, our kids are picked up at half past three by a childminder. ... So you are really taking away all that relationship building if you like.
> (Long-term settled majority ethnic man, Peterborough)

> I think that ... family cohesion or community cohesion of family relationships [in the past] were a great buffer against some of the social or economic pressures, the instabilities in life, unpredictable things like declining health, changes in physical and mental health and stuff like that. ... And for all that those social community links needed to change, the fact that in some instances they're broken altogether would make me want ... I think that people who face the consequence of that are maybe, they're the vulnerable in society ... who kind of need to rely on the goodness of other people either as individuals or collectively.
> (Long-term settled majority ethnic man, Glasgow)

In the first quote the care deficit is seen as a direct outcome of people having less time to spend with their children because of the demands of work. Time poverty is seen as impacting on the depth of relationships between parents and children and the community context in which they and their children live. In the second quote the family is presented as no longer able to respond to people's day to day vulnerabilities and requirements.

A young professional woman familiar with the realities of being a working mother, and whose young family was supported by grandparents, still felt the demands of the contemporary work/life balance to be onerous.

> I just don't think people in the past have been this busy. I mean when I compare my mother for instance, at my age ... I've obviously got a pressurised job. I'll take work home sometimes ... and then I've got the kids and I'm trying to make sure we're doing things with them ... so I think about things like that, you know and making sure they do their homework, then I'm doing my Masters as well ... my husband he goes to work all day and we're both tired at the end of the day and there's tea to get on the table.
> (Long-term settled minority ethnic woman, Leicester)

In this instance career enhancement, the demands of children's education, and cultural support for the family left space for few other concerns or activities. The heightened pressures on families to achieve, was matched by a perceived pressure for families to consume, and the greater disposable income of families was seen as another way in which work was having a negative impact on family dynamics and generational relations.

> I think that when I was little sometimes we'd get a nice pair of shoes that we really, really wanted for our birthday. Whereas my kids – you know, I am not with their dad – but he's got a big family. ... And they get huge amounts of things. If they got what I got when I was younger, they totally wouldn't be thankful for it. I think it's a very expensive world now as opposed to then. You were happy with very little then.
> (Long-term settled majority ethnic woman, Downham)

The fear that consumerism was diminishing capacities for appreciation and anticipation was echoed by many parents, who felt powerless in the face of advertising and unable to transmit to their children the pleasures of their own childhoods.

While many felt that families were locked into work because of the demands of a consumerist society, those families without work equally felt the pressures of consumerism and these often led to illegal working or the even greater pressures of debt.

> If you allow the media to force feed your kids with images and scenarios then things can get out of control ... it's a general decline in the mentality of the country, the moral standards of the country ... it just seems to be going downhill, those things that were classed as wholesome before are now classed as old-fashioned. I feel like an old man now – 'much better in the old days' – but I can see looking back it wasn't that bad in some cases in the old days.
> (Long-term settled minority ethnic man, Leicester)

> You can't blame like poor people, people from a poor background who have a poor education from taking advantage of [the system] and just getting their giro and just living from day to day and doing stuff on the side. Because that's the nature of the system, it's not a family-friendly system.
> (Long-term settled majority ethnic man, Leicester)

In the first quote the man was wary of being romantic about the good old days, a cautiousness that others repeated, but equally he wanted to appeal to an alternative way of living that did not entail families being as he saw it, bullied by consumerist culture. These understandings of transformations of the spaces of family life by the ubiquitous presence of commercially driven media and an invasive consumer culture see modern families as a diminished personal and domestic life. In much the same way that work has been identified as impinging on private domains so too culture and media are viewed as contracting a realm of emotional and interpersonal ways of being that make both intergenerational and interpersonal relations more difficult.

Transnational families experienced generational dynamics rather differently, often through the isolation of leaving families behind. This often meant that work entirely dominated the spaces of personal life in the absence of families and friendship networks.

> Because we are human beings, we are not meant to be in isolation. And that is the difficulty, when you leave home you leave everybody.

You know, for us, for people who come with their family – that makes a difference. But for people who don't bring their family it's that absolute social isolation. It takes years and years. The majority will come on their own first.

(Key informant, Glasgow)

This illustrates the privilege that settlement ensures when considering the pressures that families are subject to in post-industrialism. Transnational family dynamics are similarly subject to these altering conditions, particularly evident in the phenomenon of female migration, but in addition they mark the loss of family intimacy and consequently often utilise a different measure of the values of these relationships and the significance of these changes they are undergoing. The emotional complex of transnational family dynamics is not just about loss and distance but also about the inability to dispatch, through sharing, the many frustrations and conflicts sustained in day to day life.

The stories, experiences and narratives of our interviewees trace many, often intersecting lines of history, culture, place and distance in the formations and sustenance of homes. Two things emerged from this intricate mosaic drawn by our data: the first was how troubled people felt by the – often differently perceived – pressures on families and the impact of this on the quality of relations both within and beyond the personal sphere. The second perhaps surprising feature to emerge from the various conversations on family life was that linking these very disparate experiences of personal life was the underlying commitment that people had to their families.

Conclusion

The complexity of the connections between the altered and altering terms of housing entitlement, belonging, conditions of settlement and rights to family life mark out relations between people that are inevitably fraught and constitute challenges for social cohesion. The conditions of post-industrialism, the changing demands of work, the altering dynamics of housing markets and housing bubbles, the logics of mobility and transnational life as well as the demands of consumerism have produced many pressures on families and home making and the social connections that sustain them. The privileging and valuing of family life as central in navigating the post-industrial world of individualism and mobility attaches to disparate contemporary familial relations. This was a value shared across different kinds of families and could be a resource enabling people to recognise and negotiate common conflicts and tensions structuring the places and communities they live in.

Our findings show also a shared disquiet about the constraints on the places and spaces of families that connects people across the many different methods of home making that make up domestic life in the UK. Multicultures in the UK have provided people with comparative engagement with different family patterns and different ways of trying to work out what works and what doesn't in sustaining homes and families. The ability to recognise and share these successes and failures, often deflected by ethnonationalism and racism, is surely central to cohesiveness in the diasporic spaces of migrations and settlement that organise contemporary families and society.

5
Education and Social Cohesion

'Education, education, education' was at the forefront of New Labour's rhetoric and policies. These reproduced the predicaments and opportunities that were posed by the socio-economic transformations introduced by post-industrialism and neoliberalism. New Labour's education strategy reflects its ambivalent adoption of the liberal ideology of 'possessive individualism', according to which individuals are conceived as the sole proprietors and fruits of their capacities, society being an exchange between proprietors and the state being merely a regulator of these exchanges (Macpherson, 2010). Within (and beyond) the dimension of education therefore, New Labour's approach was structured by the utopian attempt to combine a 'possessive individualist' ethos (and middle class aspiration to a privileged education) with the Marxist ethos of universal redistribution (McKibbin, 2008). This attempt of reconciliation produced the establishment of city academies, allowing schools to be sponsored by private actors (i.e. foundations, faith groups, etc.) – while being generously funded by the state – and to be more autonomous from the curriculum and equal access criteria imposed by local educational authorities.

The way the neoliberal ethos of privatisation was applied to education is crucial for the analysis of social cohesion because it is likely to have important future consequences for the quality of education and democracy in the UK. Although under New Labour education received increased funding, its education policies represented 'an extension of the new market-state, through the transfer of public assets away from local authorities in a process of state subsidised privatisation' (Allen and Ainley, 2009). In the process, the monitoring of admission procedures and the adherence to the national curriculum was substantially 'devolved' from local public authorities to the private organisations running academies. This policy represented the privatisation of education into the hands of particular faith or elitist groups rather than its democratic restitution to a public dimension encouraging learning citizens to participate in the definition of 'the common good' (Baumann, 1999: 107). The creation of state-sponsored alliances between state responsibilities (education) and the private interests of economic and faith groups has been seen as threatening the viability of a national public sphere (McKibbin, 2006). These considerations are all the more important after the political elections held in May 2010 and the coming to power of a Conservative-Liberal Democratic coalition government which, having fully embraced the cultural logic of possessive individualism, plans to cut dramatically the overall education budget and further extend the city academy programme to all secondary and primary schools.

At a more general level, New Labour's stress on quantifiable and marketable outcomes has been seen as consistent with the neoliberal logic of 'capitalist realism', according to which 'it is *simply obvious* that everything in society, including healthcare and education, should be run as a business' (Fisher, 2009: 17, emphasis in original). Under pressure from the necessity to understand and administrate education as a 'profit making' enterprise, New Labour translated educations' unique function of public socialisation – defined as 'nonmarket cooperation between social actors' (Gough, 2002) – into a set of skills and targets to be capitalised upon on in the labour market. The process of commoditisation of education was merely intensified, not introduced, by New Labour. It needs to be contextualised by the transformed role of education within a post-industrial society. In the latter, the predominance of a manufacturing-based economy gives way to a knowledge economy, based on the provision of information, innovation and services and on the expansion of finance over production.

Since the late 1950s, the gradual transition towards the knowledge economy coincided with the collapse, together with heavy industry, of established school-work transitions and employment opportunities, as well as of individual and collective working class identities. In order to respond to the transformed needs of the knowledge economy, education was gradually commodified into an industry of certification of skills, which have become increasingly vital to secure access to the employment opportunities offered by the knowledge economy (Tomlinson, 2004). As a consequence of these dynamics, education in general and secondary education in particular assumed a more decisive role in providing access to the labour market and achieved a strategic function of social control of people's employment and employability (Mizen, 2004: 41).

These observations are particularly relevant for the study of social cohesion, as the access to 'marketable' skills through education has increasingly become a strategic passage allowing people to position themselves socially according to their perception of 'where they should be at' in their lives. As we have explained in Chapter 3, these perceptions play a key role in people's satisfaction or dissatisfaction with the place they live in and are a driving force in local experiences of social cohesion, particularly in relation to the arrival of new migrant groups. Here we do not engage with the wider debates on the role and dimension of education in society, which would be beyond the scope of our research. Rather, in this chapter, we focus on the role played by education settings in the unfolding of social cohesion, by focusing on the social relations intervening between long-term settled and newly arriving people. By education settings we mean the institutions, practices and spaces in which people learn as well as the socio-economic dimensions and the cultural meanings attached to education characterising their catchment areas.

Education is deeply implicated both in the development of social cohesion and in the emergence of social tensions. There is an important interplay between education, social cohesion and local experiences of 'being young', which are informed by the local availability of opportunities and educational provision, as well as by globalised transformations of youth and discipline. Social divisions such as class, ethnicity, gender and age influence the way educational achievement is perceived locally, in relation to established hierarchies of belonging and social mobility. In other words, in local settings, individual educational performances are involved in sociocultural perception of 'who should be here' and of which social groups should be 'doing well'. Depending on whether education is valued or not within local youth identities and wider politics of belonging, the arrival of migrant groups with educational aspirations can exacerbate existing conflicts in schools and the wider community or act as a catalyst for the improvement of the overall educational achievement. As was the case with housing and work, the arrival of new individuals and groups within education settings did not create entirely new tensions. On the contrary, new students were often caught in the deficiencies and the structural tensions that were already in place among long-term settled residents, within which they were often re-positioned as convenient 'scapegoats'. These factors are crucial when identifying the challenges and opportunities posed by regeneration initiatives in the field of education, youth, and social cohesion.

Education is embedded in the socio-economic transformations and realities of social cohesion. We will address educational settings, with particular reference to secondary schools and city academies, as a privileged vantage point for the observation and resolution of conflicts originating from the surrounding social context. Going to school is one of the key stages in people's life histories. The school emerged as a very strategic setting for the study of the interaction between long-term settled residents and new arrivals. We found that educational settings played a particular role in the unfolding of the relations between new arrivals and long-term settled residents in Downham, Leicester and Dungannon (Northern Ireland), which will be the focus of this chapter. In each of these three sites, secondary education settings were spaces where both social tensions at work in the surrounding areas and responses to address and defuse them were played out. The first two sections of the chapter will deal with social processes unfolding in Leicester and Downham, respectively, that underline the importance of social hierarchies in the emergence of social tensions in educational settings. The following section focuses on the relationship between social interventions in educational settings and their immediate neighbourhoods and the improvement of relations between different groups in Leicester, Downham and Dungannon. The final section will present our conclusions.

Hierarchies of entitlement to support and achievement in the context of education

The concept of self-representations is important again here, as we examine the specific way in which educational settings can be implicated in dynamics of social cohesion. Self-representations result from the complex interplay between hegemonic representations and their individual/collective internalisation or rejection. They emerge at the intersection between individual and collective identifications and affiliations (see discussion in Chapter 3). Self-representations play a pivotal role in the unfolding of social cohesion as they influence people's ability to negotiate the unequal exchanges of resources and the hierarchies characterising the places they inhabit in terms which they deem satisfactory. Leicester (except in Braunstone) and Downham (Lewisham/London) are differentiated by the predominance of different self-representations. These different sets of representations revolve around how people regard their social and cultural heterogeneity and the role of migration in the historical formation of their localities.

Whereas Downham is characterised by a prevailing self-representation in terms of settledness (being 'from here') and White English majority ethnic homogeneity, Leicester (except Braunstone) is characterised by a prevailing (self)perception in terms of ethnic heterogeneity and migrancy (being from other places as well as 'from here'). However, in both sites the arrival of new groups coincided with an upsurge in social antagonism between different groups of majority ethnic (Downham) and minority ethnic (Leicester) long-term settled young people, who felt that their (marginalised) positioning within local society was jeopardised in different ways.

In order to analyse the interplay between education and social cohesion in both these places we will also use the concept of 'settled backlash'. The concept refers to the way discourses of 'locality' and 'convenience' have become prevalent in the reinforcement or challenging of social hierarchies within any given place. Throughout this chapter we analyse the way different ethnic and racialised groups in different places participate in the 'settled backlash' phenomenon in the context of education. This is achieved by deploying discourses and ideologies of 'locality' (being 'from here') that express local and intersectional elements of social diversification according to race, class and ethnicity.

According to MacDonald and Mars (2005: 66, quoting Ball et al., 2000a; 2000b) subscribing to an ethos of educational achievement means engaging with local 'learner identities' which are shaped by a number of factors, including: personal perceptions of the value of learning and educational qualifications; the local experience of formal schooling; the ideological and political backgrounds of families; and the political economy of relevant neighbourhoods. The enhanced role of social control on employability and social mobility played by education within contemporary knowledge economies means that adhering to local 'learner identities' corresponds to a specific social positionings for individuals and groups living in the same place. Secondary education was often a field within which different individuals and groups maintain and/or challenge hierarchies of entitlement to social mobility which are part of the places they live in. These dynamics transcend the specificity of educational settings and highlight their relevance for the study of social cohesion as a whole. As metaphors of mobility and immobility have become key late modern discourses for the reproduction of symbolic and social forms of class distinction (Skeggs, 2004: 60), the representation of specific individuals, groups, or places as bounded and immobile becomes part of dynamics of social marginalisation. In the process education is invested with a strategic function as it is seen as having, and often has, the potential to enable an individual to be socially mobile. Because of this pivotal 'socially mobilising' role, secondary education is a privileged setting for the study of social cohesion, as it is often a place where the ability to negotiate the inequalities and hierarchies informing place are both expressed in terms of antagonism and cohesively resolved in terms which are positive for the people involved. In the next two subsections we show how different groups of young minority ethnic and majority ethnic long-term settled residents resist the arrival of new social groups on the basis of existing hierarchies 'in place'.

Leicester: Social antagonism between long-term settled minority ethnic residents and new arrivals in educational settings

The first case study refers to the conflicts that emerged between Somali newly arrived and African-Caribbean long-term settled young people, after the settlement in Leicester of a large group of Somali people (approx. 15,000) since the early 2000s. In Leicester, Gujarati East African refugees in the 1970s regenerated the declining hosiery industry. Their positive contribution to the city economy, combined with a fear that the racial riots of the 1980s might spread to Leicester prompted the council to promote the harmonious coexistence of different ethnic groups. This was achieved through a policy of funding a capillary network of grass root ethnic organisations. As a result of these policies and because of 50 years of settlement of minority ethnic people from former British colonies – the Caribbean and India, Pakistan and Bangladesh, and East Africa – Leicester has now the largest (proportionally) minority ethnic population in England and Wales and its experience of multicultural governance is often regarded as an example at a national and international level.

Most Somali families and individuals arriving in Leicester have either settled directly in Highfields, a large multicultural inner city area, or subsequently relocated there after experiences of racial attacks and harassment in more traditionally white English majority ethnic working class areas such as Braunstone. As a consequence, in Highfields, Somali people are a very visible presence and have opened a range of shops to cater for their community. Recent research on Somali young people's educational achievement emphasises their poor performance, because of the combination of insufficient language and mentoring support in the UK and of the high level of disruption of the educational system in Somalia (Harris, 2004: 43–8). However, the story in Leicester is different, as the city received a large number of Somali migrant students from Sweden and Holland, where they had settled in the early

1990s with their families, many of whom belong originally to Somalia's cultural and social 'elites'. Their position is, therefore, relatively privileged because they are documented and have the educational skills to do well in the UK.

The visibility of these Somali young people in shared public spaces in Highfields and their history of relative success in educational and other social settings gave rise to competition and antagonism with long-term settled African-Caribbean youth, whose experience of education had been marked by a long-term history of underachievement and socio-economic marginalisation (Stephen et al., 1996). In Leicester we co-operated with Soft Touch, an art co-operative that was involved in cultural mediation projects between African-Caribbean and Somali young people, among many other projects. A key informant working for Soft Touch explains how the arrival of students who were better achieving than long-term settled African-Caribbean students displaced the existing hierarchies of entitlement for receiving educational support. Up until this period these resources had been focused on disadvantaged African-Caribbean young people.

> In just a few years Somali students have outnumbered the African-Caribbean students and citizens. ... A lot of them are very ambitious in terms of what they want to do with their lives, while African-Caribbean young men have been under-achieving ... and I think in the last few years there was so much focus on other groups of young people in terms of providing services and extra support that they became aware of that and resentful. 'These people have just come to our city ... they get everything, we get nothing'. Totally untrue but that's the perception.
>
> (Key informant, Leicester)

This confrontation in an educational setting is an example of how such social antagonism is a reflection of and expresses imaginary and lived hierarchies at work in the wider social arena of Highfields. In particular, the arrival of the Somali community displaced the racialised and class hierarchies of entitlement to educational achievement and support at work in Leicester across different neighbourhoods (and council estates) and in relation to education and housing, in particular. In the process, African-Caribbean young people who saw themselves as being 'from Leicester' felt deprived of the support and attention they had received because of their recognised socio-economic marginalisation. They feared that their needs would be further overlooked because of a range of reasons, including the number and visibility of Somali young people in Highfields, their relative success in education and in other aspects of youth social mobility, and the level of support their arrival mobilised.

The animosity between African-Caribbean long-term settled and Somali newly arriving students was played out in Leicester schools but emerged within different social settings, in the forms of street fighting around issues of spatial distribution (who hangs around where) and gender (who dates whom). In the process, narratives of 'othering' emerged in relation to prevailing perceptions of who has the right to have privileged access to strategic resources such as education, income and housing (money from the Council), which became increasingly scarce because of cuts to the welfare budgets and support. A key informant from Leicester Council shows how stigmatising was a strategy to establish a hierarchy of local belonging and entitlement to resources.

> Some Somali men had a perception that African-Caribbean people had low morals, they were pimps, prostitutes, drinking alcohol ... while there was a perception the other way that Somalis were a proud African tribe who looked down on every other tribe in Africa. And think they are inferior. And they had arrived here and they were getting all this money from the Council which we never had. Again, this misperception of the privileged and the under-privileged.
>
> (Key informant, Leicester)

The key informant explains, in part, that the conflict between Somali new arrivals and African-Caribbean long-term settled residents exposes intersections of race and ethnicity and how they inform local narratives of belonging. In this case, African-Caribbean young people's use of narratives of 'being from here' both challenged and reinforced local class and racialised social hierarchies.

In Leicester, hierarchies of belonging to local areas emerged in relation to rights to receive social and educational support on the basis of class, which intersect hierarchies of 'Africanness' and 'blackness'. In this respect, 'being from here' and 'blackness' or 'Africanness' became contested fields in which new criteria for both coexistence and competition were established. The Somalis were seen by some African-Caribbean long-term settled residents as doing better than themselves. This was problematic for them, as the fact that the Somalis were also black exposed the marginalisation in terms of class and race of African-Caribbean long-term settled residents. An interview with an African-Caribbean long-term settled resident makes this link more evident. He drew a parallel between the experiences of stigmatisation endured by the first migrants arriving from the Caribbean and those faced by the Somali community today.

> What they are going through now the West Indian community went through 30 or more years ago. They were the newest community in the area and they faced the same problems. The same things my parents tell me that white people used to say about them when they first came here – you just couldn't get houses and get money – the same thing Black kids now are saying about Somali kids and Asian kids are saying about Somali kids, you know, blah blah blah they are getting all these resources. It was the general scenario really because there wasn't as many Black people in their community so it was more visible, it was more apparent. Now they have been kind of integrated into the general fabric of society. ... I think if you try and bring in people into a community that is already underdeveloped and people are coming in and they are seen as getting a disproportionate level of resources by people who are already there ... that causes resentment. Yes, it's like they are saying, money is the root of all evil, a case of why have they got it and we haven't.
>
> (Long-term settled, minority ethnic, man, Leicester)

By comparing the experience of the first African-Caribbean migrants in the 1960s with current experiences of animosity between African-Caribbean long-term settled and new groups of newcomers, this interviewee reflects on both continuities and changes. On the one hand, now as then social antagonism is fuelled by feelings of resentment emerging in relation to scarce resources such as housing, educational achievement and income support. On the other hand, in different periods and social conditions, different social groups engage in antagonism according to different ideologies of belonging. This African-Caribbean man from Leicester shows that race was a more critical marker of social antagonism in the 1960s because, as he puts it, there were not 'many Black people in their community'. However, now that African-Caribbeans 'have been kind of integrated into the general fabric of society', resentment for the arrival of new groups is expressed with the localised tenets of the 'settled backlash' phenomenon. In the process, 'people coming in' are resented by racialised Arican Caribbean young people for 'getting a disproportionate level of resources' not in racialised terms but because they are not 'from here'.

In Leicester, new arrivals' right to have access to social support is contested by minority ethnic long-term settled residents according to narratives of belonging, structured around the concept of being 'from here'. At the same time, these hierarchies of 'from hereness' are also informed by racialised hierarchies of blackness and by perceptions of entitlement to social mobility through education, which emerge at the intersection of class, race, age and ethnicity. In the next subsection, we will analyse how similar dynamics took place in Downham, a place which can be seen as reproducing in contemporary settled backlash times the racialised backlash reactions directed towards new arrivals from the Caribbean in the 1960s.

Downham: Social antagonism between majority ethnic and minority ethnic long-term settled residents/new arrivals in educational settings

Downham, is an area characterised by a symmetrically different demographic composition from Leicester (except in predominantly majority ethnic and deprived working class areas such as Braunstone). It is also symmetrically different because of its (self)representation in terms of isolation, majority ethnic homogeneity and settledness. The majority of the population in Downham are white (82 per cent, this includes all sub-sections of the white category in the 2001 Census), against a 66 per cent average in the borough of Lewisham. From the late 1990s, the arrival of Albanian and Tamil refugees into Downham coincided with an escalation of inter-ethnic social antagonism, which was fuelled and amplified by the local media. Until 2005, one of the main areas around which social antagonism emerged was the secondary school serving Downham – Malory School. This school did not secure good examination results at GCSE and was not popular as a first choice school. Consequently there were surplus places available, which were filled by new migrants. In the meanwhile, many majority (and, to a lesser extent) minority ethnic parents in Downham resorted to sending their children to different schools in neighbouring Bromley.

This second generation minority ethnic Irish young man describes how his mother participated in class-based hierarchies of educational achievement. By sending her son to a 'good school ... at the other end of Bromley', she aims to provide him with a higher degree of social mobility through educational achievement, which is an important priority for the majority of new arrivals and first generation minority ethnic long-term settled people.

> My mother wanted me to go to a good school ... at the other end of Bromley. I was travelling to a completely different place every day and I guess I insulated myself against the wider neighbourhood as a kid.

> I remember tagging along with schoolmates from primary a couple of times and they were just like awful, their whole idea of spending time seemed to revolve around being in really dodgy places and having fights with people. I never associated with the people from school except the two or three people on my road who I went to school with. We were definitely mixed and we never broke into the working class body or social networks. I think I stayed on the periphery of that.
> (Long-term settled, minority ethnic, young man, Downham)

Experiences such as the one narrated by this interviewee were far from being exceptional, as in our interviewees' accounts Bromley schools were perceived as having the potential of providing their children with 'better' educational standards, which reflected aspirations embedded within the intersection of (middle) class, (white) race and English ethnicity. The interview also illustrates how local 'working class' learner identities of 'commonness' can become a form of resistance to 'middle class' notions of educational achievement, and how they can become translated in powerful markers of 'being from here' (Evans, 2007: 10–12). In the process, minority ethnic pupils growing up with expectations of educational achievement and social mobility can be marginalised for not wanting to participate in learner identities of 'commonness'.

At the time we undertook the research, as well as Albanian and Tamil children from Downham, the minority ethnic students in Malory school also comprised long-term settled pupils from the north of Lewisham and from other London boroughs with a shortage of school places. As a result, over 45 per cent of Malory's pupils were from minority ethnic communities (both new arrival and long-term settled), which account for only 18 per cent of Downham's population. The convergence of the arrival of new groups, the long-term deprivation endured by some sectors of the local white English majority ethnic working class population, the campaigning of the British National Party (BNP) and the poor performance of the school were the background for considerable inter-ethnic tension.

Social antagonism emerged within and around the school and involved both youth from the school and from the wider neighbourhood, with local white English majority ethnic youth attacking pupils in the playground, while they were exiting the school gates and on their way to the train station. An Albanian former Malory student explains how these dynamics worked.

> Back in 1999 in Downham you only used to see white people. I came here to get my education and to plan what I do with my life. But a

lot of people back in them days they think that I am here to take their money. Malory school took a lot of Albanians and basically the English people started bullying and we had the Black people helping us. So then people started oh, why are you getting involved, blah blah, it's not good to do it. Everything started really. And every day I used to be afraid to go to school, I just run back before someone comes and beats you up or whatever.

(New arrival, Albanian, young man, Downham)

This Albanian student illustrates the complexity of the relation between race, ethnicity and local narratives of belonging. The situation he describes allowed the emergence of strategic alliances between groups perceiving themselves to share the same lower 'minority' status in relation to established hierarchies. The poor achievement record of Malory school was further compromised by the high transit ratio of the new arrival student population (also due to the dispersal and deportation initiatives promoted by the Home Office). However, in the earlier quote from the interview with the second-generation Irish young man who used to go to school in the 1990s and from the accounts of many other long-term settled residents in Downham what clearly emerges is that the school had been perceived as 'rough', unruly and underachieving long before the arrival of new immigrants in the late 1990s.

Malory had a very bad reputation, there was always fights going on up there. Academically there wasn't a lot of results got out of there. Erm, it just had one big bad reputation so that Downham kids then stopped going there. All those places at Malory, which if there is places and you've got kids that have been excluded from other schools they then go to the school where there is vacancies. So you then got kids travelling from all over the place to go to Malory. But a lot of those kids had had problems in other schools. I think it was mainly a problem of failing education.

(Long-term settled, majority ethnic, woman, Downham)

This long-term settled English majority ethnic woman living in Downham explained that Malory school's 'big bad reputation' for not providing 'results' created the vacancies that were later to be taken by migrant pupils or pupils arriving from other areas. An English majority ethnic young man from Downham recounted that Malory was often the last choice in relation to other available state or private (in this case Catholic) schools.

To be quite honest it was me parents' decision. They – at the time there was bad reputation at Malory so, erm, a lot of people didn't go to Malory ... So, erm, I think years back when I was picking my schools to, Malory was one of the bottom ones. Like you had Bonus Pastor, Sedgehill and Malory really round here. And if you couldn't get in Sedgehill or Bonus Pastor then Malory was sort of your next choice, do you know what I mean? So that's why I didn't go Malory.

(Long-term settled, majority ethnic, young man, Downham)

The last two excerpts show that long standing problems of educational achievement in Malory preceded the arrival of migrant pupils and of minority ethnic pupils from other parts of the borough. Malory's educational performance needs to be mapped onto the socio-economic and cultural co-ordinates of its immediate and extended catchment area. This was characterised by the presence of several competing primary and secondary education opportunities, whose access was structured by local hierarchies of class and by racialised cultural constructions of educational achievement. The intersection between these local hierarchies and constructions is the context which welcomed the pupils which took up vacancies at Malory school. Children from minority ethnic background, both long-term settled residents and new arrivals, report having experienced isolation, bullying and racist attacks, usually in relation to their visible and successful investment in educational achievement.

Since the 1980s in Downham, the arrival of new 'achieving' students in a context marked by anti-academic learner identities, has evidenced the way in which educational achievement and discipline were a site of implicit class struggle between different groups, their life trajectories and their stances towards an educational ethos. In turn, this can be seen as rooted in localised understandings of the relationship between belonging, local intersections of class, race and ethnicity and the entitlement to (social) mobility. This strategic intersection, in turn, informs local politics of place and belonging that needs to be 'learned' (Willis, 1977) to negotiate the rhythms and realities of everyday life and the social relations constituting any given place. As noted earlier, most white English majority ethnic local pupils seemed to have embraced a sub-culture of 'commonness' which was based on educational underachievement as a way to resist 'middle class' values of achievement and discipline. Migrants coming from contexts where attending school was a privilege reserved to the few saw free education as a unique opportunity for self-advancement.

The contrast between these opposed priorities and trajectories is what generated situations of antagonism in and around Malory school. This former student at Malory in the 1980s, a minority ethnic woman, shows these dynamics at play.

> At Malory the kids didn't really want to go to school. Erm, I mean, that was the feeling. Because my parents always brought me up, we worked really hard to come to England, back in India you've got to pay for an education, here you get a free education, you've got to make the most of it. If you are going to get a good job. So that was always emphasised by our parents. And it was the complete opposite at Mallory. It was uncool to do your homework. Our first head teacher was very strict she was always having to take action to keep the kids in the school because they kept leaving. She even had Alsatian dogs for that purpose at some stage ... as well as teachers all round the school at all the gates.
> (Long-term settled, minority ethnic, woman, Downham)

Besides highlighting the contrasting cultural understandings and experiences of educational achievement, the interviewee also underlines what was a feature of a number of accounts of former Malory pupils and teachers, that the school had difficulty exercising discipline and teaching. This under-achieving culture of 'commonness' and the associated problem of discipline are consistent with the post-industrial erosion of parental authority. As the new economy erodes even the 'poor work' (Brown and Scase, 1991) which had been available to the working class in Fordist times, the authoritativeness of parents was undermined by worklessness and their related inability to provide for the family (MacDonald and Marsh, 2005).

The situation in Downham was one in which the arrival of new groups of asylum seekers, migrants and minority ethnic long-term settled residents from other areas de-stabilised local self-perceptions of the local area as homogeneous and local hierarchies of (entitlement to) educational achievement and upward social mobility. A council employee working in Downham explains this.

> The majority of refugee kids have their own issues, in terms of language and everything else but they are basically okay kids, you get some that are traumatised, they are going to be bad, but you are going to get as you get with all the other people, you know, a certain percentage of challenging for whatever reason. So I think the truth lies somewhere in the middle. It was partly locals didn't like, locals don't like new people coming in and specifically new people from

different ethnic backgrounds. You know, the BNP stuff. I am talking about older siblings etc. And people trying to come in and causing trouble in the school. I think there is not one answer to that and it was a mess. And Malory has been going downhill for a long time. Now it's going uphill but it was going downhill for a long time.

(Key informant, Downham)

This interviewee clearly expresses the way tensions and deep seated inequalities arising from the environment surrounding educational settings infiltrate and permeate social relations between pupils and staff. What happened in Downham is of interest beyond the immediate local dimension because it shows the link between structural deprivation, social relations, poor educational achievement and place.

One of the recurring issues interviewees referred to while analysing the status of social relations in Downham was the presence of widespread deprivation, especially within the majority ethnic working class. Most key informants had a complex understanding of deprivation, encompassing low educational achievement, lack of self confidence, unemployment, intergenerational reliance on subsidised housing and income support, family breakdown, isolation and lack of aspirations. The director of a local community initiative in the education field working in Downham highlights the role of the combined lack of education and of aspiration in triggering social antagonism.

> One of the reasons that that area is considered deprived is not because of money, it is because you have several generations of people who haven't progressed in the educational sense. It's more the aspirational thing. And I think one of the reasons that there is resentment there is that migrant communities tend to be aspirational and to work very hard to improve in life. ... Because you've got families who don't know how to do that. And also don't get that a lot of them who are coming in they are coming in with education and aspirations. Like my neighbour she is from Downham, born and bred, grew up there. And she said she has difficulty going back there because she knows that people with whom she went to school there see her as having sold out.
>
> (Key informant, Downham)

Her final remark, explaining the difficulty of reconciling belonging in the community and successful social mobility, refers to the paradoxical interplay of proximity, isolation and solidarity that we found in marginalised inner city estates (Mac Donald, 2005: 883). The interplay between lack of confidence, skills, aspirations and actual employment possibilities that is reflected in the quote above is a very important factor fuelling resentment against people who are able and willing to 'move on'. The necessity to cope with unemployment, marginalisation and poverty fosters the establishment of strong kinship, friendship and community ties, which are the basis of both support for people who 'keep being from here' and resentment against people aiming at 'moving on' with their lives.

Both in Leicester and in Downham, antagonism emerged out of the challenging of social hierarchies constituted around the right and ability to obtain both educational achievement and upward social mobility. In turn, this right was argued through localised narratives of belonging (I have more rights to support because I am 'from here'). Predominant perceptions and hierarchies of what and who represented 'the local' produced place as a hostile environment for achieving newcomers, who found themselves in better conditions to meet the skills needed to 'move up' into education and employment. A majority ethnic young man expresses his frustration with the structural unavailability of housing and work characterising his place.

> I'd like to have me own car. Sort of get a girlfriend, settle down, have me own kid, get a steady job so that I have a decent income so that I can provide for the kid. Move out me mum's, get me own place. But then you have all these people coming over and they get handed cars, they get handed houses, jobs, do you know what I mean, ... being a resident in this country and I can't get no help whatsoever.
> (Long-term settled, majority ethnic, young man, Downham)

He also shows how the impossibility of 'getting his own place' and 'getting a steady job' leads him to characterise his 'being from here' in terms of his privileged right to social support and mobility. As a reaction to his lived experience of marginalisation and exclusion, he participates in collective fantasies about the superior hopes of new arrivals, who 'get handed cars, houses and jobs'.

In summary, for both white English majority ethnic long-term settled residents (in Downham) and African-Caribbean minority ethnic long-term settled residents (in Leicester) the experience of education and social mobility was characterised by lack of resources and marginalisation. In this shared situation, the arrival of aspirational and more skilled new students triggered long standing feelings of disappointment and resentment which were projected on new arrivals. However, in both contexts, the situation has improved considerably in the last four years, due to the increased ethnic pluralisation of local populations (in Downham), to their successful revitalisation of local economies, and to positive role of targeted social interventions within educational settings. This positive role will be the main topic of the next subsection, which will deal with the way educational settings can contribute positively to the improvement of the social relations unfolding in the wider social contexts encompassing them.

Social transformations and social interventions in educational settings in Leicester, Downham and Dungannon

Both in Leicester and in Downham, the tensions between different groups of long-term settled residents and new arrivals are much less significant now than in the past, as they were addressed by initiatives of social intervention and, in Downham, because of the transformation of local settings. In Dungannon, the arrival of new migrant students from Portugal and new EU (Eastern European) accession countries evidenced the lack of English language support for new arrivals. In all of these cases, the arrival of new groups of migrant posed specific opportunities and predicaments to the unfolding of social cohesion in educational settings.

Leicester

In Leicester, in response to the chain of misperceptions fuelling the tensions between Somali and African-Caribbean young people, initiatives of mediation in public areas and information campaigns in schools and other settings were set in place. These had the aim of preventing the conflict from escalating further and of providing young people with the information they needed to challenge prejudices and myths. The main strategy to forestall the development of social antagonism between ethnic groups in Leicester is a policy of 'de-ethnicisation' of the issues at stake. This operation usually involves the setting up of appropriate initiatives of mutual information and myth-dispelling enabling contending partners to navigate the inequalities and divisions of place in terms they feel they are positive. In other words, these initiatives were cohesive not because they resolved or eliminated conflicts and tensions, which would match a 'consensualist' understanding of social cohesion as marked by the absence of conflicts or segregation. They promoted social cohesion because they provided antagonised groups with the resources they needed to negotiate the conflict underpinning their locality in terms that they deemed positive, which is the understanding of social cohesion corroborated by our research findings.

Leicester council's strategy of defusing potentially antagonistic issues through their de-ethnicisation is enabled by two different strategic resources, whose availability is the consequence of the city's long-term engagement with and investment in multiculture. The first refers to the widespread awareness of the economic and social consequences of conflict and of the destructive impact the racialisation or ethnicisation of antagonism could have on the common good. This leads to a prompt response both at institutional and at an individual level. An African-Caribbean long-term settled resident expresses the necessity to not even consider the possibility of not 'coming together and put differences aside', his shorthand for social cohesion, as the only other alternative is conflict.

> We have got to face reality and work hard to make sure it works because if it don't, with the nature of race and religion and people who are coming into Britain at the moment, it will be a war. So we might as well be realistic and try and put our differences aside and work with each other discussing things with each other and come together. Because the different people who are coming into Britain at the moment are here to stay.
> (Long-term settled, minority ethnic, man, Leicester)

This minority ethnic long-term settled resident summarises one of the main findings of our research: that most people valued as cohesive the ability and possibility to negotiate what is separate and what is shared in the communities and places they lived in. He also highlights the role played by the acknowledgement of the role of migration – 'that the different people who are coming into Britain at the moment are 'here to stay', in the formation of locality. This acknowledgement, as we will analyse in more detail in Chapter 6, translates in dealing with, rather then eliminating, conflicts by accepting them 'realistically', while trying and 'put our differences aside and work with each other'. Conflicts and tensions are not the contrary of social cohesion. They are expression of the social field in which the ability to negotiate them in terms deemed positive by the people involved is deployed. The self-representation of communities and places as plural and mobile or as segregated and deprived is deeply implicated in the unfolding of social cohesion. It enhances or hinders, respectively, the cohesive ability of individuals and the communities they live in to straddle the inequalities and divisions constituting their places in ways that are deemed positive by the majority.

Secondly, the long-term policy of employing minority ethnic people in the public sector and the long-term investment in an extensive network of 'ethnic' and other 'social' organisations has resulted in the right instruments and figures of mediation being available to manage conflicts. For example, the conflict between African-Caribbean and Somali young people was also played out in local neighbourhoods, where the response was often led by the police. In Leicester, the police were able to mobilise the right figures of mediation. They decided to deploy Sikh officers. This meant that the police were not perceived as being 'on side' with either 'Muslim' Somali or with 'Black' African-Caribbean young people, while also not being associated with the 'white' majority ethnic population.

A specific issue related to the arrival of A8 migrants also emerged in Leicester, where a few young pupils recently arrived from Eastern Europe displayed a racist attitude towards black and Asian long-term settled people. This was usually attributed, by our key informants, to new arrivals' lack of experience and ignorance of racial diversity. The lack of experience with racial difference, if left unchallenged, could pose a serious challenge to existing community relations. A former director of a secondary school in Highfields shows these dynamics at work.

> Most people from Eastern Europe had never come across Black or Asian people in their countries and one of the girls said 'I don't want to sit next to a nigger.' But instead of criticising, it is better to teach children about what is right, what is acceptable and what is wrong and what gives offence, through social and personal education. It's not about, you know, blaming someone for doing something wrong. You don't sort of blame and start labelling them as racist because the reason for that is that they have not encountered that. And maybe from where those children have come from that is a word that is still being used. You know, we talk about anti-racist strategies and race equality, it might not be the case in some Eastern European countries.
>
> (Key informant, Leicester)

This key informant highlights the potential danger posed by leaving racialised conflicts unaddressed in educational settings. She also illustrates the potential key role played by schools in providing pupils with information and lived opportunities to 'unlearn' (hooks, 1986) the racialised discourses and divisions which they met in the social settings they come from. Here, again we see how tensions and problems emerging in the wider social environment were also mirrored in the context of education and how education settings can act as strategic catalysts through which these can be both expressed and successfully addressed.

In Leicester any topic which can be seen as potentially igniting dynamics of social antagonism, whether in educational or in other social settings, is discussed in transversal bodies such as the Multicultural Advisory Group, also promoted by the Council, where the best way to present it to the general public is agreed by representatives of local media, ethnic communities and key institutions. A Somali member of the multicultural advisory group explains how key information is presented in a de-ethnicised terms, in order for the problem (violence in schools) and its solution (information campaigns, mediation initiatives, police intervention and community work) to be emphasised over potentially divisive ethnicised accounts.

> I think most of the media in Leicester was very positive, in my experience. I think they are very respectful of different cultural sensitivities. If there are incidents like this they always take sensitive approach. Not promoting in terms of negativity. But looking at ways of telling the news but also being sensitive about it. What happens is that they will not mention for example that Somali and African-Caribbean students are fighting each other, but that there were incidents between different students in a college and they will have also for example talked to the teacher, talked to the parents so that they will have a complete picture and each of the contributions will be put in the picture.
>
> (Key informant, Leicester)

An interview with the Editor of the Leicester Mercury, currently the chair of the Multicultural Advisory Group, was another interesting testimony of the way potentially contentious issues are dealt with in Leicester. He stated:

> There were fights between some Somali lads and some African-Caribbean lads at one of the local colleges ... people ended up in

hospital. So that has to be reported. What we didn't say was that it was Somalis versus African-Caribbeans. Because why was that important, it was basically two groups of lads having a fight. The minute you start putting a cultural background in you are making a judgement about part of the reasons.

(Key informant, Leicester)

Harmonious relations between social groups are often the result of a careful and skilled process of monitoring and co-ordination between strategic actors. By deciding to report the conflict between groups of young people in non-ethnic terms, the newspaper acknowledged its implication in and responsibility for social cohesion. Consequently, it prioritised the harmoniousness of the social relations intervening within its readership over the potential (short-term) gain potentially offered by representing the same issue in more sensationalist and polarising ways.

Downham

In Downham, according to many long-term settled residents and new arrivals, the inter-ethnic tensions mentioned above are now less acute than four or five years ago because younger generations seem to show a different attitude to ethnic difference. Many interviewees indicated that the situation had improved in the last few years as people 'got used' to dealing with a more diverse population. However, this 16 year-old black young man from Downham describes how the relatively recent improvement of inter-ethnic relations in the area was the outcome of the renegotiation, rather than the abolition, of racial and ethnic boundaries.

> No, I can't go there. It's not wise. It's not wise. When I was about fourteen and I would have the Tavern and the Baring youths like all try and fight me and fight my boys and stuff like. Now my home boys are white folk, Black folk, mixed race folk. Up in the Tavern now there is Black folk. But they've got the white boy accent and they drink with the white boys and act white. And that's only because of people like myself, we had to walk over that land for us to not have it from them, just so that these people can walk over there safely. Do you know what I am saying? So the easiest thing for them to do is make peace with them because someone will get hurt.
>
> (Long-term settled, minority ethnic, young man, Downham)

As a consequence of the conflictive redrawing of racial and ethnic boundaries and of the relative acceptance of inter-racial and inter-ethnic relations indicated by many, particularly younger, interviewees, Downham has left the most acute years of ethnically motivated antagonism behind and is now a place where it is easier for an increasingly diverse population to find positive solutions to existing conflicts and inequalities. In other words, Downham is a more socially cohesive place. However, the tensions and conflicts that were played out in Malory school were only partially addressed by its transformation into a city academy.

In September 2005, Malory school became the Haberdashers' Aske's Knights Academy, in accordance with the current Government's policies to involve private education institutions in the restructuring of the public education sector as a means to improve education services. Although Malory came to be seen as a classic case of a 'failing school', in the last years before its transformation into a school academy it also became an interesting laboratory for the management of ethnic difference and was able to achieve a good performance with non-English speaking children and children with different educational needs. Moreover, the school had developed a successful method, based on civic education and the use of theatre, of dealing with both bullying and social antagonism between different ethnic groups. These observations corroborate critiques of the commoditised criteria used to evaluate school performance, which emphasise how many so-called failing schools deliver very high 'added value' results. These often cannot be measured by the marketable terms of achievement and skills set by neoliberal policies, even when they enable a diverse student population to learn and live together more harmoniously (McKibbin, 2008). Thus, besides not providing pupils with the skills they need to enter the knowledge economy, the main failure of schools perceived as 'failing', might be that they are not effectively publicising the intrinsic value of their contribution to social cohesion. The experience of Malory school highlights the opportunity of including schools' record of catering for the educational needs of marginalised students, alongside their academic results, in the overall evaluation of their educational achievement.

The transformation of the 'failing' Malory school into the 'high achievement' Haberdasher's Aske's academy coincided with the introduction of polarising and fragmenting changes in the selection procedures. Those now in place at Haberdasher's Aske's are seen as excluding the less achieving local pupils in favour of 'brighter' pupils from outside, with fewer 'special' needs. These local observations are corroborated by existing research, underlining how city academies in general (Gorard, 2005: 276) and Aberdasher's Aske's Knights Academy in Downham more specifically (Powell Davies, 2008: 68) improved their results by changing the nature of their intake and claiming the improvement of overall results was an outcome of improved teaching or management (Beckett, 2007). Two interviews with the representatives of a local education trust and of a theatre group with a long experience of working within Malory school show how the transformation of Malory into a city academy was experienced by people who were directly involved in it.

> Haberdasher Aske's do an entrance exam which they say is comprehensive intake. Well, they have this fifty per cent random selection, they call it ... but a lot of the random selections are apparently, seem to be in the top twenty per cent or twenty five per cent achievement. And great. The other fifty per cent come in on distance. So there is already a bit of social engineering going on there.
> (Key informant, Downham)

> The transformation was overnight. And basically it was made absolutely clear that the ESOL department was closed down. We said well, what about the new arrivals. 'There will be no more new arrivals here.' So the staff left. Erm, and there is no support in language learning there. That's the – these academies can, they are quite autonomous. And it was under the management of Haberdasher's Aske's. So yeah, absolutely they can do that.
> (Key informant, Downham)

Thus, as a consequence of the social engineering deployed by the new city academy, although local people are increasingly trying to enrol their children at the new school, only a few local pupils manage to get in. Those less likely to meet the high academic achievement standard required to enter city academies fall on less achieving surrounding schools which become at very high risk of falling into a Malory scenario. At the same time, important experiences of social mediation and educational support are scrapped overnight as they do not fit with the imperative of marketability of skills driving neoliberal educational policies in the UK.

The delivery of key and expensive infrastructures such as the £40 million state-sponsored Haberdashers' Aske's Knights Academy, the most expensive city academy according to the latest National Audit Offices report (quoted in Powell-Davies, 2008: 61), will not alone be able to overturn alone decades of neglect and deprivation and their impact on educational achievement. According to existing research (Cassen and Kingdon, 2007) only 14 per cent of the incidence of low achievement is attributable to (secondary) school performance and low achievement is strongly associated with eligibility for free school meals, neighbourhood unemployment rate and the proportion of parents with low educational qualifications; all measured in the place where the pupil lives. At the same time, addressing the long standing socio-economic problems of schools' catchment areas is not, on its own, going to improve their performance, which requires specific skills, techniques and abilities.

Dungannon

In Dungannon (Northern Ireland), the arrival of large numbers of Portuguese and Eastern European (Lithuanian and Poles in particular) migrants in the early 2000s, put an initial strain on but also revitalised local schools, thanks to organisation of voluntary schemes to cope with the demand for language classes and school places. These are now very important spaces for the establishment of non work-related forms of social participation, involving both long-term settled resident and new arrival parents and children.

As a consequence of the lack of resources to fund targeted English language provision, primary and secondary schools were under considerable strain and had to resort to voluntary schemes to cope with the demand for language classes and school places. The following is a quote from a key informant directly involved in the delivery of language courses.

> I have no money for these kids as I am funded a year in retrospect. I had a massive influx this year but I don't get the money for another year so I am living in a deficit budget.
>
> (Key informant, Dungannon)

Some schools were reluctant to enrol children from migrant workers' families, as they were not willing to face a financial deficit. However, thanks to the organisation of voluntary schemes and to the intervention of migrant rights' associations such as STEPS, our partner organisation in Dungannon. English language classes became important occasions of socialisation for new migrant groups, who found there the motivation and the opportunity to participate in local society. New arrivals who brought their family, especially young children, felt a greater need to integrate and start belonging to the community as their children were adopting local culture. One recent migrant felt that because her daughter was attending school in Dungannon from a very young age, this was enabling her to also integrate into the local community:

> My daughter she has friends here. We don't have anything where we came from. She doesn't remember and she is already like a local. She is speaking the same language.
> (New arrival, Portuguese, woman, Dungannon)

This young mother sees the acquisition of English language as the marker of her daughter's social integration into locality, where 'she speaks the same language' and 'has friends'.

Within the tertiary education sector East Tyrone College of Further and Higher Education saw a steep increase in the numbers enrolling for English language classes, which again placed pressure on the service. The college had to put in place measures to deal with this to ensure needs were being met. Extra classes were provided and partnerships established with local churches that were informally offering the service. Some younger interviewees were attending the college on a full time basis and seemed to be interacting well with their fellow students, something the college itself was endeavouring to encourage, by making sure that new arrivals would be able to attend most courses.

The value of learning English language for migrants goes beyond its usefulness for the purposes of integration. For many new arrivals, and particularly for young people from A8 countries, the motivation to migrate centred on the desire to learn English and improve their educational opportunities. In some cases, there was a realisation that for them to succeed in their own countries, being able to communicate in English would benefit their future employment opportunities. These tended to be younger migrant workers, who were taking a year or two away from their studies in an attempt to improve their English language skills, as the following two quotes from two young A8 male migrants show.

> I decided to come here because it is better to learn English in the United Kingdom than at school, it is much easier.
> (New arrival, Polish, young man, Dungannon)

> I wanted to learn the English language that's why I come to the UK.
> (New arrival, Slovakian, young man, Dungannon)

In both cases, interviewees aimed at achieving a strategic set of skill to be capitalised on in the labour market back at home and intended to stay in Dungannon for only a short period, possibly two years.

The cases presented in this subsection present different interplays between the arrival of new migrant groups in educational settings, social interventions and social cohesion. Although the case of Dungannon is a positive one, it also further highlights the lack of adequate resources and instruments to address the issue of new arrivals into the education system, as a timely response was only possible because of voluntary interventions. The case also highlights the fundamental role of educational settings as shared spaces of socialisation for new arrivals and long-term settled residents, which could lay the foundations for the development of positive social relations between individuals and social groups in the wider society.

Both Highfields (Leicester) and Downham can be seen as having deep seated issues of deprivation. However, in Highfields, the relative advantage (in terms of the education achievement ethos and the learning skills available within the family) that some asylum seekers had compared with some of the long-term settled residents was capitalised on by both the educational institution and the pupils. For example, the former director of a secondary school in Highfields explains how the ethno-cultural diversity of the student population was valued and capitalised upon by 'mainstreaming' community languages within the system of GCSE accreditation.

> To celebrate their cultural background, we entered children who came from Holland for Dutch GCSEs. The children that came from Denmark for Danish GCSEs. The children that are newly arrived for Gujarati GCSEs and so on. So the community languages were given accreditation and currency in the mainstream.
>
> (Key informant, Leicester)

The interviewee shows how in Highfield the recognition of people's cultural diversity corresponds to their accreditation with specific skills which can open up both work and socialisation opportunities within people's local and wider (diasporic) affiliations.

In Downham, minority ethnic long-term settled and new arrival students who wanted to achieve became a scapegoat for a social and educational system that failed to improve the lives of white English majority ethnic long-term settled residents, the latter, as a result claimed to be more 'from here' than others and adopted a culture of 'commonness' to resist their perception of being further marginalised by the arrival of 'achieving' newcomers. Only a minority of white English students were subscribing to a culture of academic achievement in Downham, because of the prevalence of anti-academic attitudes, which are rooted in the history of place characterised by decades of worklessness and stigmatisation as a 'white working class' neighbourhood. As a result of the structural and long standing socio-economic inequalities brought about by the convergence of post-industrialism and neoliberalism, most white English majority ethnic students saw resistance to academic achievement and discipline as an integral part of their majority ethnic localised identity. In the process, unique educational opportunities and resources are wasted and entire generations of students do not get the skills they need to move on into adulthood and independence. As we have explained, although by the mid-2000s the most acute phase of social antagonism was over in Downham, this happened mainly because of the greater number of minority ethnic people living in the area and of the coming of age of the groups of young people who were involved in violent confrontations. At the same time, the inauguration of 'state of the art' facilities such as Knight's academy, although representing signs of a new season of investment in the rhythms and realities of everyday life in Downham, appear still to exclude and marginalise those at the bottom of the hierarchy of educational and social needs.

Conclusion

Social relations between new arrivals and long-term settled residents in the context of education were heavily influenced by local 'learner identities'. These are rooted in the life trajectories and histories of new arrivals, long-term settled residents, as well as in the socio-economic realities they come from and live in. Although educational structures and practices can play a key role in helping the communities negotiate their inherent conflicts and tensions in terms deemed positive by all parties involved, they cannot do that alone. The socio-cultural and economic dynamics characterising school's catchment areas often determine both the symbolic meanings and localised identities associated with educational achievement and the overall educational performance of their students. Our findings emphasise the importance of the socio-economic environment surrounding education in its potential to facilitate the unfolding of social cohesion, that is, the ability to solve conflicts in terms deemed positive by those involved. These findings are in line with holistic approaches to inter-ethnic conflict in the context of education emphasising how tensions are more likely to emerge as a result of the interplay between unemployment, lack of housing provision, stigmatisation of new arrivals in local media and inability to address violent behaviour between pupils (Rutter, 2006: 96–7).

Our observations reflect existing concerns about the suitability of localised neighbourhood regeneration initiatives to redress the social transformations and polarisations of place introduced by the convergence of post-industrialism and neoliberalism (Cresswell, 2006). In the absence of a co-ordination of these investments with the different spatial (local, borough, urban, national, transnational, global, etc.) and economic scales and nodes of governance of place, any localised target-based intervention is likely to further polarise places and the social relations constituting them. As we have seen in the case of Downham, the introduction of a city academy can end up by further polarising and fragmenting educational settings. Overall, the outcome of such neoliberal interventions as city academies was to widen the gap between the groups and places that can be included in the neoliberal knowledge economy, and the 'wasted lives' and places simultaneously produced in the process (Baumann, 2002). While a few of the least privileged students 'from Downham' are able to get a place in the city academy which succeeded Malory school, most move to further overcrowded 'failing' educational settings in and around Downham. Moreover, in the process of dismantling of Malory school, key skills for the improvement of social cohesion, such as theatre based conflict-resolution techniques, were discarded and substituted, rather then being complemented, by skills that can be certified as marketable in the knowledge society.

Our findings show that the arrival of new migrant pupils, when properly managed, can be an opportunity for local educational settings. In Dungannon the arrival of new migrant groups exerted pressure on local educational setting, but also contributed to the revitalisation of depopulated local schools. Most importantly, after initial difficulties and resistances due to the lack of funding for English language classes, educational settings became a key socialisation catalyst fostering the social participation of migrant parents and children as well as an important meeting point for (young) long-term settled residents and new arrivals. In Leicester, schools were able to help antagonised groups of young people negotiate the tension and inequalities they lived in the places they shared. In Downham, the inequalities characterising people's experience of place, which were grounded in the structural worklessness and marginalisation of the white working class majority, impacted very negatively on the school's ability to become a catalyst for social cohesion.

As school performance can only be seen as partially responsible for the improvement of educational achievement, the real challenge is to make sure that deprivation and localised self-representations in terms of homogeneity, commonness and isolation, are addressed in a comprehensive fashion. To this end, individual academic achievement should not be separated from overall social responsibility for combating disadvantage in the local area when assessing school performance. It is only by acknowledging and valorising the complex relation between schools and the transforming social contexts they work within that 'socially cohesive' policies and actions can be identified and promoted. By allocating funding to private–public joint ventures which only guarantee a high achievement rate by 'preaching to the converted', that is by selecting the relatively most advantaged children, the structural inequalities and dynamics underpinning social antagonism are reproduced and exacerbated elsewhere. In the process, the potential for educational settings to act as catalysts for social cohesion, by providing a group of pupils whose diversity mirrors the diversity of the places they live in with the ability to positively address existing inequalities and conflicts, is further undermined.

6
Social Cohesion and the Politics of Belonging

Throughout this book, drawing on our findings, we conceptualised social cohesion as the ability of individuals and groups to negotiate the inequalities and conflicts structuring the places they live in on terms which they consider satisfactory and positive. Both narratives of belonging to place and local histories of migrancy, diversity and mobility are key to the unfolding of social cohesion. They frame the way in which individuals and groups are able to negotiate social cohesion. The following questions inform this chapter, which will explore experiences of belonging to Britain and understandings of social cohesion. How do people express their sense of belonging in Britain? How does this impact on their experiences and understandings of social cohesion? In what ways is the arrival of new migrant groups implicated in this interplay? First, we will examine belonging in Britain, in terms of the everyday experiences of the three main categories of people we have been addressing throughout the book: majority ethnic long-term settled residents; minority ethnic long-term settled residents and new arrivals. Second, we will explore the relationship between the understandings of social cohesion and the local prevalence of specific narratives and self representations.

Understandings of social cohesion are embedded in the relationship between self-representations and politics of belonging. It is important here to recap the way we conceptualise this relationship. We understand personal and social identities as forms of self-representation which are shaped by the interplay between social representations and their internalisation or rejection at an individual level. The local specificity of this interplay characterises local experiences of social cohesion. Hegemonic self-representations reproduce social divisions and the categories and narratives which can be used to negotiate local inequalities. The complex interplay between self-representation, belonging and social cohesion will be an important thread running through this chapter. We will analyse the way the internalisation or rejection of self-representations underpins people's understandings of their local, national and transnational belongings and of social cohesion.

Drawing on our research findings, we will show that the prevailing self-definition of specific places as 'homogeneous' and 'settled', rather than 'heterogeneous' and constituted by migration impacts strongly on people's understandings of social cohesion. Homogeneous narratives of belonging coincide with assimilationist understandings of social cohesion being about the ability of migrants to adapt to fixed and nationalist structures of belonging to Britain. In contrast, heterogeneous narratives of belonging coincide with pluralist understandings of social cohesion being about the ability of both migrants and long-term settled residents to negotiate conflicting and shared needs. Assimilationist and pluralist narratives of social cohesion are part and parcel of local self-representations and impact strongly on social relations. For instance, assimilationist understandings of social cohesion, together with narratives of boundedness and (social) immobility, can participate in the further stigmatisation and exclusion of individuals and groups, which in turn undermine their ability of negotiating the conflicts and tensions they share. Defining where the responsibility of social cohesion lies can become part of politics of belonging strategically emphasising the cohesiveness of some groups against the uncohesiveness of others. In contrast, drawing on our findings, we define social cohesion as a skill and ability, rather than a set of values and responsibilities that lie with particular groups of immigrants or long-term settled residents. More specifically, social cohesion is the individual and social ability to negotiate conflicts and tensions in ways which are deemed positive by all the parties involved.

In order to capture and analyse the complex interplay between narratives of belonging and social cohesion, we will first focus, in the next section, on the nexus between experiences of belonging in contemporary Britain. In the section that follows, we will examine the relationship between local understandings of social cohesion and the prevalence of specific narratives and self representations. More specifically, we will compare understandings of social cohesions prevailing in places characterised by a self-representation in terms of homogeneity, separation and settlement, with those prevailing in places characterised by the acknowledgement of the formative role of migration and of heterogeneity in the emergence and prospering of the locality. In the final section of the chapter, we will offer our conclusions.

Belongings within contemporary Britain

New arrivals and (majority and minority) long-term settled residents' feelings of belonging to Britain are characterised by similar degrees of complexity and ambivalence. Researching the way feelings of belonging unfold in people's everyday lives means engaging with a complex interplay between different (and similar) understandings of interconnected personal and social (nation, community, family, etc.) identities. As to be expected, 'belonging to Britain' has different (and overlapping) local, national and transnational meanings for the people we interviewed. Further, there are different degrees of intensity and modes of belonging to Britain for our three different groups of interviewees.

Before exploring the specific experiences and understandings of belonging to Britain we encountered, let us remember how we differentiated these three groups of interviewees. We use the term 'majority ethnic long-term settled' to indicate the population who has a majority numerical and ethno-racial positioning in their respective UK jurisdiction. In England this would be people who for example in 2001 ticked the 'White British' box. In Scotland, we use the term 'majority ethnic long-term settled' to refer to people who perceive themselves as part of the 'indigenous' population in Scotland or a foundational immigration from Ireland in the nineteenth century. In Northern Ireland the term 'long-term settled' encompasses the Catholic/Nationalist and Protestant/Unionist/Loyalist populations and others who would not ascribe to any of these labels. The term 'minority ethnic long-term settled' is used to refer to all the long-term settled residents in the UK who do not see themselves as part of these majority groups. Finally, the term 'new arrivals' refers to people who were born outside and came to live in the UK since 1997.

Majority ethnic belongings in England

Some of the white English majority ethnic interviewees' narratives of belonging to Britain can be considered as examples of what Michael Banton described as 'minus one ethnicity'. This refers to the way predominant identities tend to be naturalised as unmarked and to define all other groups as ethnically marked and different (Banton, 1998: 159). This phenomenon was reflected in the findings of our research by the fact that in most cases, majority ethnic long-term settled residents found the question about the meaning they attached to belonging to Britain hard to answer. This white English majority ethnic long-term settled woman from Downham exemplifies this difficulty, as she seems to have never questioned the basis of her belonging to Britain.

> What does Britain mean to me? Oh dear, that's a difficult one. I don't really know. Yeah, I don't really think about it to be honest with you.
> (Long-term settled, majority ethnic, woman, Downham)

Many majority ethnic interviewees, after hesitating, as if surprised by an unexpected question, referred to a 'minimalist' positive feeling of belonging to Britain because it is their home, as in this following example. The interview with another white English majority ethnic long-term settled woman, this time from Leicester, is an example of another frequent response to the question of belonging.

> It's me home, I feel proud to be British, even though there is a lot of things I don't like about it which wherever you'd be there is something that you wouldn't, you know. I mean, there is a lot of things that the governments could do to improve the living standards.
> (Long-term settled, majority ethnic, woman, Leicester)

Many white English majority ethnic people, as indeed did this woman from Leicester, combined their positive sense of belonging to Britain with a critique of government action or inaction. The existence and contraction of the welfare state were, respectively, both a recurring motive of positive identification and a concern for many white English long-term settled residents. The following woman from Peterborough explains how her positive sense of belonging in Britain is based on her feelings of safety and security, because of the existence of the welfare state and social services.

> Well, it's like my homeland. Somewhere that I feel comfortable and safe really, at the end of the day. Obviously we are really, I know that we are quite privileged here compared to people in other countries. I know, that I am always going to be looked after. I mean, I am a lucky person, I know that I have not only got family but I do feel that if I really needed help with social services or something like that I know that, well, hopefully, not that I have experienced it but you know, I do believe that I would get the support I needed.
> (Long-term settled, majority ethnic, woman, Peterborough)

The possibility of 'being looked after' by the state, through the NHS or the social services, in case of need and beyond the support offered by the family is an important aspect of this woman's positive feelings of belonging to Britain. Many white English residents associated feelings of positive belonging to Britain to the availability of support from the welfare state, with the perception of British society being fair, safe and tolerance of ethnic diversity. A man and a woman from Downham, an area which, as we have seen, was characterised by ethnically motivated social antagonism in the late 1990s, openly value multiculturalism, tolerance and equality as a way to describe their belonging in Britain.

> Umh ... yeah, that is a difficult one, isn't it!? I think it is a more kind of a multicultural country now ... I think it is good ... I think it is a good thing, it's not without its problems but ... you know, I think we're quite a tolerant country and that we do try and live with our neighbours as well as we can.
> (Long-term settled, majority ethnic, woman, Downham)

> It means, um, a fairly tolerant society, a fair society. ... Some might have more money but ... it's becoming more egalitarian, compared to when I grew up, I would like to think so anyway.
> (Long-term settled, majority ethnic, man, Downham)

This man is expressing a feeling of positive belonging in Britain and that is related to his perception of society having become more egalitarian, compared to when he was growing up. However, when the perception of Britain being a place characterised by equality, fairness or tolerance was betrayed by personal experiences that seem to show the opposite, the outcome in terms of positive belonging is quite different. For example, a white English young man, also from Dowham, provided us with a different account.

> I don't know really. Britain to me is sort of home, do you know what I mean. It will always be home. But like I say a lot of things have changed. Because the way I see it it's not our country anymore. Not like that as in whites, Blacks, things like that. But British people have sort of been pushed aside and they are not sort of thought about or recognised as British citizens. The attention and all that is on the immigrants and all that coming over.
> (Long-term settled, majority ethnic, man, Downham)

For this young man with an experience of poor education provision, unemployment, economic difficulties and family breakdown, being proud of belonging to Britain was seen as historical, since the country was now perceived as catering for the needs of new arrivals. The experiences and narrative of this young man illustrate the transition from the 'white' to the 'settled' variety of backlash. He explains that his alienation from Britain, that is, his feeling that 'Britain is not our country anymore', is due to the privileged treatment of 'immigrants and all that coming over' against the long-term settled population. He shows how in contemporary 'settled backlash' times locality (being from here), rather than race – 'the Black/White thing' – is the main discourse through which new hierarchies of people who (should) belong and receive state support are argued for. Most importantly, the interview from this young man and from the other people from Downham preceding it show how individual experiences of relative success and its contrary overrule general trends characterising localities or ethnicities regarding feelings of belonging to national and other forms of community (local, ethnic, etc.).

Although Downham is the research site where 'settled backlash' was more evident and recent compared to all the others, within Downham there are, in fact, a plurality of voices, as we showed in the chapter on place and belonging. These voices express different experiences of current social transformations and of their relations with new arrivals. However, within the polyphony of narratives composing Downham's experience of place, the particular voice of this disaffected young man bears the heritage of decades of disinvestment in the social texture of the neighbourhood. In this case, the interviewees' experience of exclusion is corroborated by locally available narratives of 'from hereness'. These are also reinforced by generalised experiences of marginalisation, which led him to perceive that Britain is no longer a place for British people.

Majority ethnic belongings in Scotland and Northern Ireland

In Scotland and Northern Ireland, long-term settled interviewees' relations to belonging to Britain were also contested, albeit in different and specific ways, when compared with England. In both Scotland and Northern Ireland people tended to explain their belonging (or not) to Britain in terms which reflected the way they negotiated their (national) identity position within it. Thus, in Scotland, the issue of belonging to Britain was seen by some interviewees as complex, as it was mediated by people's belonging to Scotland. For example, this majority ethnic long-term settled Scottish man explains his perception that for many Scottish people the negotiation of belonging in Britain was both quite complex and not meaningful, altogether.

> *What does Britain mean to you?*
> Erm, in fact I think for Scottish people it's quite a complex thing, Britain, in terms of your identity and your various identities, Scottish and British. And so, so I think it can mean quite a few things, it's not altogether quite relevant actually.
> (Long-term settled, majority ethnic, Scottish, man, Glasgow)

His comment, that the issue of belonging in Britain was seen as irrelevant by many people in Scotland, was confirmed by other interviewees, who, like the following woman, would rather relate to Scotland or not relate to any national affiliation at all.

> *What does it mean to belong in Britain?*
> [Pauses] Don't know. I only lived in Scotland.
> (Long-term settled, majority ethnic, Scottish, woman, Glasgow)

The irrelevance of the issue of belonging to Britain which emerges from these narratives needs to be read against the recurring difficulty people had in reconciling Britishness and Scottishness. The picture that emerges from the interviews we gathered in Glasgow is one in which most Scottish majority ethnic long-term settled residents do not feel that they belong primarily or at all to Britain and have much stronger and more meaningful feelings of belonging to Scotland overall.

In a parallel fashion, in Northern Ireland many majority ethnic long-term settled interviewees did not express feelings of belonging to Britain, but to Ireland and/or Northern Ireland. This depended on their ethno-religious positioning within local society. The following Catholic majority ethnic man saw himself as not belonging to Britain, which he considered as completely detached from (Northern) Ireland.

> Britain is a country that is across the water from us.
> (Long-term settled, Catholic, man, Dungannon)

Similarly, a Protestant woman considers her home country to be Northern Ireland, rather than citing Britain or the UK, but she would identify as Irish in an international context.

Well, Northern Ireland is basically my home. But again if I was abroad or working or whatever, I would say I'm Irish.
(Long-term settled, Protestant, woman, Dungannon)

In Northern Ireland people's ethno-religious position according to the Catholic and Protestant divide can shape the degree of affiliation to Britain/UK, which is refused in the first case (Catholic) and more nuanced and contextual in the second (Protestant). Whereas neither the Catholic nor the Protestant interviewee felt they belonged to Britain, in the first case this is argued by underlining geographical separation, whereas in the second case a more careful distinction is made about the feeling of belonging to Northern Ireland in the context of inter-Irish and inter-British relations and feeling more generally Irish when abroad.

In many cases, interviewees relativised the relevance of whether they felt they belonged to Northern Ireland or Ireland as an expression of their wish to leave ethno-national struggles and affiliations behind. These two catholic majority ethnic interviewees, a young woman and an elderly man in Dungannon show these dynamics in play.

What does it mean to you to be living in Northern Ireland or belonging to Ireland?
It doesn't really bother me what or where.
Where would you most like to live?
Probably somewhere hot and warm like Spain!
How do you think things could be improved in Northern Ireland?
All this RA thing (slang for IRA) and all about the PSNI (Police Service of Northern Ireland), if they would just give over and everybody just speak and stop all the rowing. Like people in the south of Ireland still think that the riots are going on up here, they think that we riot all the time.
(Long-term settled, Catholic, young woman, Dungannon)

What does Northern Ireland mean to you?
Really nothing.
Do you think it's good that the area is more multi-ethnic now?
Yes, I would say it's good to live along with your European friends, we should all be treated as one, all European, we are Europeans, we're not Irish.
(Long-term settled, Catholic, elderly man, Dungannon)

These relational dynamics, by which different local and wider affiliations become more or less relevant in different respects and contexts and change over time, are by no means exclusive to Northern Ireland, but are a structural aspect of identity phenomena. At the same time, in the case of both Scotland or Northern Ireland, for many interviewees dismissing the relevance of the issue of belonging to Britain often felt like a polite and non confrontational way to convey the sense that they felt they belonged much more to their respective jurisdictions.

In summary, majority ethnic long-term settled people tended to overlook or dismiss their belonging to Britain, but for different reasons. White English people tended to find it difficult to express the terms of their belonging to Britain. Their 'minus one' hegemonic status within Britishness meant that they had experienced their identities and belongings as naturalised as unmarked. Whereas Scottish people and people from Northern Ireland tended to dismiss the relevance of the issue of their belonging to Britain as they felt more attached to their respective jurisdictions. However, they did so according to different ambivalences and nuances, which are rooted in the histories of the geo-political and sociocultural belonging of their jurisdictions in (Great) Britain.

Minority ethnic belongings

Compared with people who are and perceive themselves to be in a position of relative majority, minority ethnic groups tended to be more openly appreciative of belonging to Britain. Many did so with reference to the possibility of enjoying the range of opportunities available for self-advancement in education and in the wider social sphere. As was the case with white English majority ethnic people, safety, often related to the existence of the welfare state and of a legal and institutional system that is accountable to and responsible for citizens was a recurring theme. A woman from Leicester and a man from Downham illustrate some of these discourses at work.

> Yes, it's a free country isn't it? I should say Britain is great! (laughs) I would say it like that. Because even if you're unemployed you get your job seekers allowance, and the NHS is there, so you're not struggling. That way it's quite good. Otherwise if we had to pay everything, then people would be like struggling, so there's no struggle. That way it's quite alright.
> (Long-term settled, minority ethnic, woman, Leicester)

> I think it is a country of opportunity. Erm, I do feel that you make of it what you will. ... It has given me a lot of opportunity. A better

standard of living than I could have expected in my own country, so you know, I do feel that, you know – and I give thanks that I am here. The place is more secure as well. I mean, there is a problem, there is a higher authority. In my country I feel that if there is a problem, there is no higher authority, you deal with the problem yourself.

(Long-term settled, minority ethnic, man, Downham)

As was the case with white English long-term settled residents, these two interviewees highlight safety and security, which they explain with the presence of the welfare state and with the democratic accountability of the state, as reasons for their positive feeling of belonging in Britain.

Feelings of appreciation of the degree of fairness and tolerance of British society were the prevailing narratives. However, as was the case with white English majority ethnic long-term settled residents, they were sometimes tempered by the critique of hierarchies of inclusion and dynamics of exclusion at work within Britain and Britishness. These were sometimes mentioned in relation to different expectations and degrees of incorporation into the 'imagined community' of the British Empire. The following two interviews, with an African-Caribbean and an Irish minority ethnic perspective, reveal the complex interplay between affiliation and separation characterising post-colonial relations and show two different individual reactions to experiences of disappointment and discrimination. Both respondents were able to incorporate these negative experiences within a feeling of positive affiliation to Britain.

Deep down in my heart I always think I belong to Britain, but I don't know if Britain thinks I belong. See? It's like two people in love, one might be in love and the other one mightn't. Britain is the motherland of a lot of the Caribbean islands, but we see it as the motherland but you come here and it's totally different this is one time you think well 'mother not looking after us!' But deep down I think Britain is a good place to live, apart from the cold. I find people of all different race and religion will find it easier to live here. Looking at what's happening in all different parts of the world, Britain seems to be the place to be.

(Long-term settled, minority ethnic, man, Leicester)

Well I would say as an Irish person here, I feel that um with the Irish and the English we are like first cousins, gibing with each other and fighting – it's stupid but at the same time liking each other. ... Now that is not to say that I haven't been subject to, when all the bombs where going off, to certain remarks that were made, which I found

hurtful but there was nothing I could do about it you know, it is part and parcel.
(Long-term settled, minority ethnic, woman, Downham)

These two interviews reveal the ambivalence between familiarity and antagonism at work within the 'British (colonial) family'. They show the deep ambivalence characterising post-colonial relations of belonging and attachment to Britain. These relations of belonging are characterised by the coexistence of feelings of proximity, experiences of disappointment or antagonism and the pragmatic appreciation of both negative and positive 'parts and parcels', such as the possibility of being subject to discrimination and exclusion, while also enjoying cultural pluralism and safety.

Many minority ethnic long-term settled residents often have a diasporic sense of belonging, articulating between Britain and their country of origin. An Indian woman from Leicester and an Irish man from Kilburn illustrate the different degrees and intensity of their multiple belongings to Britain and other places which are relevant to their in their sense of self.

Where do I feel I belong? That's a split between Britain and India. Both places, yeah. That's why I said that I'm a British Indian.
(Long-term settled, minority ethnic, Indian, woman, Leicester)

All I can say is that it's somewhere betwixt and between. I really mentally I belong at home with the option of coming back here.
(Long-term settled, minority ethnic, Irish, man, Kilburn)

For these two interviewees, and for many other minority ethnic long-term settled residents, their feeling of belonging to Britain was not in contradiction with other belongings. This diasporic multiplicity of national and ethnic affiliations was often described, as in the two examples presented above, in non-conflictive terms.

Younger generations of minority ethnic long-term settled residents show different feelings and degrees of belonging to Britain and different understandings of what constitutes political engagement. In Leicester, minority ethnic (East African) long-term settled interviewees, both parents and offspring, talked openly about young people's unavailability to subscribe to relations of authority which were established by previous generations. In particular, Asian younger people tend to refuse what they perceive as the 'colonised' pragmatism of their parents' generation and their tendency to engage in relations of 'subordination'. Their refusal takes the form of becoming more assertive and confrontational vis-à-vis the cases of injustice and discrimination they experience or witness in Britain. The representative of an organisation working with majority and minority ethnic young people in Leicester explains how this more assertive stance poses both opportunities and predicaments, as younger generations who refuse to negotiate risk being excluded from the political debate.

> Yeah, I think that the older generations are more prepared to accept what was there. And there were elements there who were prepared to negotiate and did negotiate and did change things. I think our generation is less tolerant to having things being done to them. I think unfortunately that we have lost that skill to be able to engage and have those conversations in my generation for the vast majority of people. ... And if you don't engage with people in policy you are automatically accepting yes, I should disenfranchise and accept what is given to me.
>
> (Key Informant, Leicester)

This view, that the more assertive stance of new minority ethnic generations could offer a greater potential for resistance and affirmation at an individual level, is therefore contextualised by the fear that it might also lead to the exclusion of minority ethnic young people from collective forms of social participation.

It was a view voiced to us also by the representative of an Asian business association in Leicester. He analyses the different positions he and his son occupy in relation to Britishness and the different ways in which they would react in a situation of racist abuse. These observations prompt him to then express his concern about young Asian people's recourse to violence, which he sees as a consequence of isolation.

> My sons consider themselves as totally British, they have got nothing to do with Africa or the Indian sub-continent. If somebody calls me 'You Paki, go home' or – I will say thank you very much. But if you say the same to my son you will get a slap, he will retaliate. Because he is British, he's born here, this is home, he wants to live here, he's been educated here. And he doesn't see anything else. That's the worry that I have. You see the way the media portrays the Asian community in some cases and also what's happening in Bradford and the 7th of July is that particularly the Muslim groups have been isolated

> I think. The fear that I have, you know, that my son will not be treated as equal by the mainstream and that will cause resentment for the future. I mean, that's not a very positive thing but that's what happens in reality.
>
> (Key informant, Leicester)

These last two interviews show an interesting interpretation of Asian young people's recourse to violent behaviour as an outcome of a combination of factors: a closer experience of belonging to Britain and a contradictory experience of isolation. Thus, the increase in assertiveness and antagonism of some young minority ethnic long-term settled residents can be seen as an expression of their feeling of belonging in Britain and as a reaction to their marginalisation and exclusion.

In summary, minority ethnic long-term settled residents shared with their majority ethnic fellow citizens, except in Scotland and Northern Ireland, a feeling of positive appreciation of Britain as a place of safety and fairness. This was often linked to the presence of the welfare state and to the democratic accountability of institutions. The feeling of positive appreciation of their experiences of belonging to Britain were equally mediated by their individual and collective experiences – as members of a minority ethnic group – of inclusion and exclusion within British society.

New arrivals

Appreciations of Britain as a place of security, fairness and opportunity were pronounced in interviews with new arrivals, both asylum seekers/refugees and migrants. New arrivals in particular expressed their gratitude for the level of and opportunities for self-improvement they could secure by living in Britain, which they also linked to a wider degree of dignity and freedom. A Somali man from Leicester, and two Czech interviewees, a woman and a man from Kilburn and Peterborough, respectively, appreciate the combination of safety, multicultural openness and the opportunities 'to be successful' they found in the UK.

> I think it is very open, multicultural. Everyone has opportunity to be successful. Community members feel more confident to be successful in this country compared to Scandinavian countries. I feel other countries should learn from this country and I feel very pleased to be here.
>
> (New arrival, Somali, man, Leicester)

You know about England, I like really their rules and laws and rights, because it's very useful and it's for everybody you know. Everybody has got their own rights and responsibilities and everything. So I like these systems, social system I think is the best. In Czech Republic is worse.
(New arrival, A8, woman, Peterborough)

What do I think? Big country, lots of chance to get what you want. For me it's nice that they support the education, that they give you some money for it. That's very nice, no one give you in my country. Or the state just pays you basics, you know. And what's – what else? Opportunities to earn, that's good in here, you know.
(New arrival, Czech, man, Kilburn)

Besides the appreciation of the accountability of state institutions and of the opportunities for self-advancement, some new arrivals, including the Czech man from Peterborough quoted above, particularly appreciate the availability of support for education as a way to express their belonging to Britain. Often, as in the case of the Somali man from Leicester quoted above, the regime of rights and responsibilities and the level of security available in Britain are compared favourably to the situation in the country of origin, even when new arrivals refer to countries such as Sweden and Holland. Another Somali man, who obtained both refugee status and citizenship in Sweden feels that he is more able to express his identity in the UK than in Sweden, where he felt more 'foreign' and less accepted as a Swedish citizen, which prompted him to move on to the UK.

It's my fourth year over here and from day one nobody ever dared called me a foreigner. But in Sweden, I mean, our kids are going to be the fourth generation over there and ... we have a terminology in Sweden called 'third generation foreigner'. And erm, and even at times like you say I am a Swede, it's like no, you are not. Yes, I am. No, but you are not because you don't look like a Swede. ... So I felt like listen, I am not going to progress, carry on. So I need to go somewhere which is more English speaking. ... I felt like now the best country in the whole of Europe in order to experiment would be England. Because it's an English speaking country, it's tolerant, very well integrated. In Peterborough we have a mosque over here, we know people from far away so at least now, they are not relatives but I mean, know them, their family knows our family. So you know, yeah, why not. Let's try it, this city.
(New arrival, Swedish-Somali, man, Peterborough)

As did other Somali onward migrants from the Netherlands and Sweden, this man underlined the wider degree of pluralism and social participation he can enjoy in 'English speaking' and 'well integrated' UK. He finds it easier to live according to his chosen lifestyle and enjoy a sense of belonging to a Somali diasporic community, living in Britain.

Many refugee interviewees and migrant new arrivals were adamant in expressing and acknowledging their loyalty and gratitude to Britain, although this did not prevent them from criticising the racialised connotations attached to the label of 'asylum seekers' or other specific aspects of British society. A Kurdish-Iraqi refugee from Peterborough expresses both his gratitude and loyalty towards the UK for 'embracing him' and supporting him in tragic circumstances. However, he is critical of the stigmatisation of asylum seekers and of the drinking culture in Britain.

> The country is good, the Government is good for, to be honest, the Government is good but there are people, people for example, the people in this country maybe they will blame the foreigner, like asylum or immigration, because the name is not good you know when you say asylum ... because there is a kind of you know, a racism inside. When I escaped from my country, in the terrible time, I found myself here, and this country embraced me, and I am not disloyal against this country. I belong to and I support this country, but I have my own opinion, I am not supporting everything which happens in this country with people. ...I don't like the drink culture for example. ... But at the end of the day, I am, I have to be loyal to this country.
> (New arrival, Kurdish-Iraqi refugee, man, Peterborough)

Remarks such as these show that, as was the case with white English majority ethnic and minority ethnic long-term settled residents, new arrivals' feelings of appreciation of and belonging to Britain are mediated by their experiences of inclusion and exclusion within British society, as well as by specific aspects of their way of life.

As far as a sense of where they belonged is concerned, most new arrivals felt that they belonged both to the country of origin and their new place of resettlement. This Albanian young man explains the hierarchy of affiliation structuring his sense of belonging to both Albania and the UK.

> If someone asked me, I am saying an example, if someone asked me, choose quick, quick, quick I would say Albania. But probably

I'd say England as well because as long as I have the right to go to Albania whenever I want I would live here. Yes, if I have rights, I will be here.

(New arrival, Albanian, young man, Downham)

This young man's condition of belonging in between his countries of origin and re-settlement mirror the situation of minority ethnic long-term settled residents for whom transnational relations are important and usually non conflictive. At the same time, he refers to the way his plural belonging is influenced by the right to legally reside in the UK. In doing this, he underlines the role played by power, regulating the legal and sociocultural dimensions of residing and belonging to place, and the possibility to express multiple or critical belongings in the UK. We will explore more in depth the implication of power in people's experiences of belonging in the next section, which will sketch out some concluding observations about local and wider politics of belonging in contemporary Britain.

Politics of belonging in contemporary Britain

New arrivals' and majority and minority long-term settled residents' feelings of belonging to Britain are characterised by similar and comparable degrees of complexity. White English majority ethnic interviewees in England tended to find it difficult to explain their feelings of belonging to Britain, because they perceived them as self-evident. Majority ethnic interviewees in Scotland and Northern Ireland explained how they felt they belonged more to their respective jurisdictions than to Britain, although most Northern Irish respondents also seemed to want to move on and away from previous patterns of divisive ethno-national belongings. Finally, minority ethnic long-term settled residents and new arrivals were overall more aware and explicit than all of the other groups about the positive reasons for their feelings of belonging in Britain and about their experience of belonging between different places, which they tended not to see in contradiction to their belonging to Britain. In addition, minority ethnic long-term settled residents and new arrivals particularly valued the opportunities of social mobility they enjoyed by living in the UK.

Most interviewees, across all groups, particularly valued as positive aspects of belonging in Britain the existence of the welfare state, the public accountability of institutions and the possibility of living in a safe and multicultural society. However, across all of the places and groups we studied, people's appreciation of their belonging in Britain was mediated by their experience of inclusion and exclusion as individuals and as members of specific social groups. When the contrast between the expected and the actual degree of inclusion and participation was stark, hierarchies of British 'from hereness' were mobilised to express the desire for a 'better' social positioning. This would be 'better' because it would correspond to individual understandings of social self-representations. This was true whether people were minority or majority ethnic long-term settled residents, according to their perception of their desirable and expectable degree of inclusion and belonging to British society.

These dynamics of belonging are the expression of Britain's contemporary sociocultural and economic settings. However, our findings both encompass and transcend contemporary debates on the multiplicity and relationality of identities and belongings (Brah, 1996; Fortier, 2000; Anthias, 2006). We add a sensitivity to the structuring role of whiteness and Englishness within the British identity constellation in regard to the hegemonic project of the multinational state; arguing that there is a direct relation between England's 'minus one' naturalisation, its hegemonic position within the UK, and the ethnicisation as 'different' of its formerly subaltern jurisdictions: Scotland, Northern Ireland and Wales. The invisibilisation of hegemonic identities does not only happen around the dimension of ethnicity. It is structured by the intersection of categories of social differentiation – class, ethnicity, race, gender – which have particular resonances in different places. In this respect, as we have explained in Chapter 3, power can be seen as residing in the possibility to naturalise and invisibilise prevailing interests, values and practices while at the same time framing as 'different' or 'ethnic' or 'working class' those falling outside its strategically negotiated boundaries (Skeggs, 2004: 4).

White English majority ethnic residents' difficulty in defining the basis of their attachment to Britain is the result of the naturalising and hegemonic positioning of Englishness within Britishness. It is also partially due to the combined effect of devolution, the cultural diversification introduced by immigration, Europeanisation and globalisation (Perriman, 2009; Hickman, 2000). The power dynamics taking place between the different (infra)national positionings and places constituting Britain were observed at a more structural and general level. We found that the more people felt safe in their right to reside, work and express themselves in Britain, the more they allowed themselves to be openly critical about British society and its predicaments. In this respect, minority ethnic long-term settled residents and new arrivals' open appreciation of the advantages of being here can be seen as having a potentially negative implication. It can be seen both as a sign of appreciation of the opportunities available in the UK and a marker of the degree of vulnerability they perceive themselves to be subject to.

The resentments of some young second and third generation minority ethnic people, but also of 'deprived' majority ethnic long-term settled residents is rooted in their experiences of the interplay between power, social inclusion and belonging to place ('where they are from'). The two cases of the deprived white English young man from Downham and of the relatively privileged Asian young man from Leicester are emblematic examples in this respect. They illustrate the ways in which the betrayal of the expectation to belong in British society informs the potential recourse to antagonism to obtain a higher degree of social participation. In other words, white English and Asian majority ethnic young people's recourse to antagonism can be seen as a strategy to negotiate a higher degree of inclusion and participation in British society, which corresponds to the contradictory and differential ways in which they are included and excluded within it. Antagonistic understandings and experiences of social life are part and parcel of social cohesion, as they express the inequalities which are negotiated locally and constitute people's experiences of place. However, in the process, narratives framing specific groups and social trajectories as inherently separate and homogeneous might start 'making more sense' than those accepting the inherent porosity and interdependence of places and of the people inhabiting them.

These homogenising and polarising narratives of 'separatedness' are a potential threat to social cohesion as they strongly limit the ability of individuals and groups to negotiate the inequalities structuring the places they inhabit in terms they themselves consider positive and successful. For this reason, in the next section of the chapter we will focus on the strategic relationship between the local prevalence of narratives of separatedness and commonality and the emergence of specific understandings and experiences of social cohesion.

Local histories and understandings of social cohesion

Many research participants had an intuitive and complex understanding of the meaning of social cohesion. Most tended to associate the concept of social cohesion with the willingness to understand and engage with other people constructively and with the ability to appropriately negotiate separateness and commonality. In other words, most interviewees thought that social cohesion was about the ability to draw a fine line between what we understand as 'our own' and 'shared'. The contextual and nuanced understandings of social cohesion emerging from our findings contrast with the predominantly 'consensualist' (Zetter et al., 2006) interpretation of social cohesion, framing it as being about togetherness and sharing rather than about being able to negotiate an appropriate balance between unity (interdependence) and separation.

These six interviewees, one for each of the research settings, explain in their own words how they see social cohesion as the 'willingness to get along' while 'being private and together as well', in order to 'get the best out of the benefits that each other can bring'. All of the six interviewees are majority ethnic long-term settled residents, with the significant exception of the first one, from Leicester, where minority ethnic groups are likely to form the majority within the next ten years.

> It is about sort of live and let live. It's not about total integration, it is about people being able to feel free and able to make up relationships with individuals depending on similar interests and things. It is about people recognising that you know, that we have our own ways of doing things.
>
> (Long-term settled, minority ethnic, woman, Leicester)

> Well, personally ... it means understanding, not wanting to stay in your own little box and not wanting to get involved. That doesn't mean that you come out of your box and that you become something else than what you are.
>
> (Long-term settled, majority ethnic, man, Kilburn)

> I think ... people being as integrated as they want to be but not being forced to be integrated, certainly not allowing ghettos to form. It's got to be that people can live alongside each other and tolerate each other's differences and try to get the best out of the benefits that each other can bring from their experience.
>
> (Long-term settled, majority ethnic, man, Downham)

> People living in harmony, being together, being private as well but being able to work together as a whole. Not 'them and us' and etc. But that's my idea of social cohesion, as a city we work together.
>
> (Long-term settled, majority ethnic, woman, Peterborough)

Social Cohesion? A community of people that know each other and at least respect each other ... if not like and get on with each other. The most important immediate element of social cohesion is that people know each other and they are genuinely part of a community rather than people living in boxes separated from each other.
(Long-term settled, majority ethnic, man, Glasgow)

I suppose a willingness to get along, a willingness to integrate and to be more accepting and ... shared community beliefs.
(Long-term settled, majority ethnic, man, Dungannon)

Most interviewees, across all settings and groups understood social cohesion to be about the choice and possibility, and sometimes the duty, to reach out to people, whenever the appropriate occasion arises. This 'contextual' and 'relational' idea of social cohesion is congruent with Peter Mann's 'latent neighbourliness' concept (quoted in Buonfino, 2006: 14), referring to the ability of members of a neighbourhood to give support to each other in the case of an emergency or of a specific event, while remaining more private and withdrawn in their everyday routines. Thus, social cohesion unfolds in places where people are able both to be 'private' and to work 'together' in order to negotiate their diverse and potentially conflictive needs and priorities. As we will explain below, places characterised by a 'consensualist' emphasis on what is 'together' over what is 'private' tends to be ones in which people and groups find it more difficult to negotiate their specific needs and priorities in terms which they deem successful.

The quotes from the two long-term settled residents from Kilburn and Downham above also show how the metaphor of 'boxes' or 'ghettoes' are sometimes used to indicate what many interviewees consider to be the opposite of social cohesion, social segregation, which is seen as potentially conducive to antagonism. A successful entrepreneur from the Gujarati East African minority ethnic community in Leicester introduced a similar perspective. According to this interviewee the fact that ethnic communities tend to live in ethnic 'silos' (separatedness) is a lost opportunity to find a 'common purpose and sense of belonging' (interdependence). This is something that he sees as promoting social cohesion, which needs to encompass a socio-economic as well as a 'mental' dimension.

What does the idea of social cohesion mean to you?
It's a very misused term, I think in a given time, a set of values, making people co-exist together, with a common purpose and a common

sense of belonging, without silos. Leicester for example has silos, you got the Belgrave silo which is Gujarati, you got the Highfields silo which is Muslim, and you got further up Knighton which is Punjabi silo. So social cohesion is more than that, it is also the mental part and a social economic phenomenon. I think we have to get back to our core values of why we came to this country, any group of immigrants, including Anglo-Saxons who came across from over there to here.

(Long-term settled, minority ethnic, man, Leicester)

However, he explains that this deeper 'mental' dimension of a common experience of belonging can only be achieved through a self-reflective effort on the part of all of the groups composing localised and national communities, whether they are or see themselves as 'from here' and/or from somewhere else. By counting Anglo Saxons, the supposed (white) ancestors of the British genealogy, among the many migrant groups contributing to contemporary experiences of social cohesion in Britain, he challenges the way hegemonic understandings of being 'from here' erase the fact that migration and heterogeneity are part and parcel of the historical establishment of local and national communities.

Although most people saw social cohesion as the ability to negotiate the fine line between separatedness and commonality along the lines we presented above, we identified four interrelated aspects differentiating their understandings of social cohesion:

- responsibility for cohesion (who should make an effort),
- its direction (in terms of what should be learnt by whom),
- the role of separateness in hampering/promoting social cohesion,
- the acknowledgment of the historical role of migration in the emergence of localities.

Moreover, the way the responsibility for cohesion, its direction, and the positive and negative role of separateness in social cohesion were understood, changed consistently across the research settings in relation to some strategic aspects, including:

- the degree of public and individual acknowledgement of the role of migration in the constitution, evolution and survival of local social environments; and
- the local governance of complex local social environments.

The combination of all of these sets of factors shaped different local understandings and experiences of social cohesion across the sites, as we shall explain in more detail below.

In Kilburn and Leicester (except Braunstone), which are characterised by the acknowledgement of the role of migration and of the structural heterogeneity of society, people's understanding of social cohesion tends to refer to a minimised expectation of commonalities, the acceptance of cultural pluralism and the acknowledgement of the necessity to pro-actively understand and adapt to the social changes introduced by the arrival of new groups. Two people living in 'pluralist Kilburn', a majority ethnic long-term settled woman and a new arrival man, had similar responses about how the concept of social cohesion could help improve relations between different social groups. Both emphasised the importance of listening and learning from other people and avoided identifying a specific responsibility or direction for the flow of information, whether this is from the long-term settled to the new arrival group or vice versa.

> I think it can help to bring people together. And trying to listen to people. And not being judgemental because you don't know what everyone is carrying, you don't know what everybody is going through. People have all sorts of baggage. But if we are trying to be patient, listening and accommodate each other, things could be better.
> (Long-term settled, minority ethnic, woman, Kilburn)

> Erm, it's maybe like in some social centres where people meet, they meet and talk about everything and about problems like we are talking now. This is social cohesion. To start talking to strangers. I think this is what a social centre should be for. To teach people how to find just the sociology of the people, you know, how to find out that there is no stranger on the street if you know the people.
> (New arrival, Czech, man, Kilburn)

Both of these people highlight key factors in play within the local unfolding of social cohesion. These factors have important implications in relation to how the encounter between new arrivals and long-term settled residents is experience at a local level. The first is the ability and willingness to operate some 'willing suspension of disbelief' towards newcomers, by empathising with their potential difficulties and needs. And also by accepting that relations between long-term settled and new arrival groups will only improve by mutual listening and accommodation. The second is about being willing to 'talk to strangers', in order to learn more about and become familiar with them and their stories.

In contrast, in Downham and Braunstone (Leicester) as well as in Dungannon, Sighthill (Glasgow) and Peterborough, initially, the predominant self-representation of place as 'owned' by people who are 'from here' translated into 'social cohesion' being about the willingness on the part of newcomers to adopt ethnocentric canons of neighbourliness. In the process, the burden of social cohesion tends to be placed on the shoulders of newcomers, rather than on those of all subjects involved in community relations. The following example from Dungannon shows how explanations and solutions for conflicts emerging in relation to the arrival of new groups can be primarily sought and found in the behaviour of newcomers. In this specific case, the negotiation of common values and neighbouring practices takes for granted that the direction of learning is from the long-term settled to the new arrival groups, rather than an exchange between the two.

> What we say to our migrant workers is that there are things that they can do that would help your own situation and your own acceptance within the community. I tell them open the curtains, because they have an awful habit of keeping their curtains closed. Open the windows, cut the grass of the house. Because a lot of people really resent, especially if they are in middle class semis, all the locals are trying to keep their gardens tidy etc, but the migrants don't open the curtains, don't cut the grass. So I tell them to do these, maybe pick up some litter, and also to say hello to your neighbour.
>
> (Key informant, Dungannon)

This last interview was with a respondent who was involved personally in social interventions aimed at fostering social cohesion. In trying to mediate between the perceptions of long-term settled residents and the lifestyles and habits of new arrivals, she implicitly places the responsibility for the development of cohesive social relations on the latter. Therefore, the prevailing message is that it is new arrivals, rather than long-term settled residents, who should 'make an effort' to cohere according to fixed criteria and expectations of behaviour that defined localised understandings of belonging.

Understandings of social cohesion and their relationship to the responsibilities and abilities of individuals and groups inhabiting a place are influenced by the convergence of a number of interrelated factors. Local understandings of social cohesion tend to be more oriented towards a pluralist and reciprocal interpretation in places characterised by

- a higher degree of social inclusion and participation from all groups;
- a public and individual acknowledgement of the role of migration in the historical formation of the local area, and
- effective social interventions in the management of heterogeneous social environments.

In contrast, places will be more oriented towards a non-reciprocal interpretation of social cohesion in terms of the responsibility lying with the newcomers to adapt to fixed and local notions of neighbourliness when

- they are characterised by the presence of significant dynamics of social exclusion and marginalisation;
- the majority of residents do not acknowledge the role of migration in the historical formation of their locality;
- they lack the appropriate social interventions or skills to manage heterogeneous local environments.

The acknowledgement of the inherent and historical diversity of places and of the need to invest in multiculture emerge as key factors within the prevalence of 'pluralist' rather than more homogeneous understandings of social cohesion. However, there is also an important direct correlation between local histories of migration and relative socio-economic progress. In all of the six areas the arrival of new migrant groups coincided with a relative improvement of local socio-economic settings. In this context, the most relevant difference is between

- places where the positive contribution of migrants to the local social and economic texture is accepted as part and parcel of the rhythms and realities of everyday life and capitalised upon; and
- places where the arrival of new groups is seen as a disruption of the rhythms and realities of everyday life and becomes an occasion to blame newcomers for long seated problems and tensions.

In the first case the predominant expectation is that good social relations are based on mutual acceptance and understanding of different needs and values. In the second, the onus of negotiation tends to be placed on the shoulders of newcomers, who are in the difficult position of cohering according to models of neighbourliness which are not known to them and which are often highly disputed and ambivalently implemented by long-term settled members of the receiving society.

In each of the places we studied, we gathered accounts that refer to understandings of local societies both in terms of homogeneity and settlement and in terms of heterogeneity and migration. The trends and factors we presented in this section above are not intended to be read as the establishment of typologies of response to change associated with any specific area. On the contrary, our observations are meant to underline the way different communities and individuals were subject to place-specific experiences of deeply transforming socio-economic dynamics. In order to understand and navigate these transformations, which involved their family, working and private lives, most people needed new skills and narratives, which were not equally available locally. In the absence of these key resources, such as an understanding of societies as made of migrancy, and of the skills to find employment according to the requirements of the knowledge economy, sometimes people tended to blame their exclusion from British society on the arrival of new migrant groups. In the same circumstances, social cohesion tended to be seen as the responsibility on the part of new migrant groups to adopt fixed identities and practices demarcating what it means to be 'from here', rather than the shared responsibility to address the diverse needs and priorities defining a place.

The prevalence of narratives and self-representations in terms of homogeneity and settledness in places should not be seen as fixed or unchangeable. For instance, each of the sites we studied had already moved away from an initial and acute phase of resistance and refusal of heterogeneity and diversity, what we called settled backlash, mostly associated with the arrival of new groups of migrants and minority ethnic long-term settled residents. However, not all sites had the same socio-economic resources, the same logistical infrastructure to foster social inclusion and participation, the same historical experience of migration and the same degree of people recognising themselves as migrants or recognising the structural role of migrations and exchanges in sustaining local societies. The interplay between this factors and dimensions, as we will explain more 'cohesively' in the last conclusive section, made a significant difference in the responses to the arrival of new groups in past and recent times.

Conclusion: Social cohesion as both relational and structural

We would like now to establish a link between the politics of belonging in Britain and the understandings of social cohesion, both of which we observed at a local level. We will do so by highlighting the role played by neoliberal policies in reorganising places and the socio-economic and cultural resources which are available to the people and social relations places are made of. There is a doubly articulated and interlinked naturalisation uniting the role of Englishness in structuring invisible hierarchies of Britishness and the role of neoliberal policies in reordering places according to its 'capitalist realist' – that is, profit making (Fisher, 2009) priorities. In other words, people's belonging to Britain and the resources they have available are structured by the parallel invisibility of Englishness and neoliberalism. This invisibility is embedded within the cultural logic of hegemony, which naturalises and produces further inequalities and differences out of diverse and already unequal places. The dissimulation of diversities and inequalities under naturalised hierarchies of Britishness and inclusion into the neoliberal knowledge economy makes it more difficult for people to be able to negotiate them in terms which they 'cohesively' deem successful and positive. This double-edged process of invisibilisation of power conceals the ethnic and class basis of the hierarchies restructuring places in contemporary times, which does not allow for the recognition of specific and shared political responsibilities in the development of social cohesion. In the process, places and people which were marginalised by the convergence of post-industrialism and neoliberalism and who perceived themselves as being entitled to privileged inclusion insofar as they were white English, tended to blame newcomers instead of the social hierarchies and economic dynamics excluding them.

As we have seen, against prevailing governmental understandings of social cohesion as being about the negotiation of 'commonality', many of our interviewees actually understood social cohesion to be about being willing and able to negotiate a difficult line between commonality and separation. This more nuanced and interdependent understanding of social cohesion as a process and as an ability, rather than as a functionalist output, resonates with Lyn Layton's analysis (2008) of the psychological sustainability of a 'democratic' subjectivity. This is based on the ability to negotiate and recognise the need for separatedness and interdependence (commonality), in neoliberal times, which are marked by increased socio-economic insecurity, because of the demise of the welfare state and of the increased precariousness of work.

7
Conclusions

In a challenge to prevailing conceptions of social cohesion we asked: do people have to get on well together? We also asked the question: how do people live together? In this concluding chapter we aim to draw the threads of our analysis together in order to answer these and other questions. First we consider the implications of our evidence demonstrating that the prevailing understandings of social cohesion in public policy are out of step with the rhythms and realities of everyday life. Second, we consider local and national narratives framing cohesion and their implication in the unfolding of the dynamics of social cohesion and suggest ways to move on. Finally we examine the import of our research for practices of social intervention in the field of social cohesion.

Social cohesion in the UK

We found that a majority of the long-term settled, across the UK, understood social cohesion to be about a willingness and ability to be able to negotiate a difficult line between commonality and separation. Most people do not live with an expectation that living locally means being surrounded by people who have the same values as themselves. What many people welcome, again across all places we visited, is the opportunity to meet people in their area at social occasions or at cultural events and at festivals, and to be able to exercise the choice of, selectively, getting to know people better, or not. Although many of the long-term settled shared broadly congruent notions of what social cohesion is about this did not mean they were agreed on how it was to be achieved. One of our most significant findings – about narratives of belonging – helps explain this further. It highlights a specific aspect of the relationship between place and belonging that does not always get the attention this research suggests it warrants.

One of our conclusions, therefore, is that the dominant 'consensualist' sensibility informing current policies of social cohesion, with its implication that immigration threatens a cohesive national identity and emphasis on identifying processes that can ensure social cohesion, is out of step with the rhythms and realities of everyday life on two grounds. First, this 'consensualist' sensibility is at variance with our finding that most of the long-term settled understand social cohesion to be about the negotiation of the right balance between separateness and unity, rather than about having consensus on shared values and priorities. Second, the 'consensualist' sensibility implicitly overlooks the deep-seated social divisions and transformations shaping the everyday life experiences of both the long-term settled and the new arrivals. These transformations emerge from structural processes (individualisation, post-industrialism, globalisation) at work locally, nationally and transnationally. They necessitate that individuals and groups have the ability to manage the inequalities, differentiations and tensions intervening within and between them in terms that they perceive as positive and successful in order to negotiate social cohesion.

Our over-riding message is that in order to ensure the cohesion of the social fabric of society it is necessary to address both relational and structural issues. That is, we need to consider how people relate to each other as well as address fundamental issues of deprivation, disadvantage and discrimination. This research suggests that in addressing the relational aspects of the dynamics of immigration and social cohesion it is necessary to enable and support both expressions of *difference* and of *unity* in local areas. Both are opportunities for people to learn about each other and relate to each other if they so wish. The public events and public spaces that enable people to mix are welcomed by most, if not all, people. In addressing the structural aspects of the dynamics between immigration and social cohesion it is necessary to ensure that the benefits of investment in local places accrue to both the long-term settled (majority ethnic and minority ethnic) and new arrivals.

The dynamics of social cohesion are framed by particular national identities and projects of unification and these involve the elisions necessary to achieve the imagined community of national coherence. We have argued throughout the book that histories of ethno-national and religious identities, disparate antagonisms, and the social and political hierarchies embedded in national formations continue to frame and interact with the politics of belonging in contemporary societies and influence national navigations of what has been called the era of migration. The taken-for-granted understandings of cohesion that we outlined at the beginning of the book frame the management of migration flows and these intersect with these histories of national formation to produce distinctive social relations. In the formative narratives of nation and national belonging, as in contemporary renditions, the politics of difference, the power to designate who is included and excluded makes up much of the substance and structure of social solidarities that become taken-as-given. These social solidarities are negotiated by people in their everyday lives and constitute, we have argued, what social cohesion is about: the ability within the individuals and groups informing a social field to manage the inequalities, differentiations and tensions intervening within and between them in terms that they perceive as positive and successful.

Many of the features of life in the UK that we have addressed in this book are shared by other OECD countries that in a similar way discursively invoke the merits of a normative understanding of social cohesion to stabilise the social disruptions of post-industrialism, globalised migrations, neoliberal markets, and changing demographies. The widespread adoption of social cohesion policies in the West, although adopted with different enthusiasms, marks the troubled realities of national stabilities and borders in a globalised and migratory world. In the UK public and political debates about social cohesion tend to be defined through the governmental agenda of community cohesion. This is a functionalist understanding, based on a Durkheimian model of mechanical solidarity, of a cohesive society as one which is devoid of conflicts and tensions because key values are shared by the ethnic groups composing local communities. In the process, places that are marginalised by the new economy are often defined as deprived and as inherently lacking community cohesion. These understandings of social cohesion need to be challenged in the name of the complex ways in which people understand and navigate their places in times of heightened social change. The risk is that social cohesion, rather than an ability which is socially and historically grounded in the specific history of places, becomes just another exclusionary category differentiating places that are able to participate in neoliberal knowledge economies from those that are left out.

The prevailing self-definition of specific places as 'isolated', 'homogeneous' and 'inward looking', rather than 'multicultural', 'pluralist' and 'diverse' is part of the establishment of social and spatial hierarchies which are embedded within neoliberal imperatives of mobility

(Skeggs, 2004). Assimilationist understandings of social cohesion, by prescribing what positive social relations are and who is responsible for them, can also participate in the discursive marginalisation of individuals and groups 'within a field of unequal power relations' (Cresswell, 2006: 55). In defining social cohesion as an ability within people to negotiate the social conflicts they meet in terms that they themselves consider positive, we acknowledged that conflicts and inequalities are not its opposite. They are the obstacles across which people's cohesive ability can negotiate resolutions they deem acceptable. Our definition of social cohesion as an ability, that is, in processual and relational terms, is the result of our 'emic' approach, addressing 'life as it is experienced and described by the members of a society themselves' (Eriksen, 2001: 36). In other words, our approach 'from below' allows for the ways in which local UK social settings negotiate the structural conflicts and inequalities highlighted by the arrival of new immigrants to emerge in their full complexity.

Although we found a broad understanding of what constitutes social cohesion across the UK, we found differences of view about immigration and about who is responsible for social cohesion. Migration is an entrenched characteristic of the economy and is as pertinent to understanding changing family forms and the accelerating need for care workers as it is to grasping the extent to which the engine of economic growth depends on immigrant workers being willing to work long hours for low wages. We have argued that a crucial aspect of understanding the dynamics of immigration and social cohesion is the identification of the dominant narratives that are a key part of the complexity of different places, to this we now move.

Local and national narratives framing cohesion

Dominant narratives in local settings are key to understanding how new immigrants will be perceived and addressed and have an important impact on the unfolding of social cohesion. The dominant narrative can either be that of a population who views the locality as 'our place' or it can be one where no one ethnic group is in the ascendancy, either numerically, culturally or politically. If the dominant narrative has strong elements of perceiving the local area as comprised of people who are 'the same' or 'like us' until new immigrants appear, then the likelihood of a more negative response to new arrivals is heightened. Alternatively if the dominant narrative is one that recognises the history of immigration to the area and the mixture of residents in terms of a range of social divisions and sees no ethnic group as having a claim on the area then the likelihood of an accepting response towards new immigrants is correspondingly heightened.

We found that these narratives were a key part of the complexity that underpins the relationship between new immigration and social cohesion. For example, broadly similar definitions of social cohesion were in circulation in Downham and Kilburn but different narratives of history, immigration and belongings characterise each place. These different narratives produce differences in who is held responsible for achieving social cohesion in each place. In Downham, Braunstone (Leicester), and (initially) in Dungannon and Peterborough, the self-representation of local areas in terms of homogeneity and 'settledness' generates expectations among the long-term settled that the burden of achieving social cohesion lies with the new immigrants. We identified the phenomenon of 'settled backlash' in these places, referring to the way narratives of 'being from here' subsumed the intersections of race, ethnicity and class structuring belonging to place. This, as we have seen, can involve the long-term settled minority ethnic population as well as the long-term settled majority ethnic population. In Kilburn, Leicester (except Braunstone) and Glasgow (though not initially) – places that are characterised by an acknowledgement of histories of immigration, the existence of many transnational families and the heterogeneity of the local area – the burden of achieving social cohesion is a shared one. The long-term settled populations' understanding of social cohesion in these places tends to include a minimalised expectation of commonalities, the acceptance of cultural pluralism and the acceptance of the necessity to adapt to the social changes introduced by the arrival of new groups. These are two broadly different narratives and we found them repeated across the six sites of the research. They are nevertheless fluid narratives that are susceptible to change. In certain areas where the long-term settled felt 'this is our place', there has been a shift that has allowed an acceptance, and valuing, of heterogeneity to be represented.

Local narratives are also framed by wider national understandings of the role of migration in the structuring of the national population in the past and in the present. In England, the New Labour government was generally perceived to be pro-immigration. For some long-term settled majority ethnic people, especially, but not solely, in older age groups, this represented the government's greater concern with the interests of globalised business than with them and gave rise to feelings of betrayal. The implementation of multiculturalist policies in England from the 1980s onwards has come to be perceived as neglectful of this group. On the one hand, this was partly because minority ethnic groups (who were assumed to be black) became the object of the social interventions which multiculturalist policies inspired. On the other hand, it was because much of the professional and political rhetoric about multiculturalism did not recognise the white population as constituted ethnically. In other words the term 'white' was stripped of ethnic content. For example, a survey of the Irish in England in the mid-1990s found that a majority thought they were a minority ethnic group, but a large minority did not think they could be because they were white (Hickman and Walter, 1997). This assumed homogeneity of the white population reinforced the idea that ethnicity was the property of historical immigrations and not of the majority ethnic group, the English/British. This has made it all the more difficult in a period of renewed immigration, this time on a bigger scale and drawn from across the globe rather than Britain's former colonies, to open up the 'box' of Englishness. If this 'box' could be opened up it would enable the variety of experiences of those who identify as English to come to the fore and enable them to participate equally in contemporary heterogeneity.

This could happen if first there was a full acknowledgement of England's hegemonic (and invisibilised) capitalisation on the interconnecting processes of (post)colonialism, (post)industrialisation and neoliberalism, in the context of the two hegemonic projects of British national formation: empire and the multinational state. What could follow is that Englishness, as separate from and interdependent on the British system of national identities, could be re-negotiated in progressive and non-'individually possessive' terms. Recognising the way in which England's economic, political and cultural hegemony and prosperity has been based on its privileged (inter)dependence within a system of circulation of people, resources and knowledge that far exceeded its geographical boundaries would be an important step in this direction. For instance, it could introduce a narrative of responsibility and accountability for the current and past inequalities engendered by industrialisation, post-industrialisation and neoliberalism, not to mention (post)colonialism, which could search for (and find) solutions in globally 'cohesive' redistributive policies. The paradox of Englishness' is its syncretic capacity to incorporate and classify alterity into a naturalised form of its own hegemony. This subsumes both 'what worked' and 'what did not work' within the two hegemonic projects of British national formation. It is at the root of Englishness's ability to accept and manage ethnic and cultural diversity, while disowning the deeply entrenched inequalities and differential exclusions emerging in the process. Finally, this turn to introspection and responsibility might allow Englishness, as opposed to cities in England such as Leicester and London, to capitalise on this same cultural syncretism as a key aspect of its culture.

In Scotland, motivated by the economic need to raise the numbers in the work force the political leadership began to actively promote immigration as a solution to the problems of a small country with a declining population and to recognise that integration at a local level was an important factor in the retention of migrants (see Curran, 2005). We found in Glasgow that this political and economic imperative to secure new populations refigured the frame of belonging. The political leadership assumed a degree of ownership of the problems of new arrivals coming to settle in the city, and consequently solving the problems of cohesion and integration is seen as a collective political responsibility. The motivation in part at least stems from recognising that immigrants can leave just as they can arrive. Therefore policy development is based on acknowledging that immigrants are a constituent element of the settled population with equivalent claims of rights and entitlements. The issue for cohesion from this standpoint is not immigration but addressing the distribution of rights and entitlements of both long-term residents and new arrivals. The key point we take from what we found in Scotland is that proactive political leadership on the subject of the necessity and benefits of immigration was able to effect some changes in policy direction that have contributed to a greater acceptance of immigrants and the lowering of certain tensions.

In Northern Ireland we found concerns about how the society was adapting to significant immigration for the first time and about the welfare of new arrivals in a difficult context of social transformation due to both global and local reasons. In Dungannon the interviews revealed a high degree of similarity with other areas of the research, in particular Peterborough, in terms of initial response to immigrants, the nationalities of the new arrivals, the jobs that they are doing, the gradual acceptance of immigrants by many and the usefulness of social interventions. As in Scotland we found little interest in discussing the meaning of belonging to Britain among the long-term settled but we found significant evidence of a wish to leave a divisive past behind. Methods of expressing antagonism towards immigrants, especially on some relatively deprived housing estates, mirrored those used during decades of ethno-religious conflict – exclusions of specific groups from pubs, gangs 'putting out' families from their homes during the night – although it was clear that long-term settled residents and new arrivals alike could be subject to these hostilities. There is evidence that projects of social intervention in Northern Ireland have a role in diminishing anxiety and fear by providing avenues for socialisation (Hughes et al., 2007) and our study would suggest that the implications and impact of new immigration should be a central aspect of these interventions.

There is no intrinsic link between deprivation and the prevalence of homogenising discourses framing the relation between place and belonging. However, places where narratives of 'from hereness' and homogeneity defined local politics of belonging tended to be characterised by intergenerational worklessness and social exclusion, as individuals and communities were marginalised from the benefits of the post-industrial knowledge economy. In these circumstances, the evidencing of migrants' contribution to the local economy made more visible, and 'reactivated', long-standing dynamics of exclusion. This interplay potentially forms the socio-economic basis for the phenomenon of 'settled backlash' and the resurgence of localised identities celebrating homogeneity as a category of belonging. However, we found instances of 'settled backlash' in areas, such as 'leafy suburbs', which were not at all marginalised. In turn, only a minority of people living in deprived areas in Kilburn and Leicester deployed 'being from here' as a strategic discourse to defend rights and entitlements they saw under threat.

Our findings highlight the complexity of the interplay between socio-economic marginalisation and the emergence of 'settled backlash' narratives of 'being from here'. The acknowledgement of the constitutive role of migration for the sustainability of locality is key in the unfolding of social cohesion. People's awareness of the way migration structured their communities and made them demographically and economically sustainable often provides them with the ability to negotiate conflicts and inequalities in terms they deem positive. However, it is also important to understand that when people are aware of the role of migration in the formation of their localities, they perceive and experience migration as an asset. Places in which the arrival of new migrants was either welcomed, accepted or seen as part of everyday life, like Kilburn and Leicester (except Braunstone), were those where the arrival of migrants evidently fuelled the local economy and/or where migrant labour and skills were able to de facto reconnect the local economy with the new economy. In the same way, in places where relations between migrants and long-term residents improved, such as in Dungannon, Peterborough and Sighthill (Glasgow), this happened because the role of migrants in actually revitalising and guaranteeing the well-being of place was evidenced as an effect of targeted social interventions, which we now turn to.

Social interventions on social cohesion

The demands of the neoliberal post-industrial order impact lived relations and collective belongings in myriad ways. Migration is an entrenched characteristic of the economy because of a wide range of social, economic and cultural transformations that the UK is undergoing. The unfolding of social cohesion can be particularly challenging in areas of heightened poverty and multiple inequalities. Most of these challenges are not related to immigration. What the arrival of new immigrants can highlight, depending on the area, is either the continuing resilience within deprived communities or the existence of profound disconnections between people, groups and institutions. We found that deprived communities can work internally through shared narratives of homogeneity or heterogeneity. However, as we have seen, these discourses have different consequences on the cohesive ability to negotiate conflicts and inequalities in terms deemed positive by the people involved.

In places where there is an antagonistic response to new immigrants, sustained investment in the infrastructure and in social interventions that are redistributive and available to the long term settled and new arrivals alike is very important. In areas of deprivation that either welcome or adapt easily to accommodate new immigrants investment is also required so that there are resources sufficient to integrate (often large numbers of) new arrivals and rectify existing inequalities. These latter places are the ones that many new immigrants seek out due to family ties or friendship networks or because they are known to be more secure and tolerant multi-ethnic places. Most of the projects and policies delivering social cohesion we examined managed to improve relations between communities, by offering mediation services or promoting shared resources and opportunities of socialisation and co-operation. They addressed the relational aspect of conflicts and inequalities. However, because of their relational focus and short-term duration, they could not intrinsically address the structural inequalities and marginalisations structuring these conflicts and inequalities, brought about by the convergence of post-industrialism and neoliberalism.

In order for social relations between long-term residents and/or new arrivals to become positive, there needs to be concrete reasons for this transformation. It needs to be socio-economically sustainable in the long term. In other words, there needs to be a real redistribution of actual, enduring and structural socio-economic opportunities underpinning societal hope, which is about 'one's sense of the possibilities that life can offer' (Hage, 2003: 20). As we completed this book, the consequences for social cohesion of the unequal distribution of societal hope introduced by neoliberalism became evident. London and many other urban centres in the UK became the scene of massive social disturbances between 6 and 11 August 2011. These disturbances, which later became known as 'the riots', had nothing to do with immigration. Rather, 'the riots' mapped established places of exclusion in which settled communities were already marginalised, racialised and confronting a world of diminishing employment prospects. The still emerging profile of 'the rioters' is, to date at least, of a young, poorly educated population living in places marked by structural worklessness and where their already limited access to social resources had been further reduced by recent, strategically targeted neoliberal reductions in social spending. In Tottenham and Hackney, where the disturbances were ignited, the rhythms and realities of everyday life were not only marked by a structural polarisation and diminishing of societal hope, they were also characterised by relational failures of communication, as the Metropolitan Police initially refused to address community concerns about the police killing of Mark Duggan, a young local black man. This specific failure of communication evidenced other longer-term relational failures, as racialised stop-and-search interventions by police were part of daily life in the communities and places which were most involved in 'the riots' in London (Laville, 2011).

The ability to negotiate conflicts and inequalities across social divisions mirrors the ability to recognise and accept the constitutive interdependence of individuals, groups, places and histories. Both of these cohesive abilities reflect a degree of introspection and self-awareness that is sustainable within a regime of relative sociocultural and economic stability and security. In fact, under the pressure of heightened social change and the feeling of instability and precariousness this produces, individuals tend to retreat from heterogeneous and complex ways of thinking and adopt narrower and more limiting perceptions of their social worlds (Cooper and Lousada, 2005). These dynamics are also, in turn, linked to the issue of the acknowledgement of individual and collective responsibility for the positive development of the social relations informing places.

People's awareness of the constitutive role of migration in the formation of local societies also influences deeply the viability of social cohesion. Our work shows that education can be a catalyst for social cohesion and mobility. In this respect, it would be fundamental to re-write and re-teach national and local histories starting, in line with Eric Wolfe (1982), from the acknowledgement of migration, trade and cultural and exchange as the propellers of the formation of 'settled' societies, cultures and nations, rather than assuming that these and the places they coincide with, emerged separately. The comparative study of the experiences of migrancy of new arrivals and established minority ethnic groups (Reed, 2005) should not be limited to intercultural initiatives mobilised ad hoc in relation to acute cases of ethnic antagonism. Ideologies of settledness and homogeneity should be problematised by default as part of the national education curriculum and discussed with particular emphasis in local social settings which are particularly immobilised by ideologies of homogeneity and anti-educational ideologies of 'commonness'.

To answer our original question: everyone does not have to get on together. Most people we spoke to did not want to be told what they should be doing in this respect. They want safe, secure and convenient neighbourhoods in which they have reasonable neighbours, among whom they can choose to get to know some more than others; and they want good public services especially in housing and schools. If problems arise, particularly with neighbours, they want responsive local structures that can either mediate effectively or can identify the structural cause of the problem and deliver a solution. The nearest to a picture of social cohesion that can be generated by this research is one where people are able to negotiate the inequalities and conflicts they meet in their everyday lives, in terms they themselves deem positive. It is in the economic and cultural sustainability of these cohesive abilities that social cohesion lies.

Appendix: Aims, Sites and Methods of the Research

This book is informed by the findings of a research project – 'Immigration and Social Cohesion in the UK: The Rhythms and Realities of Everyday Life' – which was the flagship project of the Immigration and Inclusion programme (of the Joseph Rowntree Foundation). The project was delivered in 2008 and its fieldwork undertaken between 2006 and 2007.

Aims and objectives

The study aimed at understanding the relationship between recent immigration and social cohesion in the context of other social and economic transformations that affect everyday life for everyone living in the UK. It responded to public debates that often associated increasing ethnic diversity resulting from immigration with the erosion of social cohesion.

Our aims in delivering the projects were to provide evidence about the supposed causal relationship between new immigration and the emergence of social antagonism. In order to do so we gathered the voices of all subjects included in these social dynamics, that is, both new immigrants and long-term residents. Unrelated to immigration, we also considered the role of deprivation, disadvantage and long-term marginalisation and how this effected the way people relate to each other, within dynamics of social cohesion. Our objectives were to:

- capture the voices of long-term settled residents and new immigrants;
- outline the contours of belonging and marginalisation in the UK;
- understand 'what works' – that is, how people are trying to make their lives work, negotiating the flows and contradictions of everyday life, in a time of rapid social transformations;
- mobilise memories of migration and settlement to illustrate how complex patterns of inward and outward migration make up the history of the UK;
- assess the role of social interventions in achieving social cohesion;
- give examples of successful strategies of social cohesion;
- suggest policy areas that need to be re-examined in the light of our findings.

Sites

To analyse the interface between people, communities and structures and ground the research in the lived experiences of long-term residents and new migrants we decided to explore and record these experiences and interrelationships in six sites across the UK:

- England: Leicester;
- England: London, Downham;

- England: London, Kilburn;
- England: Peterborough and Thetford;
- Northern Ireland: Dungannon;
- Scotland: Glasgow.

The sites were chosen for their specific and different compositions of long-term residents and new migrant populations and because, between them, they illustrate the heterogeneous contexts of social cohesion in the UK.

Each of the research sites offers a privileged focus on a spatially (urban/rural), socioculturally (multi-ethnic/homogeneous) or economically defined (agriculture/industry/services) experience of the relationship between social cohesion and new immigration. The two sites in London focus on symmetrically different experiences of the relation between urban long-term residents and new migrant groups. Glasgow enabled us to engage with the interconnection between gender, work and social cohesion through a study of health and care practitioners in the public and private sectors. Leicester and one of the two London sites problematised dynamics perceived as 'positive' and 'successful' in the interplay between migration and social cohesion. Dungannon, Peterborough and Thetford also enabled a focus on work (the food-processing sector) as a factor shaping the conditions and experiences of social cohesion in two rural/small city contexts marked by the recent arrival of new migrant groups.

Leicester (Belgrave, Braunstone and Highfields areas)

With a population of approximately 280,000 Leicester is one of the East Midlands' three major economic, social and cultural centres. It is a major site of commercial and manufacturing industry, and known more for the diversity of its trade than for its dependence on a single industry. The city of Leicester was selected because of its successful performance in relation to issues of social cohesion and multiculturalism, and because of the centrality of family migration within the migratory patterns of its new and old migrant, asylum-seeking and refugee groups. After over 50 years of settlement of people from former British colonies, the Caribbean, India, Pakistan and Bangladesh, and East Africa, Leicester has now the largest (proportionally) minority ethnic population in England and Wales, while its multi-generational Indian community is the largest in the country outside London. In the last ten years, these established minority ethnic groups witnessed the arrival of significant numbers of Polish and Romanian migrants, and of Albanian and Somali asylum seekers and refugees. While some of these arrivals coincided with an increase in social antagonism, they highlighted pre-existing and structural issues and were dealt with successfully by a range of public and non-governmental initiatives. In Leicester, we focused our research on three areas which are characterised by the prevalence of majority ethnic (Braunstone) and different minority ethnic populations (Belgrave and Highfields).

Downham

Downham is a local authority ward located in the southern part of the Borough of Lewisham in south-east London. One characteristic of the area is a series of post-First World War social housing estates that were built to re-house people from Deptford and Bermondsey, both areas of acute housing shortage. The area has been in gradual economic decline since the 1960s, with the closure of many community facilities. There are a higher number of economically inactive people than the national or Lewisham averages, a poor educational record – especially in secondary schools, an older-than-average population and a high percentage of people renting from the council. Downham was selected because it is characterised by a perception of self-containment and majority ethnic sociocultural homogeneity. The arrival of (mostly Albanian and Tamil) refugees, asylum seekers and East European migrants in the late 1990s and early 2000s concurred with a significant increase in racialised social antagonism. This was particularly acute within and around the underachieving local secondary school, Malory, whose surplus places were filled by pupils from new migrant groups and established minority ethnic communities. As a response to the upsurge in racially aggravated crimes, in the last three years, the area has been targeted by a range of social intervention initiatives. These were implemented by local authorities and non-governmental organisations and contributed to a significant decrease in racialised social antagonism in the area.

Kilburn

Kilburn, centrally located in London's North West, is divided by Kilburn High Road, which separates it into its major local authority jurisdictions of Brent and Camden. Kilburn has high unemployment, high levels of overcrowding and housing need, low levels of home-ownership, high levels of teenage pregnancy and very high levels of crime. In both Kilburn wards, the majority ethnic population is under 50 per cent; 17 per cent of the overall Kilburn population is Irish-born (accurate figures on the second generation are not available), the African-Caribbean population is 13 per cent of the Brent ward and 3 per cent in the Camden ward. Another very significant group is the black African community, of whom the Somali population form the largest proportion. Kilburn is therefore part of London's celebrated cosmopolitan core and is defined by historically multi-layered and intersecting migratory flows, notably of a Jewish population, migrants from the Caribbean and a large Irish settlement from the 1950s onwards. New migrant groups from Eastern Europe (Albania, Poland, Romania), Africa (Morocco, Somalia), South-East Asia (Philippines) and Latin America (Colombia, Peru) in the past ten years seemingly have been able to merge into hybridised patterns of everyday life. The research aimed to engage with Downham and Kilburn comparatively by exploring the way in which the historical experience of migrancy and hybridity (or its lack) can be a factor sustaining (or hindering) social cohesion.

Peterborough (and Thetford)

Peterborough is an ancient cathedral town of approximately 170,000 people. From being a transport hub and centre of the brick-making industry, it became a centre of engineering industries in the early twentieth century, but much of this had declined by the 1960s. A major change was heralded by the designation of Peterborough as a new town when, between 1970 and 1988, the population doubled. During this period, it developed a greater range of employment opportunities, especially in the service sector. Since the late 1990s, the arrival in Peterborough of migrant workers, at first from Portugal and more recently from Eastern Europe, to work predominantly in nearby agriculture and food-processing industries (notably in Thetford, which was an adjunct research site), has had a significant impact on the town's population, and has created new challenges for the local delivery of accommodation, health provision and social services. There is evidence of exploitative practices, which have targeted the undocumented migrant population. The long-term resident population's response to the arrival of this new group of workers has not been uniformly positive and indeed there were reports of physical attacks on migrant workers. However, the city has been the site of significant social interventions in response to the situation and this is one of the main reasons it was selected for inclusion in the study.

Dungannon

Dungannon is a rural town of approximately 11,000 people located 40 miles west of Belfast. During the Troubles, it occupied one corner of the infamous murder triangle, an area comprised between the Tyrone and Armagh counties which saw a very high concentration of conflict and violence. In recent years, it has experienced the arrival of large numbers of migrants (first Portuguese, then Polish, Lithuanian and other East European nationals, also some migrants from Brazil), who were recruited to work in the local food-processing factories. Some animosities between long-term residents and new arrivals had been reported. A range of statutory and voluntary organisations and initiatives was set up, providing needed support and information services. Dungannon was chosen as a site of the research because of the potential it offers to explore in some depth the way these organisations and initiatives were able to respond to a context of rapidly changing socio-economic and linguistic demographics. We were also interested to see if the issues about new immigration and social cohesion were similar in Northern Ireland to the rest of the UK or very different, in that migrants could potentially be subject to a process of polarised integration into already antagonistic local communities.

Glasgow

Glasgow is a city in the south-west of Scotland that has a population of approximately 592,000. The city was hit hard by the economic restructuring of the1970s and 1980s when many of its traditional industries declined or disappeared. Since then, it has successfully regenerated itself through investment and development of the service sector, and a wide-ranging cultural programme of restoring Glasgow's considerable wealth in museums, galleries and architectural monuments. Prior to the twentieth century the largest immigration to Scotland was that of the Irish and much of it was concentrated in south-west Scotland. Twentieth-century migrants to Scotland continued to come from Ireland but also from Italy, China and Pakistan. The research specifically investigated the experiences of overseas nurses working in the NHSS and the private health sector. The nurses came mainly from the Philippines, India and Africa. We decided to focus on work and its relationship to social cohesion in Scotland because the Government in Edinburgh is targeting increased immigration to offset a declining work-age population. In Glasgow, we also paid particular attention to issues in relation to the settlement of refugees and asylum seekers, as there had been initial problems with their dispersal to the city, which were successfully addressed by public and non-governmental social interventions.

Methods

The research was conducted between autumn 2005 and autumn 2007. The methodological approaches used responded to Joseph Rowntree Foundation's wish to explore the relation between social cohesion and new migration by focusing on the way this is embedded into the rhythms and realities of everyday life, and on the strategies people deploy to meet their perceived priorities and needs. Therefore, although the research design was customised to meet the specificities of each neighbourhood, at core, each site incorporated the following methods:

- ethnographic observation of the rhythms and patterns of everyday life in the contexts under examination;
- 15 in-depth, semi-structured interviews with key respondents of local structures and institutions;
- 40 biographical interviews with local residents in each site (20 in Glasgow).

These methods were selected because of their complementary nature and manageability, their appropriateness for exploring the impact of macro-level trends in people's lives and their suitability for including the voices of marginalised groups. Life-narrative accounts enable us to describe and understand the realities of life through the textures and weaves of new migration flows; contemporary social transformations; local experiences of social cohesion and civic association; and across the social divisions of ethnicity, gender, class and social status. The interviews took place between February 2006 and May 2007.

In each of the research sites, we co-operated with local partner organisations in the implementation of the research. They assisted us in contacting research participants and in developing our understanding of the complexity of the histories and social dynamics of each research site. These were our project partners in each area:

- Leicester: Soft-Touch Arts
- Downham: Lewisham Refugee Network and Lewisham Youth Service
- Kilburn: Church of the Sacred Heart Quex Road Community Centre and Al-Khoei Foundation
- Peterborough and Thetford: New Link and MENTER (East of England Black and Minority Ethnic Network)
- Dungannon: Institute for Conflict Research (ICR) and STEP (South Tyrone Empowerment Programme)
- Glasgow: Overseas Nurses Network (ONN)

Our project partners were actively involved in the analysis and dissemination of the findings of the research. This was an occasion for them to reflect on the opportunities and predicaments posed by social interventions targeting the relationship between new immigrations and social cohesion. The research was also an opportunity for project partners to gain more insight into the intricate relationship between migration and social cohesion. The dissemination of the research findings involved the organisation of cross-site exchange meetings in which research participants, partner organisation members, key stakeholders and policymakers discussed the effectiveness of different social interventions on social cohesion. In Downham the research focused on the experiences of young people and its findings informed a youth theatre workshop, which was run by 'The Complete Works' theatre company and facilitated by the Lewisham Youth Services. The play that resulted from the workshop was then performed at the Tricycle Theatre in Kilburn and involved young research participants, partner organisations members, key stakeholders and policymakers from both sites.

Glasgow was a partial exception to these methods because of our decision to focus on the experiences of overseas nurses working in the NHSS and the private health sector. Our partner organisation, the Overseas Nurses Network (ONN), provides, through the workplace and supported by UNISON (public sector trade union), a network for migrant health workers and does not require union membership. It includes 600 nurses from all over Scotland (predominantly women, but some men) and the nurses are from India, the Philippines, South Africa, West Africa and China. Focus groups were conducted within the meetings of the network to explore the personal, institutional and cultural experiences of the nurses and care workers. A small group was invited to keep diaries committing to a minimum of twice-weekly entries over a six-month period or weekly entries over 12 months. The discussion groups and diaries substituted for 20 biographical interviews, otherwise the methods used were the same as in the other sites. In Dungannon, our research partner, the Institute for Conflict Research (ICR), Belfast, conducted the research on our behalf. There were meetings between the London-based research team and ICR, the director of ICR was on the Steering Group of the project and 10 of the 55 interviews in Dungannon were undertaken by a member of the London team to ensure full familiarity with the local area.

We used a non-random, stratified, quota-sampling method drawing on the statistical profile of demographic and socio-economic characteristics of each site, and the majorities and minorities within it. Specific attention was given to ensuring equal numbers of men and women, and an appropriate age profile and distribution of people in work and not employed. The aim was to ensure that important variations in the local profile were represented in the overall sample, rather than to produce statistical representativeness. Our two core categories of interviewees were long-term settled residents and new arrivals, paying attention to country of origin in the latter case. Accordingly, across all sites, a sample profile was created by mapping the key demographic and socio-economic dimensions in terms of the issues we were focusing on in each area. For example, in Downham, the main issues we aimed to investigate were the (self-)perception of the area in terms of majority ethnic homogeneity, claims of 'unruly' youth behaviour and inter-ethnic conflicts in the context of education. In order to address the main ethnic and social dimensions of these key issues in this particular place, we decided to interview 30 long-term residents, of whom 18 were white British and 12 minority ethnic, of whom four were of Irish background, four Asian and four black Caribbean. The remaining ten biographical interviewees were new arrivals selected in order to be able to examine the migration experiences of the three main groups of new arrivals, Tamil and Albanian refugees (six and two, respectively) and Eastern European A8 migrants (two). An appropriate age and gender balance was aimed at in each area. But, for example, the fact that youth and education were issues to be investigated in Downham meant that the age distribution of the sample here was purposely skewed to a relative over-representation of young people.

In each place, the sample profile was discussed and refined with our partner organisations. They suggested people who would fit the required profiles or indicated appropriate associations and contacts when they were unable to do so directly. In all sites, we only allowed ourselves to rely on a particular 'entry point' to obtain a maximum of 20 per cent of our sample. In this way, the samples of the local population for the biographical interviews were identified through a combination of the snowball technique, starting from existing contacts within key local structures and institutions, random calls and other methods, including contacts resulting from our ethnographic fieldwork. We are very grateful to our partner organisations in each place for the ways in which they helped us to access divergent networks and spaces in each of the localities. We are also grateful to all those who generously participated as interviewees in our research. The final act of our research was to deliver public presentations of our research findings in all the areas that participated.

Bibliography

Ahmed, S. (2000) *Strange Encounters: Embodied Others in Postcoloniality* (London: Routledge).
Alexander, C. (2007) 'Cohesive Identities: The Distance between Meaning and Understanding', in M. Wetherell, M. Laflèche and R. Berkley (eds), *Identity, Ethnic Diversity and Community Cohesion* (London: Sage).
Allen, M. and Ainley, P. (2009) *Education Make You Fick, Innit?: What's Gone Wrong with England's Schools, Colleges and Universities and How to Start Putting It Right* (London: Tufnell Press).
Amin, A. (2002) 'Ethnicity and the Multicultural City: Living with Diversity', 34, 959–80.
Anderson, B. (1991) *Imagined Communities* (London, Verso).
Anthias, F. (2006) 'Belongings in a Globalising and Unequal World: Rethinking Translocations', in N. Yuval-Davis, K. Kannabiran and U. M. Vieten (eds), *Situating Contemporary Politics of Belonging* (London: Sage).
Appadurai, A. (2001) *Globalisation* (Durham, NC: Duke University Press).
Back, L. (1996) *New Ethnicities and Urban Culture: Racism and Multiculture in Young Lives* (London: UCL Press).
Balibar, E. (2004) *We, the People of Europe? Reflections on Transnational Citizenship* (Princeton & Oxford: Princeton University Press).
Ball, S., Maguire, M. and Macrae, S. (2000a) *Choice, Pathways and Transitions Post-16: New Youth New Economies in the Global City* (London: Routledge).
Ball, S., Maguire, M. and Macrae, S. (2000b) '"Worlds Apart" – Education Markets in the Post-16 Sector of One Urban Locale 1995-8', in F. Coffield (ed.) *Differing Visions of a Learning Society: Research Findings Volume 1* (Bristol: Policy Press).
Balls, E. (2010) 'We were Wrong to Allow so Many Eastern Europeans into Britain', *The Observer*, Sunday 6 June: http://www.guardian.co.uk/commentis free/2010/jun/06/ed-balls-europe-immigration-labour.
Banton, M. (1998) *Racial Theories* (Cambridge: Polity Press).
Bauman, Z. (1999) *In Search of Politics* (Cambridge: Polity Press).
Bauman, Z. (2000) *Liquid Modernity* (Cambridge: Polity).
Bauman, Z. (2002) *Wasted Lives: Modernity and Its Outcasts* (Cambridge: Polity Press).
Beck, U. (2002) 'The Terrorist Threat: World Risk Society Revisited', *Theory, Culture and Society*, 19 (4), 39–55.
Beckett, F. (2007) *The Great City Academy Fraud* (London: Continuum).
Bell, D. (1973) *The Coming of Post-Industrial Society: A Venture in Social Forecasting* (New York, Basic Books).
Ben Tovim, G. (2002) 'Community Cohesion and Racial Exclusion: A Critical Review of the Cantle Report', *Renewal*, 10 (2), 43–8.
Black, L. (2001) *Consensus or Cohesion?: The State, the People and Social Cohesion in Post-War Britain* (Cheltenham: New Clarion Press).
Blair, T. (2000) 'The E-Generation is with us,' *The Guardian*, 7 March.

Blair, T. (2006) Speech on Multiculturalism, Downing Street, 8 December. See report at http://news.bbc.co.uk/1/hi/uk_politics/6219626.stm.
Brah, A. (1996) *Cartographies of Diaspora: Contesting Identities* (London: Routledge).
Brah, A. (2002) 'Global Mobilities, Local Predicaments', *Feminist Review*, 70.
Brenner, N. (2004) *New State Spaces: Urban Governance and the Rescaling of Statehood* (Oxford: Oxford University Press).
Brenner, N. and Theodore, N. (2003) *Spaces of Neoliberalism: Urban Restructuring in North America and Western Europe* (Oxford: Blackwell).
Brewer, M. (1999) 'The Psychology of Prejudice: Ingroup Love or Outgroup Hate? *Journal of Social Issues*, 55 (3), 429–44.
Brown, G. (2006) Speech to the Fabian Society, 14 January. See report at http://news.bbc.co.uk/1/hi/uk/4611682.stm.
Brown, P. and Scase, R. (eds) (1991) *Poor Work* (Milton Keynes: Open University Press).
Brown, W. (2006) *Regulating Aversion* (Princeton and Oxford: Princeton University Press).
Buonfino, A. and Mulgan, G. (eds) (2006) *Porcupines in Winter. The Pleasures and Pains of Living Together in Modern Britain* (London: The Young Foundation).
Burnett, J. (2004) 'Community, Cohesion and the State', *Race & Class*, 45 (3), 1–18.
Cameron, D. (2011) Speech on Radicalization and Islamic Extremism, the Munich Security Conference, 5 February. See full text at http://www.newstatesman.com/blogs/the-staggers/2011/02/terrorism-islam-ideology.
Cantle, T. (2001) *Community Cohesion: A Report of the Independent review Team*, chaired by Ted Cantle, Home Office.
Cantle, T. (2008) *Community Cohesion: A New Framework for Race and Diversity* (London: Palgrave Macmillan).
Cassen, R. and G. Kingdon (2007) *Tackling Low Educational Achievement* (York: Joseph Rowntree Foundation).
Clarke, J. and Newman, J. (1997) *The Managerial State* (London: Sage).
Clarke, S., Gilmour, R. and Garner, S. (2007) 'Home, Identity and Community Cohesion', in M. Wetherell, M. Laflèche and R. Berkley (eds), *Identity, Ethnic Diversity and Community Cohesion* (London: Sage).
Cohen, P. (1988) 'The Perversions of Inheritance: Studies in the Making of Multi-Racist Britain', in P. Cohen and H. S. Bains (eds), *Multi-Racist Britain* (London: Macmillan).
Colquhoun, G. (2005) 'The Changing Structure of the UK Economy: Implications for the Current Account', Oxford Economic Forecasting, St Aldates: Oxford.
Commission on Integration & Cohesion (2007) Our Shared Future, www.integrationandcohesion.org.uk (accessed 23 April 2008).
Cooper, A. and Lousada, J. (2005) *Borderline Welfare* (London: Karnac Press).
Crenshaw, K. (2003) 'Mapping the Margins: Intersectionality, Identity Politics and Violence Against Women of Colour', in L. Martin Alcof and E. Mendieta (eds), *Identities: Race, Class, Gender and Nationality* (Oxford: Blackwell).
Cresswell, T. (2006) *On the Move* (London: Routledge).
Crick, Bernard (ed.) 1991 *National Identities: The Constitution of the United Kingdom* (Oxford: Blackwell).
Crompton, R. (2006) *Employment and the Family: The Reconfiguration of Work and Family Life in contemporary Society* (Cambridge: Cambridge University Press).

Cruddas, J. (2010) 'Hand on heart, I do not want to be Labour leader', *The Guardian*, 18 May, can be accessed on http://www.guardian.co.uk/commentis free/2010/may/17/labour-leadership-jon-cruddas.

Curran, M. (2005) Opening Address by the Minister for Communities, Scotland, Irish Presidency Conference, 'Reconciling Mobility and Social Inclusion – the Role of Employment and Social Policy', Bundoran, Ireland, 1–2 April.

Delanty, G. (2003) *Community* (London: Routledge).

Dench, G., Gavron, K. and Young, M. (2006) *The New East End. Kinship, Race and Conflict* (London: Young Foundation).

Denham, J. (2010) *Labour and Cohesive Communities* (London: Runnymede Trust).

Denham, J. (2011) *Labour and Cohesive Communities* (A Runnymede Platform Publication) (London: Runnymede Trust).

Dilnott, A. (2011) *Fairer Care Funding*, Report of the Commission on Funding of Care and Support, http://www.dilnotcommission.dh.gov.uk/2011/07/04/commission-report/.

Dorling, D. (2011) *So You Think You Know About Britain?* (London: Constable and Robinson).

Dreier, P., Mollenkopf, J. and Swanstrom, T. (2004) *Place Matters: Metropolitics for the Twenty-first Century* (Lawrence, Kansas: University Press of Kansas).

Elliott, A. and Lemart, C. (2006) *The New Individualism: The Emotional Costs of Globalisation* (London: Routledge).

Eriksen, T. H. (2007) 'Complexity in Social and Cultural Integration: Some Analytical Dimensions', *Ethnic and Racial Studies*, 30 (6), 1055–69.

Eriksen, T. H. (2010) *Small Places, Large Issues: An Introduction to Social and Cultural Anthropology* (London: Pluto).

Esping-Anderson, G. (2009) *The Incomplete Revolution: Adapting to Women's New Roles* (Cambridge: Polity Press).

Evans, G. (2007) *Educational Failure and Working Class White Children in Britain* (Basingstoke: Palgrave Macmillan).

Fanning, B. (2011) *Integration and Social Cohesion in the Republic of Ireland* (Manchester: Manchester University Press).

Ferree, M. Marx, Lorber, J, Hess, B. B. (eds) (1999) *Revisioning Gender* (New York: Sage).

Finlayson, A. (2003) *Making Sense of New Labour* (London: Lawrence & Wishart).

Finney, N. and Simpson, L. (2009) *'Sleepwalking To Segregation'?: Challenging Myths About Race and Migration* (Bristol: Policy Press).

Fisher, M. (2009) *Capitalist Realism: Is There No Alternative?* (New York: O Books).

Ford, R. (2007) 'Motivated Immigrants Fill Skills Gap and Solve Labour Shortages', *The Times*, 17 October, p. 4.

Forrest, R. and Kearns, A. (2001) 'Social Cohesion, Social Capital and the Neighbourhood', *Urban Studies*, 38 (1), 2125–43.

Fortier, A. (2000) *Migrant Belongings: Memory, Space, Identity* (Oxford: Berg).

Fortier, A. (2005) 'Pride, Politics and Multiculuralist Citizenship', *Ethnic and Racial Studies*, 28 (3), 559–78.

Friedkin, N. E. (2004) 'Social Cohesion', *Annual Review of Sociology*, 30, 409–25.

Gedalof, I. (2007) 'Unhomely Homes: Women, Family and Belonging in UK Discourses of Migration and Asylum', *Journal of Ethnic and Migration Studies*, 33, 1.

Gilchrist, A. (2004) *The Well-Connected Community: A Networking Approach to Community Development* (Bristol: Policy Press).

Gilroy, P. (1993) *The Black Atlantic: Modernity and Double Consciousness* (Harvard: Harvard University Press).
Gilroy, P. (2004) *After Empire: Melancholia or Convivial Culture?* (London: Routledge).
Gilroy, P. (2006) Multiculture in Times of War, Professorial Lecture, London School of Economics, 10 May.
Gilroy, P. (2005) 'Multiculture, Double Consciousness and the War on Terror', *Patterns of Prejudice*, 39(4), 431–43.
Glick-Schiller, N. (2009) 'A Global Perspective on Transnational Migration: Theorizing Migration without Methodological Nationalism', *COMPAS Working Paper No. 67*, University of Oxford.
Glucksman, M. and Lyon, D. (2008) 'Comparative Configurations of Care Work across Europe', *Sociology* 42, 1, 101–18.
Goodhart, D. (2004) 'The Discomfort of Strangers', *Prospect Magazine*, 24 February.
Goodhart, D. (2011) 'A Tale of Three Cities', *Prospect Magazine*, 22 June.
Gorard, S. (2005) 'Academies as the "Future of Schooling": Is this an Evidence-Based Policy?' *Journal of Education Policy*, 20 (3), 369–77.
Gray, B. (2007) 'Migration Integration Policy: A Nationalist Fantasy of Management and Control?', *Translocations: Migration and Social Change*, An Irish Inter-Disciplinary Open Access E-Journal, 1 (1). Available at http://www.translocations.ie.
Grillo, R. (2007) 'An Excess of Alterity? Debating Difference in a Multicultural Society', *Ethnic and Racial Studies*, 30 (6), 979–98.
Guidance on Community Cohesion (2002) (London: Local Government Association).
Hage, G. (1998) *White Nation: Fantasies of White Supremacy in a Multicultural Society* (Annandale, NSW: Pluto Press).
Hage, G. (2003) *Against Paranoid Nationalism* (London: Pluto Press).
Hales, G, with the assistance of Daniel Silverstone (2005) *Gun Crime in Brent*, A report commissioned by the London borough of Brent Crime and Disorder Reduction Partnership (http://www.brent.gov.uk/communitysafety.nsf/Files/LBBA-5/$FILE/Brent%20gun%20crime%20research.pdf).
Hall, C. (2000) 'The Rule of Difference: Gender, Class and Empire in the Making of the 1832 Reform Act', in J. Blom, K. Hagerman and C. Hall (eds), *Gendered Nation. Nationalism and Gender in the Long Nineteenth Century* (Berg: London).
Hall, S. (2001) *The Multicultural Question*, Pavis papers in Social and Cultural Research, no. 4 (Milton Keynes: The Open University).
Hall, S. and Du Gay, P. (eds) (1996) *Questions of Cultural Identity* (London: Sage).
Hannerz, U. (1996) *Transnational Connections* (London: Routledge).
Harris, H. (2004) *The Somali Community in the UK. What We Know and How We Know It* (London: Information Centre about Asylum and Refugees in the UK).
Harvey, D. (1991) *The Condition of Postmodernity: An Inquiry into the Origins of Cultural Change* (Oxford: Wiley-Blackwell).
Harvey, D. (2005, 2007) *A Brief History of Neoliberalism* (Oxford: Oxford University Press).
Hesse, B. (1997) 'White Governmentality: Urbanism, Nationalism, Racism', in Westwood, S. and Williams, J. (eds) *Imagining Cities: Scripts, Signs, Memories* (London: Routledge).
Hewitt, R. (2005) *White Backlash and the Politics of Multiculturalism* (Cambridge: Cambridge University Press).

Hewstone, M., Tausch, N., Hughes, J. and Cairns, E. (2007) 'Prejudice, Intergroup Contact and Identity: Do Neighbourhoods Matter?' in M. Wetherell, M. Laflèche and R. Berkley (eds), *Identity, Ethnic Diversity and Community Cohesion* (London: Sage).
Hickman, M. J. (1995) *Religion, Class and Identity* (Aldershot: Ashgate).
Hickman, M. J. (2007) 'Immigration and Monocultural (Re)Imaginings in Ireland and Britain,' *Translocations: Migration and Social Change*, An Irish Inter-Disciplinary Open Access E-Journal, 2 (1), Summer. Available at http://www.translocations.ie.
Hiebert, D. (2002) 'Cosmopolitanism at the Local Level: Immigrant Settlement and the Development of Transnational Neighbourhoods', in S. Vertovec and R. Cohen (eds), *Conceiving Cosmopolitanism* (Oxford: Oxford University Press).
Hills, John (2007) *Ends and Means: The Future Roles of Social Housing in England* (London: Centre for Analysis of Social Exclusion, London School of Economics and Political Science).
Hills, J., Sefton, T. and Stewart, K. (eds), (2009) *Towards a More Equal Society?: Poverty, Inequality and Policy since 1997* (Bristol: Policy Press).
Himmelweit, S. and Land, H. (2008) *Reducing Gender Inequalities to Create a Sustainable Care System* (York: Joseph Rowntree Foundation).
Hollander, N. and Gutwill, S. (2006) 'Despair and Hope in a Culture of Denial', in L. Layton, N. Hollander and S. Gutwill (eds), *Psychoanalysis, Class and Politics: Encounters in the Clinical Setting* (Hove and New York: Routledge).
Hollinger, D. (2002) 'Not Universalists, Not Pluralists: The New Cosmopolitans Find Their Own Way', in S. Vertovec and R. Cohen (eds), *Conceiving Cosmopolitanism* (Oxford: Oxford University Press).
hooks, b. (1986) 'Sisterhood: Political Solidarity between Women', *Feminist Review* 23, 125–38.
Hope Cheong, P., Edwards, R., Goulbourne, H. and Solomos, J. (2007) 'Immigration, Social Cohesion and Social Capital: A Critical Review', *Critical Social Policy*, 27 (1), 24–49.
Hughes, J., Campbell, A., Hewstone, M. and Cairns, E. (2007) 'Segregation in Northern Ireland: Implications for Community Relations Policy', *Policy Studies*, 28 (1), 33–53.
Huq, R. (2005) *Beyond Subculture: Pop, Youth and Identity in a Postcolonial World* (Abingdon: Routledge).
Hutton, W. (1995) *The State We're In* (London and New York: Random House).
Hutton, W. and Giddens, A. (eds) (2000) *Global Capitalism* (London: The New Press).
IPPR (2010) Exploring the Roots of BNP Support, London: IPPR.
Jacobs, J. M. and Fincher, R. (eds) (1998) *Cities of Difference* (New York and London: The Guildford Press).
Jeannotte, M. S. (2003) 'Singing Alone? The Contribution of Cultural Capital to Social Cohesion and Sustainable Communities', *International Journal of Cultural Policy*, 9 (1), 35–49.
Jenkins, R. (1996) *Social Identity* (New York: Routledge).
Johnson, N. (2007) 'Building an Integrated Society', in M. Wetherell, M. Laflèche and R. Berkley (eds), *Identity, Ethnic Diversity and Community Cohesion* (London: Sage).
Joppe, C. (2005) 'Exclusion in the Liberal State: The Case of Immigration and Citizenship Policy', *European Journal of Social Theory*, 8 (1), 43–61.
Kearney, H. (1989) *The British Isles: A History of Four Nations* (Cambridge: Cambridge University Press).

Khan, O. (2007) 'Policy, Identity and Community Cohesion: How Race Equality Fits', in M. Wetherell, M. Laflèche and R. Berkley (eds), *Identity, Ethnic Diversity and Community Cohesion* (London: Sage).

King, R. (2002) 'Towards a New Map of European Migration', *International Journal of Population Geography*, 8 (1): 89–106.

Kirton, G. and Greene, A. (2010) *The Dynamics of Managing Diversity – A Critical Approach* (Oxford: Elsevier).

Laville, S. (2011) 'Met Commissioner Says Stop and Search Must Be Used in a Smarter Way', *Guardian*, 15 September.

Layton, L. (2008) 'What Divides the Subject? Psychoanalytic Reflections on Subjectivity, Subjection and Resistance', *Subjectivity*, 22, 60–72.

Lazaridis, G. and Williams, A. M. (2002) 'Editorial Introduction: European Migration: Flows, Structures and Regulation', *International Journal of Population Geography*, 8, 2, 83–7.

Lefebvre, H. (1991) *The Production of Space* (Oxford: Blackwell).

Levitt, P. and Glick Schiller, N. (2004) 'Conceptualizing Simultaneity: A Transnational Social Field Perspective on Society', *International Migration Review*, 38 (3), 1002–39.

Levy, C., Sissons, A. and Holloway, C. (2011) *A Plan for Growth in the Knowledge Economy: A Knowledge Economy Programme Paper* (London: The Work Foundation).

Lewis, G. (2004) 'Racialising Culture is Ordinary', in E. B. Silva and T. Bennett (eds), *Contemporary Culture and Everyday Life* (Durham: Sociology Press).

Littlejohn, R. (2006) 'Is it any Wonder Britons are Leaving in Droves?' *Daily Mail*, 28 July, 15.

Lockwood, D. (1992) *Solidarity and Schism* (Oxford: Clarendon Press).

Lutz, H. (2008) *Migration and Domestic Work: A European Perspective on a Global Theme* (Aldershot: Ashgate).

Maan, B. (1992) *The New Scots: The Story of Asians in Scotland* (Edinburgh: Donald).

MacDonald, R. and Marsh, J. (2005) *Disconnected Youth? Growing up in Britain's Poor Neighbourhoods* (Basingstoke: Palgrave Macmillan).

Mackay, S. (2009) Employment Agencies and Migrant Workers (London: Institute of Employment Rights).

Macpherson, C. B. (2010) *The Political Theory of Possessive Individualism: Locke to Hobbes* (Oxford: Oxford University Press).

Malik, K. (2005) Multiculturalism has Fanned the Flames of Islamic Extremism. *The Times*, 16 July. Accessible at http://www.timesonline.co.uk/tol/comment/columnists/guest_contributors/article544443.ece.

Mann, M. (1970) 'Social Cohesion of Liberal Democracy', *American Sociological Review*, 35, 423–39.

Massey, D. (1994) *Space, Place and Gender* (Minneapolis: University of Minnesota Press).

Massey, D. (2005) *For Space* (London: Sage Publications).

McClintock, A. (1995) *Imperial Leather: Race, Gender and Sexuality in the Colonial Context* (New York and London: Routledge).

McDowell, L. (1991) 'Gender Divisions in a Post-Fordist Era: New Contradictions or the Same Old Story', *Transactions of the Institute of British Geographers*, 16, 4.

McDowell, L. (2002) 'Unsettling Naturalisms', *Signs*, 27, 3.

McGhee, D. (2003) 'Moving to "our" Common Ground – a Critical Examination of Community Cohesion Discourses in Twenty-First Century Britain', *The Sociological Review*, 51 (3), 376–404.
McGhee, D. (2005) *Intolerant Britain? Hate, Citizenship and Difference* (Milton Keynes: Open University Press).
McKay, S. and Winkelmann-Gleed, A. (2005), *Migrant Workers in the East of England*, (London: Working Lives Research Institute, London Metropolitan University).
McKibbin, R. (2001) 'Foreword', in L. Back (ed.), *Consensus or Cohesion?: The State, the People and Social Cohesion in Post-War Britain* (Cheltenham: New Clarion Press).
McKibbin, R. (2006) 'The Destruction of the Public Sphere', *London Review of Books*, 28 (1), 3–6.
McKibbin, R. (2008) 'An Element of Unfairness: The Great Education Disaster', *London Review of Books*, 30 (13), 7–10.
McLaughlin, E. and Neal, S. (2007) 'Who Can Speak to Race and Nation? Intellectuals, Public Policy Formation and the Future of Multi-Ethnic Britain Commission', *Cultural Studies*, 21 (6), 910–30.
Mizen, P. (2004) *The Changing State of Youth* (Basingstoke: Palgrave Macmillan).
Modood, T. (2005) *Multicultural Politics: Racism, Ethnicity and Muslims in Britain* (Edinburgh: Edinburgh University Press).
Moriarty, J., Manthorpe, J., Hussein, S., and Cornes, M. (2008) 'Staff Shortages and Immigration in the Social Care Sector', paper prepared for the Migration Advisory Committee (London: Migration Advisory Committee).
Morley, D. and Robbins, K. (1995) *Spaces of Identity: Global Media, Electronic Landscapes and Cultural Boundaries* (London: Routledge).
Mouffe, C. (1996), 'Democracy, Power and the "Political"', in S. Benhabib (ed.), *Democracy and Difference* (Princeton: University Press).
Ong, A. (1999) *Flexible Citizenship* (London: Duke Press).
Osbourne, G. (2009) Speech at the Conservative Party Conference 2009. See report at http://news.bbc.co.uk/1/hi/8292680.stm.
Pahl, R. E. (1991) 'The Search for Social Cohesion: From Durkheim to the European Commission', *European Journal of Sociology*, 32, 345–60.
Parekh Report (2000) *The Future of Multiethnic Britain* (London: Profile Books).
Parekh, A., MacInnes, T. and Kenway, P. (2010) *Monitoring Poverty and Social Exclusion* (York: Joseph Rowntree Foundation).
Parekh, B. (2007) 'Reasoned Identities: A Committed Relationship', in M. Wetherell, M. Laflèche and R. Berkley (eds), *Identity, Ethnic Diversity and Community Cohesion* (London: Sage).
Perriman, M. (2009) 'A Jigsaw State', in M. Perriman (ed.), *Breaking up Britain: Four Nations after a Union* (London: Lawrence and Wishart).
Perrons, D. and Fagan, C., McDowell, L. and Ray, K. and Ward, K. (eds) (2006) *Gender Divisions and Working Time in the New Economy: Changing Patterns of Work, Care and Public Policy in Europe and North America* (Cheltenham: Edward Elgar).
Phillips, T. (2005) *Notions of Identity in a Multicultural Society*, talk given at Canada House, London, 20 October.
Pierson, P. (1998) 'Irresistible Forces, Immovable Objects: Post-Industrial Welfare States Confront Permanent Austerity', *Journal of European Public Policy*, 5(4), 539–60.

Pierson, P. (2001) *The New Politics of the Welfare State* (Oxford: Oxford University Press).
Pierson, C. (2006) *Beyond the Welfare State?: The New Political Economy of Welfare* (Cambridge: Polity).
Pillai, R. with Kyambi, S., Nowacka, K. and Sriskandararjah, D. (2007) *The Reception and Integration of New Migrant Communities* (London: Commission for Racial Equality).
Pitcher, B. (2009) *The Politics of Multiculturalism. Race and Racism in Contemporary Britain* (London: Palgrave Macmillan).
Poole, R. (1999) *Nation and Identity* (London: Routledge).
Powell-Davies, M. (2008) 'Haberdashers'Aske's: The Campaign against Academies in Lewisham', *FORUM* 50 (1), 61–9.
PSNI (Police Service of Northern Ireland) (2007) PSNI Statistical Report 2006–2007 (Belfast: NISRA).
Putnam, R. D. (2007) 'E Pluribus Unum: Diversity and Community in the Twenty-first Century', The 2006 Johan Skytte Prize Lecture, Scandinavian Political Studies, 30, 2, 137–74.
Putnam, R. D. (2000) *Bowling Alone: The Collapse and Revival of American Community* (New York and London: Simon and Schuster).
Reed, K. (2005) 'Comparing New Migration with Old: Exploring the Issue of Asylum and Settlement', in C. Alexander and C. Knowles (eds), *Making Race Matter: Bodies, Space & Identity* (Basingstoke: Palgrave Macmillan).
Robinson, C. (1983) *Black Marxism* (London: Zed Press).
Robinson, D. (2005) 'The Search for Community Cohesion: Key Themes and Dominant Concepts of the Public Policy Agenda', *Urban Studies*, 42 (8), 1411–27.
Robinson, D., Reeve, K. and Casey, R. (2007) *The Housing Pathways of New Immigrants* (York: Joseph Rowntree Foundation).
Rogaly, B. and Taylor, B. (2009) *Moving Histories of Class and Community: Identity, Place and Belonging in Contemporary England* (Basingstoke: Palgrave Macmillan).
Rose, N. (1999) *Powers of Freedom: Reframing Political Thought* (Cambridge: Cambridge University Press).
Ruhs, M. and Anderson, B. (eds) (2010) *Who Needs Migrant Workers: Labour Shortages, Immigration and Public Policy* (Oxford: Oxford University Press).
Rutherford, J. (2007) *After Identity* (London: Lawrence & Wishart).
Rutherford, J. (2010) 'Labour's Good Society', *Social Europe Journal*, 28 October. Available at http://www.social-europe.eu/2010/10/labours-good-society/.
Rutter, J. (2006) *Refugee Children in the UK* (Buckingham: Open University Press).
Rutter, J. and Latorre, M. (2009) *Social Housing Allocation and Immigrant Communities* (London: Equalities and Human Rights Commission).
Salmon, H. (2002) 'Social Capital and Neighbourhood Renewal', *Renewal*, 10 (2), 49–55.
Sassen, S. (2001) *The Global City: New York, London, Tokyo* (Princeton: Princeton University Press).
Simpson, L., Purdam, K., Tajar, A., Fieldhouse, E., Gavalas, V., Tranmer, M., Pritchard, J. and Dorling, D. (2006) *Ethnic Minority Populations and the Labour Market: Analysis of the 1991 and 2001 Census*, Research Report 333, Department of Work and Pensions.
Skeggs, B. (2004) *Class, Self, Culture* (London: Routledge).

Sloane, P. J., O'Leary, N., Watson, D. (2005) *The Long Tail of Low Skills in Wales and the UK – A Review of the Evidence*, Report to the Economic Research Unit Welsh Assembly Government http://www.arsyllfadysgu.com/uploads/publications/781.pdf.

Smart, C. (2007) *Personal Life: New Directions in Sociological Thinking* (Cambridge: Polity).

Soja, E. W. (1999) *Postmodern Geographies: The Reassertion of Space in Critical Social Theory* (London: Verso).

Somerville, W. and Sumption, M. (2009) *Immigration and the Labour Market: Theory, Evidence and Policy* (London: Migration Policy Institute and Equality and Human Rights Commission).

Stephen, L., Banyon, J., Garland, J. and McClure, A. (1996) 'Education Matters: African Caribbean People and Schools in Leicestershire', Scarman Centre, University of Leicester, available online at https://lra.le.ac.uk/bitstream/2381/9451/1/ACPL%20EM.pdf.

Stolcke, V. (1995) 'Talking Culture: New Boundaries, New Rhetorics of Exclusion in Europe', *Current Anthropology*, 36(1), 1–24.

Tam, H. (2007) 'The Case for Progressive Solidarity', in M. Wetherell, M. Laflèche and R. Berkley (eds), *Identity, Ethnic Diversity and Community Cohesion* (London: Sage).

Theodore, N. (2007) 'New Labour at Work: Long Term Unemployment and the Geography of Opportunity', *Cambridge Journal of Economics*, 31, 927–39.

Thomas, B. and Dorling, D. (2007) *Identity in Britain: A Cradle to Grave Atlas* (Bristol, Policy Press).

Timesonline (2010), 'Transcript: Gordon Brown's Exchange with Gillian Duffy', 28 April, www.timesonline.co.uk/tol/news/politics/article7110540.ece.

Tomlinson, S. (2005) *Education in a Post-Welfare Society* (Buckingham: Open University Press).

Vertovec, S. and Cohen, R. (eds) (2002) *Conceiving Cosmopolitanism* (Oxford: Oxford University Press).

Vertovec, S. and Wessendorf, S. (eds) (2010) *Backlash against Multiculturalism? European Discourses, Policies and Practices* (London and New York: Routledge).

Walter, B. (1995) 'Irishness, Gender, and Place', *Environment and Planning D: Society and Space* 13(1):35–50.

Webster, W. (2005) *Englishness and Empire 1939–1965* (Oxford: Oxford University Press).

Williams, F. (2004) *Rethinking Families* (London: Calouste Gulbenkian Foundation).

Williams, F. (2011) 'Markets and Migrants in the Care Economy', *Soundings*, 47.

Willis, P. (1977) *Learning to Labour: How Working Class Kids Get Working Class Jobs* (New York: Columbia University Press).

Wolf, E. (1982) *Europe and the People Without History* (Los Angeles: University Press).

Wood, T. (2010) 'Good Riddance to New Labour', Editorial, *New Left Review*.

Worley, C. (2005) 'It's not about Race. It's about Community: New Labour and Community Cohesion', *Critical Social Policy*, 25, 4.

Young, I. M. (1990) *Justice and the Politics of Difference* (Princeton: Princeton University Press).

Younge, G. (2006) 'At Least in America they Understand the Notion of Cultural Difference', *Guardian*, 11 December.
Yuval-Davis, N. (1997) *Gender and Nation* (London: Sage).
Yuval-Davis, N., Anthias, F. and Kofman, E. (2010) 'Secure Borders and Safe Haven and the Gendered Politics of Belonging: Beyond Social Cohesion', *Ethnic and Racial Studies*, 28: 3, 513–35.
Zetter, R., Griffiths, D., Sigona, N., Flynn, D., Pasha, T. and Beynon, R. (2006) *Immigration, Social Cohesion and Social Capital: What are the Links?* (York: Joseph Rowntree Foundation).

Index

A8 migrants
  Britain's acceptance of, 69
  in Dungannon, 110
  English language skills, 157
  in Leicester, 151
Act of Union, 1707, 50
'affective citizens', 48
affluent suburban areas
  satisfaction/dissatisfaction with place (criteria/experiences), 93–5
  see also place, belongings to
affordable housing, 21, 120
  contraction of, disruptions/instabilities due to, 117
  demand for, 114
  new arrivals in, 115–19
  shortage of, 119
African-Caribbean, 171
  conflict with Somali in Leicester, 138–42, 149–53
  discrimination/migration of, 107–8
agencies
  accessing housing through, in Dungannon/Peterborough, 120–1
  in Dungannon, 73
  migrant workers, 70
  in Peterborough, 67–8, 69
Ahmed, S., 4
Ainley, P., 133
Albania, 176
Albanian refugees, 142, 143–4, 204
Alexander, C., 44, 47
Al-Khoei Foundation, 203
Allen, M., 133
'all our people' notion, 57
alterity, 3, 13, 60, 193
Amin, A., 43
Anderson, B., 17, 18, 33, 58, 66, 73
Anglo Saxons, 182

antagonism, 21, 35, 85, 103, 179, 181, 194
  localised discourses and, 85
  migration-related, 109
  negative dynamics of, 104
  religion-based, 84
  social, see social antagonism
Anthias, F., 178
Appadurai, A., 80
Asian young people
  experience of isolation, 174
  recourse to violence, 172–3
assimilation, 34
assimilationist understandings, of social cohesion, 163, 191
asylum seekers, 42, 69–70, 75, 95, 99, 118–19, 176
  belongingness in Britain, 176
  see also migrant workers
Audit Commission, 38

Back, L., 80
backlash
  against multiculturalism, 2–3, 5, 32–55
  settled backlash, 75, 81, 102, 103, 109, 110, 111, 137, 141, 142, 167, 186, 192, 195
  white backlash, 81, 111
Balibar, E., 80
Ball, S., 137
Balls, E., 22
Banton, M., 164
Bauman, Z., 20, 41, 46, 134, 160
Beck, U., 7
Beckett, F., 155
'being from here', 88, 102, 110, 192
  as category of social differentiation, 83–7
  Downham, 143, 148
  Leicester, 140, 141–2
  as marker of belonging to locality, 81, 82

216

Index

'being mobile'
  as marker of belonging to locality, 81, 82
Belfast
  Good Friday Agreement in, 33
Belgrave
  arrival of new social groups, 103
  research site, 200
Bell, D., 16
belongings, national
  heterogeneous narratives, 163
  homogeneous narratives, 163
  'locally positive' narratives of, 85
  majority ethnic belongings in Scotland/Northern Ireland, 164, 167–70
  'minimalist' positive feeling of, 165
  'minority ethnic long-term resident', 164, 170–4
  negotiation of, 168
  new arrivals and, 174–7
  placing, 80–3
  politics of, 162–86
  relations of, 172
  within contemporary Britain, 164, 177–9
  see also place, belongings to
Ben Tovim, G., 43
Bermondsey, diversity in, 104
Birmingham, 37
Black, L., 48
Blair, Tony, 52, 53, 56–7, 58
  about citizen's duties, 52
  on definition of Britishness, 52, 53
  on revitalisation of Britishness, 52
Blears, H., 1, 40
BNP, *see* British National Party (BNP)
Bradford, 14, 35, 43
Brah, A., 23, 33, 176
Braunstone (Leicester), 111, 200
  arrival of new social groups, 103
  death rate, 96–7
  life expectancy in, 97
  locality in, 84, 85
  research site, 200
  self-representations in, 184, 192
  social cohesion, understanding of, 184
  social deprivation, 100

Brenner, N., 8, 19, 80, 81
Britain, 6, 32, 36, 51, 53, 54, 57, 69, 78, 93, 108
  as welfare state, 177–8
  belongings to, 164–87
  community cohesion policies in, 41
  drinking culture in, 176
  emigration in, 24
  ethnic diversity of, 21
  family life in, 128
  housing shortage in, 115
  knowledge economy of, 58
  norms and values, 53
British Council, 38
British National Party (BNP), 143
  education and, 143
Britishness, 35, 41, 187
  definition of, 52
  and diversity, 54–5
  hyphenated, 34
  New Labour government and, 52–5
  possibilities/impossibilities of, as social glue, 49–52
Britishness under New Labour, 33–4
British politics
  immigration role in, 1–2
Brown, G., 1, 22, 52, 53
Brown, P., 146
Brown, W., 53
Buonfino, A., 46, 181
Burnett, J., 44
Burnley, 14, 35, 43

Cairns, E., 195
Cameron, D., 1, 52, 55
Campbell, A., 195
Cantle, T., 11, 36, 37, 38, 44, 92, 93
Cantle Report, 34, 36–7
  assimilationist policies, 43
  vs. Commission on Integration and Cohesion (CIC) report, 40
  critique of, 43–5
  influence of, 39
  on achieving community cohesion, 37
  on dramatic change in 1950s and 1960s, 36
  on need of the country, 37
  'parallel lives', idea of, 37

218 *Index*

Cantle Report – *continued*
  vs. Parekh Report, 38–9
  publishing of, 38
  racial harassment and racial segregation in, 43
  terms of reference of, 36
'capitalist realism', 134
care industry, 66
  in Glasgow, 73–6
  in Kilburn, 73–8
  new arrivals in, 74
Cassen, R., 156
casualisation, 62
Catholic populations, long-term settled, 164, 168, 169
CEHR, *see* Commission on Equality and Human Rights (CEHR)
Chicago School's model, 45
Church of the Sacred Heart Quex Road Community Centre, 203
CIC report, *see* Commission on Integration and Cohesion (CIC) report
citizens, duties of, 52
citizenship
  definition of, 21
civility, in place, 88
Clarke, J., 46
Clarke, S., 52
class, 1, 3, 11–12, 20, 45, 75, 84, 85, 89, 98, 102, 104, 108, 134, 135, 137, 140, 142, 178, 187, 192
  as category of social differentiation, 83, 84–5, 86
'close knit', 105
coalition government, 1, 21–2, 43, 134
Cohen, P., 8, 9, 50
cohesive community
  definition of, 37–8
cohesive group
  definition of, 11
Colquhoun, G., 17
Commission for Racial Equality (CRE), 39
Commission on Equality and Human Rights (CEHR), 39
Commission on Future of Multi-Cultural Britain, 33

Commission on Integration and Cohesion (CIC) report, 39
  vs. Cantle Report, 40
  proposals for building integration and cohesion, 39
Commission on the Future of Multi-Ethnic Britain, 34
  aim of, 34
commonality, 6, 47, 92, 180, 182, 183, 187
'commonness', 143, 158, 198
  education and, 145, 146
communitarianism, 21, 45
  and community cohesion, 45–8
  social theory of, 45
  supporters of, 38
'communities of similarity', 46
community, 12, 14, 17, 21, 26, 28, 29, 33, 41, 46, 47
  as form of governmentality, 47
  language, in neoliberalism, 47
  self-representations, 82–3, 151
community cohesion
  achieving, 37
  building, CIC principles to, 39–40
  communitarianism and, 45–8
  definition of, 37–8
  destabilisations and, 41–3
  Durkheimian model of, 14
  framework, 36, 37
  limitation of, 47
  racism/inequalities, 43–5
  and social cohesion, 6
community cohesion framework, 11, 44
  achieving consensus within, 37
  assumptions, 36
community cohesion paradigm
  dominance of, 35
community cohesion policies, 44
  critiquing, 41
    destabilisations, 41–3
    racism and inequalities, 43–5
  development of, 34–41
  governmentality and community, 45–8
'community identity', 47
'community of communities' report, 35

conflict(s), 72, 84
  around housing, 117, 119
  between African-Caribbean and Somali young people, 151
  between Kurdish and Iraqi refugees, 69
  between new arrivals and settled residents, 123, 138, 140
  between Portuguese and East Timorese seasonal workers, 69
  between Somali/African-Caribbean in Leicester, 138–42
  diversity as a source of, 40
  hierarchies of class and, 75
  inequalities and, 73, 76, 191, 196
  migrant workers, 69, 104
  negotiating, 111, 150, 163, 191, 195, 197
  over scarce resources, 98, 104
  pluralism and, 12, 13
  racialised, 151–2
  resolving, 64, 82
  response to, 26
  in work/life balance, 6
'consensualist' sensibility, 6, 150, 180, 181, 189
Conservative government, 51, 114
  on immigration, 1
Conservative-Liberal Democratic coalition government, 134
  education and, 134
Conservative party, 1, 36, 51, 114
consumerism, 30, 46, 129–30, 131
contemporary societies, 3
  heterogeneities of, 3
convenience, locality and, 83–7
  cultural constructions of, 87, 89–90, 91
  experiences/discourses, 86
  politics of, 87
  requirements of, 88–9
  'settled backlash', 137
  'street conviviality', 86
  see also place, belongings to
conviviality, 63, 71, 72, 86
Cooper, A., 197
corporatism, 36
cosmopolitanism, 8–9, 32
  with universalism, 9

CRE, *see* Commission for Racial Equality (CRE)
Crenshaw, K., 82
Cresswell, T., 160, 191
Crick, Bernard, 50
Crompton, R., 113
Cruddas, J., 59
cultural constructions, 10, 86, 93, 94, 106, 145
  of locality and convenience, 87, 89–90
cultural diversity, 74, 92–3, 102, 104, 158, 193
  in Downham, 104
cultural pluralism, 53, 106, 172, 183, 192
Curran, M., 194

Daily Mail, 24
Daily Telegraph, 1
  on Parekh Report, 35
de-ethnicisation, 149, 150
deindustrialisation, 14, 16, 57, 96, 126
Delanty, G., 45, 46, 47
Dench, G., 21
Denham, J., 12
deprived populations, 12, 109
'deprived' majority ethnic long-term settled residents, 179
deskilling, in migrant job, 60–1, 77
destabilisations and community cohesion policies, 41–3
differences, 32, 34, 38
Dilnott, A., 74
diversity, 4–5, 36, 39, 40, 44, 54–5, 57
  in Bermondsey, 104
  concept of, 4–5
  cultural/social, 92–3, 104
  ethnic, 21, 44, 106, 166
  resolving, 40
  as a source of conflict, 40
dominant narratives, 55, 191–2
Dorling, D., 12
Downham, 27, 111, 179, 200–1
  arrival of new social groups, 103
  conflicts in, 153–4
  cultural/social diversity in, 104

Downham – *continued*
  educational settings, 136, 142–9, 153–6
  and experience of pluralisation, 104
  labour markets in, 64
  long-term settled majority ethnic in, 64–5, 101–2, 129, 166, 180
  long-term settled minority ethnic in, 61, 143, 146, 153, 171, 172
  long-term settled residents vs. new arrivals in educational settings, 142–9
  majority ethnic belongings, 165, 166
  Malory School, 142–9, 153–6
  minority ethnic belongings, 170
  new arrivals in, 176–7
  people's satisfaction with place (experiences), 101–2
  research site, 200–1
  self-representations, 136–7, 142, 192
  sense of belonging to Britain, 165, 166
  'settled backlash', 167
  skilled sector in, 61–2
  social cohesion, understanding of, 180, 184
  social deprivation, 98–9
  social reformation in, 108–9
  social transformations/interventions in educational settings, 153–6
Dreier, P., 20
Du Gay, P., 82
Duggan, Mark, 197
Dungannon, 27, 111, 202
  accessing housing through landlords/agencies in, 120–1
  arrival of new social groups, 103
  catholic populations, long-term settled, 169
    sense of belonging to Britain, 168
  economic downturn, 73
  educational settings, 136, 156–9
  food industry in, 67–73
  food industry in, 67–73
  language differences, 72
  locality in, 84
  long-term settled majority ethnic in, 72, 124, 181
  long-term settled minority ethnic in, 123
  minority ethnic belongings, 170–4
  neighbourhood relations in, 121–6
  neighbouring practices, 184
  new arrivals in, 71, 72
  overcrowding, 120–1
  protestant populations, long-term settled
    sense of belonging to Britain, 169
  research site, 202
  self-representations, 184, 192
  social cohesion in, 72–3, 181
  social transformations/interventions in educational settings, 156–9
Durkheim, 7
  notions of solidarity, 14
  sociology, 7
dysfunctional communities, perceived, 38

East Tyrone College of Further and Higher Education, 157
economic individualism, 57, 59
economy, 18
  economic downturn, 73
  local economy, 111, 195
  manufacturing-based, 16–17, 134
  migration in, 191, 196
  service sector, 66, 73
  see also knowledge economy; new economy
education, 133
  achievement, 137
  commoditisation of, 134
  'commonness' and, 145, 146
  in Downham, 136, 142–9, 153–6
  see also Downham
  in Dungannon, 136, 156–9
  see also Dungannon
  'learner identities', 137
  in Leicester, 136, 138–42, 149–53
  see also Leicester
  locality and, 135, 137, 150, 157
  long-term settled vs. new arrivals, social antagonism, 138–49
  multiculturalist policies in, 32
  New Labour government and, 133–4

overview, 133–6
privatisation of, 133–4
secondary, 137–8
settings, 135
social cohesion and, 133, 198
social divisions and, 135
social hierarchies in, 136–8
socialisation, 134
social mobility and, 137, 142–3, 143, 146, 148–9
socio-economic transformations and, 136
tertiary, 157
Elliott, A., 15
emigration
in Britain, 24
England, 27
Downham, see Downham
Kilburn, see Kilburn
Leicester, see Leicester
London, see London
long-term settled
majority ethnic, 28
minority ethnic, 28
Peterborough, see Peterborough
Thetford, see Thetford
English language, learning, 156, 157
Englishness, 23, 48–55, 178, 187, 193–4
see also Britishness
entitlement
hierarchies of, in education, 136–49
housing scarcity and, 115–19
to social housing, 114
to social mobility, 95, 102
Equalities and Human Rights Commission, 52
equality and diversity, values of, 57
Eriksen, T. H., 3, 191
Esping-Anderson, G., 126
estates, inner city, 95–102
see also place, belongings to
ethnic deficit/penalty
in skilled sector, 61–2
ethnic exoticism, 32
ethnicity, 35
as category of social differentiation, 83, 84–5, 86

ethnic differences, positive evaluation of, 106–7
'ethnic minorities', 35, 44, 62
ethnic residents vs. new arrivals, 138–49
ethnic 'silos', living in, 181
'ethnic' food and fashion, 32
ethno-cultural identities, 90–1
see also identity(ies)
ethno-national relations, 50
European societies, 3
Evans, G., 143
eventual acceptance, see tolerance
'excess of alterity', 3
exclusion(s), 59, 104, 163, 171, 194, 195, 197
categories of, 57
deskilling of new arrivals, 61
socio-economic, 81, 108
of working life, 65
experience of isolation, 174
of Asian young people, 174

'failing school', 154
family
in Britain, instabilities, 114
housing and, 113–31
life in Britain, 128
relations, post-industrialism and, 113
social infrastructures of, 113
transnational, 130–1
welfare and gender regimes, 113
Fanning, B., 7
'fear of difference', 37
Fenian rebellion in Ireland (1867), 50
Ferree, M., 17
Fincher, R., 4, 5, 33, 45
Finlayson, A., 38
Finney, N., 12
Fisher, M., 134, 187
food industry, 66
in Dungannon, 67–73
in Peterborough, 67–73
Ford, R., 21
Forrest, R., 11, 12, 19, 45
Fortier, A., 35, 40, 44, 48, 55, 178
France, 17
freeborn Englishman, 50

Freidkin, N. E., 11
'from here', 87, 95, 105, 109, 141, 142
'from hereness', 142, 167, 178, 195
Future of Multi-Cultural Britain, 33
  Runnymede Trust on, 33
Future of Multi-Ethnic Britain, The, 34

Gedalof, I., 113
gender, 3, 18, 20, 25, 27, 81, 85, 87, 89–90, 94, 113, 135, 140, 178
  as category of social differentiation, 83, 84–5
Germany, 16–17
Gilchrist, A., 13
Gilroy, P., 2, 23, 32, 44
Glasgow, 27, 109, 110, 112, 192, 194, 202–3, 204
  care industry in, 73–8
  locality in, 90–1
  long-term settled majority ethnic in, 100, 117, 128, 168, 181
  long-term settled minority ethnic in, 90, 91
  low-skilled care workers in, 74
  majority ethnic populations, 168
  new arrivals in, 109, 118
  public housing in, 117–18
  research site, 202–3
  skilled overseas nurses in, 74–5
  social cohesion, understanding of, 181
Glasgow Housing Association, 117
Glick Schiller, N., 8, 9, 10, 15
globalisation, destabilising effects of, 41–3
global migration, 2
global terrorism, 2
Glucksman, M., 114
Good Friday Agreement in Belfast, 33
Goodhart, D., 14, 21
Gorard, S., 154
governmentality and community cohesion policies, 45–8
Gray, B., 47, 54
Greene, A., 58
Grillo, R., 3
Guidance on Community Cohesion, 37, 38, 40
Gutwill, S., 42

Haberdashers' Aske's Knights Academy, 154–5
Hackney, 107
  disturbances in, 197
Hage, G., 53, 75, 197
Hall, C., 50
Hall, S., 5, 82
Hannerz, U., 3
Harris, H., 138
Harvey, D., 8, 15, 80
Hesse, B., 81
heterogeneity, 25, 28, 136, 137, 163, 182–183, 186, 192, 193, 196
  of contemporary societies, 3, 29
Hewitt, R., 81
Hewstone, M., 12, 46
Hickman, M. J., 35, 50, 54, 178, 193
Hiebert, D., 8
Highfields (Leicester), 85, 89, 90, 138, 139, 140, 151, 158, 182
  arrival of new social groups, 103
  locality in, 91
  research site, 200
  Somali families in, 138
Hills, J., 114, 115
Himmelweit, S., 66, 74
Holland, 175
Hollander, N., 42
Hollinger, D., 8
Holloway, C., 58
home making, 30, 115, 126–31
homogeneity, 10, 13, 46, 95, 110, 111, 137, 161, 163, 186, 192, 193, 195, 196, 198
hooks, b., 152
Hope Cheong, P., 43
'host white community', 36
housing, 21, 98, 99, 101, 200–1
  accessing, new arrivals, 119–21
  affordable, demand for, 114
  and family, 113–31
  impact of migration on, 115–16
  in inner city multicultural areas, 90
  instabilities, 114
  personal life and, 113
  scarcity/entitlement, 115–19
  shortage in, 115, 116
  social, *see* social housing

social infrastructures of, 113
transformations of, 114
Hughes, J., 195
Hume, David, 35
Huq, R., 33
Hutton, W., 17
hyphenated Britishness, 34

ICR, *see* Institute for Conflict Research (ICR)
identity(ies)
  civic, 51
  community, 47
  cultural, 4–5
  group, 53
  local, 106
  markers, 81
  national, 2, 35, 49, 51, 167
  self-representation and, 82
imagined community, 171, 189
immigration, 6, 32, 164
  benefits, 18
  and contemporary multiculture, 23–5
  economy and, 191, 196
  as election issue, 1
  histories of, 23–5
  and housing, 115–16
  and minority ethnic groups, 2
  role in British politics, 1–2
  social antagonism and, 138–49, 142–9, 199–205
  to UK, 24
Immigration Acts, 36
inclusion, and community cohesion, 44
Independent Review Team (IRT), 35, 36
Indian National Uprising (1857), 50
individualisation, 42
individualism, 3, 7, 12, 15, 18, 30, 38, 42, 53, 57, 59, 113, 131
industrialisation, 7–8, 12, 16, 57, 193
inequalities, 14, 21, 42, 95, 100, 102, 107, 154, 160, 162, 187, 190, 194
  in care sector, 74, 76, 78
  and community cohesion policies, 43–5

and conflicts, 73, 191, 196
racism and, 43–5
inner city estates
  satisfaction/dissatisfaction with place (criteria/experiences), 95–102
  social deprivation, 97–101
  see also place, belongings to
inner city multicultural areas, 90–3
  characteristics, 90
  long-term settled residents in, 91–2
  satisfaction/dissatisfaction with place (criteria/experiences), 90–2
  see also place, belongings to
Institute for Conflict Research (ICR), 203, 204
Institute for Fiscal Studies, 43
institutionalised racism in police force, 33
interdependence, 180, 181
intersection, 81–2
intersectionality
  and belongings to place, 81–2
in-work poverty, 60, 65, 78
IPPR, 108
IRT, *see* Independent Review Team (IRT)
Italy, 16–17

Jacobs, J. M., 4, 5, 33, 45
Jeannotte, M. S., 7, 10
Jenkins R., 82
Johnson, N., 39
Joppe, C., 2, 53
Joseph Rowntree Foundation, 199, 203

Kearney, H., 49
Kearns, A., 11, 12, 19, 45
Kelly, Ruth, 39
Khan, O., 46
Kilburn, 27, 107, 183, 192, 201
  acceptance of new arrivals in, 63–4
  arrival of new social groups, 103, 107–8
  care industry in, 73–8

Kilburn – *continued*
  entitlement to housing, 118–19
  ethnic difference, positive evaluation of, 107–8
  informal economy of, 63
  long-term settled majority ethnic in, 115, 180
  long-term settled minority ethnic in, 76, 89, 96, 97, 107, 116, 118, 172, 183
  low-skilled sector in, 62–4
  migration/low-skilled work in, 62–4
  migration and housing, 115–16
  minority ethnic belongings, 172
  new arrivals in, 76, 77, 175
  research site, 201
  satisfaction/dissatisfaction with place (criteria/experiences), 88–9, 90
  social cohesion, understanding of, 180, 183
  social deprivation in, 97–9
King, R., 8
Kingdon, G., 156
Kirton, G., 58
knowledge economy, 56, 58, 59, 134
  definition of, 57–8
  low wage sector, 58
  policy intervention in, 58
  see also new economy
Kofman, 17

labour
  demand, in service sector, 66
Labour government, 114
labour markets, 18, 29, 56, 62, 70, 76
  in Downham, 64
  inclusions/exclusions in, 59
  in Kilburn, 63
  migrant workers and, 58–9
  niche, 65–78
Land, H., 66, 74
landlords
  accessing housing through, in Dungannon/Peterborough, 120–1
language, 27, 36, 38, 47

differences, 72
difficulties, new arrivals and, 124–5
learning of, 157
migrant workers, 72
late modernity, characteristics, 80
'latent neighbourliness' concept, 181
Latorre, M., 114
Laville, S., 197
Lawrence, S., 33
Layton, L., 42, 187
Lazaridis, G., 18
'learner identities', 30, 137, 143, 145
Lefebvre, H., 19
Leicester, 27, 37, 65, 106–7, 179, 183, 192, 200
  A8 migrants in, 151
  arrival of new social groups, 103, 106–7
  conflicts between Somali/African-Caribbean, 138–42, 149–53
  educational settings, 136
  ethnic difference, positive evaluation of, 106–7
  locality in, 85–6
  long-term settled majority ethnic in, 65, 89, 92, 94, 100, 130, 165
  long-term settled minority ethnic in, 84, 86, 94, 96, 97, 127, 129, 130, 141, 150, 170–1, 172, 180, 182
  majority ethnic belongings, 165, 166
  minority ethnic belongings, 170, 172
  minority ethnic young people in, 173
  new arrivals in, 174
  racialised conflicts in, 151–2
  research site, 200
  satisfaction/dissatisfaction with place (criteria/experiences), 89–90, 93–5
  self-representations, 136–7
  sense of belonging to Britain, 165
  social cohesion, understanding of, 180, 181–2, 183
  social transformations/interventions in educational settings, 149–53
Leicester Mercury, 152

Lemart, C., 15
Levitt, P., 8, 9
Levy, C., 58
Lewis, G., 44
Lewisham Refugee Network, 203
Lewisham Youth Service, 203
liberal democracy, 13, 53
Liberal Democrats
  on immigration, 1
liberal equality, 53
liberal individualism
  tolerance and, 53–4
lifestyles, 52, 86, 91, 125, 184
  and place, 88
'liquid modernity', 46
Lithuanian workers, 69, 71, 72, 122–3, 156
Littlejohn, R., 24
locality(ies)
  as category of social differentiation, 83–7
  convenience and, *see* convenience, locality and
  cultural constructions of, 87, 89–90, 91
  discourse of belonging, 81
  education and, 137, 150, 157
  self-representations and self-identities, interplay between, 82
  shared cultural traits, 85
  see also place, belongings to
local narratives, 192–3
local socio-economic settings, improvement of, 185
Lockwood, D., 7
London, 27, 32, 33, 39, 107, 108, 143
  research site, 200–1
  riots in, 197
long-term settled majority ethnic, 28
  in affluent suburban areas, 93
  in Downham, 64–5, 101–2, 129, 166, 180
  in Dungannon, 72, 124, 181
  in Glasgow, 100, 117, 128, 168, 181
  in Kilburn, 115, 180
  in Leicester, 65, 89, 92, 94, 100, 130, 165
  vs. new arrivals, 122–6, 196–7
  in Downham, 142–9
  in Leicester, 138–42
  in UK, 24
  in Peterborough, 61, 69, 117, 120, 124, 125, 128, 165, 180
  in Scotland/Northern Ireland, 164, 167–70
long-term settled minority ethnic, 28, 90, 138, 192
  in affluent suburban areas, 93
  in Braunstone, 96
  in Downham, 61, 143, 146, 153, 171, 172
  in Dungannon, 123
  in Glasgow, 90, 91
  in Kilburn, 76, 89, 96, 97, 107, 116, 118, 172, 183
  in Leicester, 84, 86, 94, 97, 127, 129, 130, 141, 150, 170–1, 172, 180, 182
Lousada, J., 197
low-skilled sector, 58
  in care industry, 73, 74
  in Kilburn, 62–3
  migrant workers in, 58–9
  migration of, 58–9
Lutz, H., 74, 126

Maan, B., 50
MacDonald, R., 137, 146
Mackay, S., 66
Macpherson, C. B., 133
MacPherson Report, 33
majority ethnic long-term resident, 28, 45, 51, 63, 64, 89, 90, 92, 93, 120, 125, 128, 144, 162, 180, 183
  in Britain, 164
  in educational settings, 142
  in England, 164
  in Northern Ireland, 167–70
  in Scotland, 167–70
  white English, 164–5
Malik, K., 53
Malory School, Downham, 142–9, 153–6
  educational performance, 145
Mann, M., 52
Mann, P., 181
manual labour, 57–8

manufacturing-based economy, 134
Marsh, J., 137, 146
Massey, D., 19, 82
McClintock, A., 113
McGhee, D., 46, 47
McKay, S., 67
McKibbin, R., 41–2. 49–50, 133, 134, 154
McLaughlin, E., 35
media
  on Parekh Report, 35
migrant workers, 58, 59, 118–19
  agency constructions of, 70
  and care industry in Kilburn/Glasgow, 73–8
  care workforce, 73–4
  category of, 60–1
  conflicts between, 69
  and food industry in Peterborough/Dungannon, 67–73
  housing options for, 116
  language differences, 72
  low pay/unsecured rights of, 73
  in niche markets, 66
  rental revenue and, 116
  social life, 77
  see also immigration
migration, 1–2, 5–6, 14, 24, 191
  analysis of, 5–6
  politics of, 14
  wages policy, 62
minorities, 95
minority ethnic long-term settled, 162, 164. 170–4
  in Britain, 164
  younger generations of, 172–3
'minus one ethnicity', 164
mixophobia, 46
Mizen, P., 135
mobility
  significance of, 81
  social, 88, 93–5
  see also place, belongings to
Modood, T., 51
  as supporter of multiculturalism, 51
'mongrel people', 35
Morant Bay rebellion in Jamaica (1865), 50
Moriarty, J., 73

Mouffe, C., 13
Mulgan, G., 46
Multicultural Advisory Group, 152
multiculturalism, 4
  backlash against, community cohesion and, *see* Community cohesion
  Britain, 93
  'community', 33
  education, policies in, 32
  overview, 32
  policies, development of, 32
  public diagnosis of, 35
  Tariq Modood on, 51
  tolerance and, 53
  in UK, 2
Muslims, 14, 45, 89
  Cantle Report and, 38
mutual empathy, 5

narratives
  of belonging, 85, 102, 141–2, 162, 163, 164, 188
  dominant, 191–2
  local, 192–3
  national, 191–6
  see also specific entries
national allegiance, 34
National Assembly for Wales, 33
National Audit Offices, 155
national belonging
  and social cohesion, 48–55
  see also Britishness
national boundaries, 9
national identity, 51
national narratives, 191–6
Neal, S., 35
negative belonging, in Britain, 166–7
neighbourhood, 11, 25, 27, 38, 40, 47, 48, 84, 85, 91–2, 94, 96, 119–31
  importance of, 91
  relations
    disruption to, 125
    in Dungannon/Peterborough, 121–6
    see also neighbourhood: relations
  'street conviviality' and, 86
neighbourliness, 88

neoliberal depoliticisations, 81, 83
neoliberal individualism, 57
neoliberalism, 42, 43, 57, 62, 65, 84, 101, 105, 106, 159, 187
  definition of, 15
  individualisation characteristic of, 42
  language of community in, 47
  and post-industrialism, 78
neoliberal policies, 43, 99, 187
  economic policies, 42
  neoliberal welfarism, 114
the Netherlands, 176
new arrivals, 119, 162, 164, 174–7
  acceptance of, in Kilburn, 63–4
  accessing housing for, 119–21
  in Britain, 164
  educational settings, 141–2, 145–8
    see also education
  housing scarcity and, 115–19
  language difficulties and, 124–5
  neighbourhood relations and, 121–6, 196–7
  racism against, 122
  settled residents, conflict, 122–4
  see also social groups, new
new economy
  'all our people' notion, 57
  care industry, 66
    in Glasgow, 73–6
    in Kilburn, 73–8
  competitiveness, 58, 63, 64, 73
  demand for skilled workers in, 58
  deskilling in, 60–1
  food industry, 66
    in Dungannon, 67–73
    in Peterborough, 67–73
  labour shortages in, 66
  niche labour markets, 65–78
  overview, 56–60
  post-industrialism and, 56
  'revolutionary' nature of, 57–8
  settlement strategies, 70
  shortages in, 66
  social cohesion in, 56–78
  structural divisiveness of, 58
  values of, 56, 57
  working lives, changes in, 60–5
  work relations in, 59

New Labour government, 1, 33, 34, 192
  about citizen's duties, 52
  'all our people' notion, 57
  Britishness, revitalisation of, 52–4
  and Britishness project, 42–3, 52–5
  Britishness under, 33–4
  education strategy, 133–6
  new economy, structural divisiveness of, 58
  policy reviews, 36
  'possessive individualism', 133
New Link, 69, 110, 124, 126, 203
Newman, J., 46
NGO, see Non-governmental organisation (NGO)
niche labour markets, 65–78
  care industry, 73–8
  characteristics of, 67
  food industry, 67–73
non-governmental organisation (NGO)
  and migrant workers, 69
Northern Ireland, 23, 27, 28, 67, 72, 178, 194–5
  Dungannon, see Dungannon
  long-term settled majority ethnic groups
    Catholic populations, 164
    Protestant populations, 164
  long-term settled minority ethnic groups, 164
  majority ethnics belongings, 167–70
  new arrivals, 164
Northern Ireland Assembly, 33
'not being from here', 103

oil crisis of 1973, 16
Oldham, 14, 35, 43
Ong, A., 9
ONN, see Overseas Nurses Network (ONN)
onus of negotiation, 185
optimism, spirit of, 33
Osborne, G., 14
'our people' notion, 57
overcrowding, 115–19
  high rents and, 120–1

Overseas Nurses Network (ONN), 76, 203, 204
Pahl, R. E., 7, 26
'parallel lives' idea, Cantle Report, 37
Parekh, A., 96
Parekh, B., 51
Parekh Report, 34, 35, 38, 51
   Cantle Report vs., 38–9
   furore over, 35
   media response on, 35
   reception of, 35
Perriman, M., 178
Perrons, D., 16, 113
Peterborough, 27, 95
   accessing housing through landlords/agencies in, 120–1
   agencies, bad practices in, 67–8
   arrival of new social groups, 103
   food industry in, 67–73
   housing in, 118
   Kurdish-Iraqi refugee expression from, 176
   locality in, 86
   long-term settled majority ethnic in, 61, 69, 117, 120, 124, 125, 128, 165, 180
   majority ethnic belongings, 165, 166
   neighbourhood relations in, 121–6
   new arrivals in, 60, 61, 69, 175–6
   overcrowding, 117, 120–1
   research site, 201–2
   self-representations in, 192
   sense of belonging to Britain, 165
   settlement strategies, 70
   skilled worker in, changes in life of, 60–5
   social cohesion, understanding of, 180, 184
   'street conviviality', 86
Phillips, T., 52
Pierson, C., 16, 17
Pillai, R., 21
Pitcher, B., 3, 36, 38, 43, 47
place, belongings to, 5–6, 10–11, 18–20
   affluent suburban areas, 93–5
   ethno-cultural identities, 90–1
   importance of, 19, 20
   inner city estates, 95–102
   inner city multicultural areas, 90–3
   intersectionality and, 81–2
   locality and convenience, 83–7
   negative/positive reactions to arrival of new migrant groups, 104–11
   neighbourliness/civility, 88
   new economy, marginalised by, 190
   overview, 80–3
   politics of, and arrival of new groups, 102–11
   safety, 88
   satisfaction/dissatisfaction with (criteria/experiences), 88–102
   self-definition of specific, 190–1
   self-representations, 82, 83–7
   'settled backlash', concept of, 81
   significance of, 81
   socio-economic security of, arrival of new groups and, 106
   socio-economic transformations, 81–2, 83, 109–10
   'white backlash', 81
pluralisation, 8, 104
pluralism, 110
   conflicts and, 12, 13
   cultural, 53, 106, 112, 172, 183, 192
   social, 41, 112, 172
polarisations, 29, 59, 78, 80, 109
police force
   and conflict in Leicester, 151
   institutionalised racism in, 33
   racism in, 33
Police Service of Northern Ireland, see PSNI
Polish workers, 62–3, 69, 70, 71, 72, 157
political issue
   social cohesion as, 1
politics
   of belonging, 162–86
   and self-representations, 162–3
   and social cohesion, 162
   within contemporary Britain, 164, 177–8

of convenience and locality, 87
of immigration, 1
of migration, 14
of place/arrival of new groups, 102–11
Poole, R., 8
populations, 28
  density of, 96, 104
  urban, categorisation of, 46
positive belonging, in Britain, 165–6
'possessive individualism', 133
post 11 September 2011, 54
post-colonial melancholia, 44
post-industrialism, 15, 16–17, 48, 101, 106, 159
  care sector and, 73, 75
  changes of, 114
  characteristics, 113–14
  conditions of, 30
  family relations and, 113
  and neoliberalism, 65, 78
  and new economy, 56
  'settled backlash', 75
  transformations of, 113
post-national multiculturalism, 35
Powell-Davies, M., 154, 155
privatisation, of education, 133–4
Protestant populations, long-term settled, 164
  in Dungannon, 169
  in Northern Ireland, 168, 169
proximity, solidarity and, 100
PSNI (Police Service of Northern Ireland), 110, 169
Putnam, R. D., 12, 42

race/racism, 35, 36, 50, 103
  against new arrivals, 122
  anti-racist and egalitarian movements (1960s), 81
  as category of social differentiation, 83, 84–5
  and community cohesion policies, 43–5
  and inequality, 41, 43–5
  institutionalised, 32
  in police, 33
  'settled backlash', concept of, 81
  in skilled sector, 61–2
  and threat perceptions, 43–4
  'white backlash', concept of, 81
race relations, promoting, 36–7
Race Relations Acts, 36
Reed, K., 198
relations
  family, post-industrialism and, 113
  neighbourhood, *see* neighbourhood: relations
  time poverty, family and, 128–9
rent levels, dealing with, 120–1
re-racialisation, 95
research project (Immigration and Social Cohesion in the UK), 199–205
  aims and objectives, 199
  methods, 203–5
  sites, 199–203
riots, 32, 45, 107, 138, 197
Robinson, C., 2
Robinson, D., 11, 99
Rogaly, B., 8, 47, 48, 85, 98, 101
Rose, N., 47, 96
Ruhs, M., 18, 58, 66, 73
Runnymede Trust, 33
Rutherford, J., 21, 42, 55
Rutter, J., 114, 159

safety, of place, 88
Salmon, H., 37
sameness, 4, 5, 53, 54, 92
Sassen, S., 9
satisfaction/dissatisfaction
  with place (criteria/experiences), 88–102
  see also convenience, locality and
scarcity, housing, 115–19
Scase, R., 146
Scotland, 27, 49, 50, 51, 164, 194
  diversified migrations of, 74
  Glasgow, *see* Glasgow
  long-term settled
    majority ethnic, 28
    minority ethnic, 28
  long-term settled majority ethnic in, 164, 167–70
  majority ethnics belongings, 167–70
  population of, 74

Scotland – *continued*
  referendums in, 33
  sense of belonging to Britain, 168
  trade with England, 50
Scottish Parliament, 33
secondary education, 137–8
  in Downham, 136, 142–9, 153–6
  in Dungannon, 136, 156–9
  in Leicester, 138–42, 149–53
  in Malory School, 142–9, 153–6
self-identities
  and self-representations, interplay between, 82
  see also identity(ies)
self-representations, 136–7, 142, 178, 184
  of belongings to place, 83–7
  community, 82–3, 151
  hegemonic, 162
  internalisation/rejection of, 163
  and self-identities, interplay between, 82
  see also identity(ies)
separateness, 2, 37, 92, 179, 180, 181, 182, 187
'settled backlash', 75, 81, 102, 103, 110, 137, 167, 192, 195
Sheffield, 37
Sighthill (Glasgow)
  arrival of new groups in, 99–100, 103
  self-representation of place, 184
  social cohesion, understanding of, 184
Simpson, L., 12, 62
Sissons, A., 58
Skeggs, B., 20, 81, 87, 137, 178, 191
skilled new arrival, 75
skilled workers
  demand for, 58
  deskilling, 60–1
Sloane, P. J., 58
social antagonism, 91, 99, 103, 107, 137, 138–42, 152, 159, 166, 199–205
  in Downham, 142–9
  in Leicester, 138–42
social cohesion, 45, 102
  assimilationist understanding of, 163, 191

Beck, Ulrich on, 7–8
commonality, 180
in contemporary social settings, 103
crisis of, 46
definition of, 7–12, 106, 163, 191
disruptions to, 63
Durkheim on, 7
dynamics of, 189–90
education and, 133–61, 198
as election issue, 1
functionalist models of, 10
golden era of, 12
and immigration, 1
local histories/understandings of, 179–86
local/national narratives in, 191–6
local understandings/experiences of, 182, 190
meaning of, 7
national belonging and, 48–55
  see also belongings, national; Britishness
negative impact on, 74
new arrivals for, 119
newspaper comments on, 1
non-reciprocal interpretation of, 185
normative models of, 10
as political issue, 1
and politics of belonging, 162
as relational and structural, 186–7
as resolving conflict, 12–13
separateness, 180
social interventions on, 196–8
sociological research and analysis, 25–9
in UK, 82, 188–91
understandings of, 162
and work/life balance, 6
social deprivation
  inner city estates, 97–101
  negative social reactions and, 101
social differentiation, 178
social diversity, 92–3
  in Downham, 104
social divisions, education and, 135
social field
  Bourdieu's concept of, 9
  definition of, 9–10
social groups, new

accessing housing, 119–21
attacks on, 122–3
and belongings, 164, 174–7
in Downham, 145–8
in Leicester, 141–2
negative/positive reactions to, 104–11
and neighbourhood relations, 121–6
politics on, 102–11
see also new arrivals
social hierarchies in educational settings, 136–8
social housing
altered entitlements to, 114
entitlement to, 118
partial privatisation of, 114
social integration, 7
social interventions, 73, 83, 103, 110–11, 136
in Downham, 153–6
in Dungannon, 156–9
in Leicester, 149–53
on social cohesion, 196–8
socialisation, education and, 134
sociality, 46, 68, 86, 94
social life, for migrant workers, 77
social mobility, 93–5
education and, 137, 142–3, 143, 146, 148–9
and place, 88
social pluralism, 41, 112
social reformation, in Downham, 108–9
social relations, 10, 68
social segregation, 181
social solidarities, 15, 78, 100, 190
social transformations
in Downham, 153–6
in Dungannon, 156–9
in Leicester, 149–53
social uncohesiveness, 10–11
socio-economic insecurity, 187
socio-economic marginalisation, 139–40, 195
socio-economic security
place, arrival of new groups and, 106
socio-economic transformations, 5, 6, 15, 21, 26, 82, 109–10, 111

education in, 136
influences on place, 83
Soft-Touch Arts, 139, 203
Soja, E. W., 82
solidarity, and proximity, 100
Somalia, 176
Somali people
conflict with African Caribbean in Leicester, 138–42, 149–53
South Tyrone Empowerment Programme (STEP), 110, 156, 203
STEP, *see* South Tyrone Empowerment Programme (STEP)
Stephen, L., 33, 139
Stolcke, V., 5
Straw, Jack, 33
'street conviviality', 86
structural redundancy, 57
'Sus laws', 32
Sweden, 175, 176
system integration, 7

Tam, H., 39
Tamil refugees, 142, 143, 204
Taylor, B., 8, 47, 48, 85, 98, 101
tertiary education sector, 157
Thatcher, M., 15, 48, 114
Theodore, N., 80, 81
Thetford, 201–2
'The Troubles', 33, 67, 122
third generation minority ethnic people, 179
Thomas, B., 20
time poverty, 128–9
Timesonline, 22
tolerance, 44, 53–4
and liberal individualism, 53–4
multiculturalism, 51
Tomlinson, S., 134
Tottenham
disturbances in, 197
transnational family, 130–1
transnational social fields, 10
tube trains bombing, London, 39

United Kingdom (UK)
condition of belonging in, 176–7
economic preeminence, 16

United Kingdom (UK) – *cotinued*
  emigration in, 24
  employment
    industrial sector, 16–17
  employment law, violation of, 68
  family life in, 128
    see also family
  housing shortage in, 115, 116
    see also housing
  immigration in, 24
  long-term settled, 24, 28–9
  migration analysis of, 5–6, 24–5
  multiculturalism, impact of, 2, 93
  national immigration policy, 2
  research project on, 199–205
  social cohesion in, 188–91
United Kingdom of Great Britain and Northern Ireland, 49
universalism and cosmopolitanism, 8–9
urban populations, 46
USA
  employment
    in manufacturing sector, 16–17
  'white backlash' in, 81

Vagrancy Act of 1824, 32
Vertovec, S., 2, 3, 8, 9
vulnerabilities, of migrancy, 67, 69, 70, 73, 129, 179

wages policy, in old economy, 62
Wales, 33, 49, 138, 178
Walter, B., 113, 193
welfare state, 2, 6, 19, 20–3, 113–14, 165, 170, 171, 174, 177, 187
Wessendorf, S., 2, 3
western individualism, 3–4
Westminster's response, 51
'white backlash', 81
white English majority ethnic
  long-term resident, 164–5, 178
  feelings of positive belonging, 166
'white host communities', 36
Williams, A. M., 18
Williams, F., 74, 114, 126
Willis, P., 20, 145
Winkelmann-Gleed, A., 67
Wolf, E., 198
women workers
  in care sector, 73, 74, 76
  in waged work, 66
Wood, T., 58, 63
work
  deskilled work, 60
  low skilled work, 18, 57, 63
  skilled work, 58
  work practices, 66
working life, changes in, 60–5
work/life balance, 6
Worley, C., 36

Young, I. M., 5
Younge, G., 53
Yuval Davis, N., 113

Zetter, R., 180